AN INTRODUCTION TO AGENCY AND PARTNERSHIP

By

MELVIN ARON EISENBERG
Koret Professor of Law,
University of California at Berkeley

SECOND EDITION

Westbury, New York
THE FOUNDATION PRESS, INC.
1995

 TEXT IS PRINTED ON 10% POST CONSUMER RECYCLED PAPER

PREFACE

This book is designed to be used either as a supplement, in courses on business organizations, to casebooks that focus primarily on Corporations, or for short courses on Agency and Partnership. A full treatment of agency and partnership is beyond the scope of this book. Rather, this book presents a working introduction to those subjects. Chapter 1 provides a brief sketch of those principles of agency law that are most salient to the study of business organizations: authority, and the agent's duty of loyalty. Chapter 2 is a somewhat more detailed introduction to the law of partnership.

The following conventions have been used in the preparation of this book:

(1) Omissions within a statutory or Restatement section or official comment, are indicated by ellipses (. . .). The omission of an entire statutory or Restatement section or official comment is not so indicated. However, in the case of the Uniform Partnership Act, the Revised Uniform Partnership Act (1994), and the Uniform Limited Partnership Act, the omission of an entire section is indicated in the Table of Contents by an asterisk following the title of the omitted section.

(2) Editorial insertions in the text are indicated by brackets. In some cases, the official text includes bracketed material, but the context usually makes clear whether bracketed material consists of editorial insertions or original text.

———

I thank the authors, publishers, and copyrightholders who permitted me to reprint all or portions of the following works:

American Law Institute, Restatement (Second) of Agency.

National Conference of Commissioners on Uniform State Laws, Uniform Partnership Act, Revised Uniform Limited Partnership Act (1994), and Revised Limited Partnership Act.

MELVIN A. EISENBERG

June, 1995

*

iii

TABLE OF CONTENTS

CHAPTER I. AGENCY

CHAPTER II. PARTNERSHIP

vii

TABLE OF CONTENTS

APPENDIX

TABLE OF CASES

Principal cases are in italic type. Non-principal cases are in roman type. References are to Pages.

ix

TABLE OF CASES

AN INTRODUCTION TO AGENCY AND PARTNERSHIP

*

Chapter I
AGENCY

SECTION 1. INTRODUCTION

Courses in corporations or business associations are, in large part, courses in organizational law. Among the most common forms of business organization in this country are the sole proprietorship, the corporation, and the partnership. Based on tax filings, as of 1991 there were 15,181,000 sole proprietorships in the United States, 3,803,000 corporations, and 1,515,000 partnerships. U.S. Bureau of the Census, Statistical Abstract of the United States 540-43 (Tables 835, 837, 840) (1994).

A sole proprietorship is a business owned by one individual. It might be thought that the term "organization" is an inappropriate characterization of a form that involves only a single owner. That terminology can, however, be justified on at least two grounds.

First, a business enterprise owned by an individual is likely to have a degree of psychological and sociological identity separate from that of the individual. This separateness of a sole proprietor's enterprise is often expressed by giving the enterprise its own name, like "Acme Shoe Company." Furthermore, a sole proprietor usually will consider only a certain portion of his property and cash as invested in the business, and will keep a separate set of financial records for the enterprise as if the enterprise's finances were separate from her own.

Thus, if Alice Adams begins a new business in 1995—say, Acme Shoe Company—she is likely to issue a balance sheet for the business that does not show all of her assets and liabilities, but only those assets dedicated to, and those liabilities arising out of, the enterprise's operations. (See Section 4, An Introduction to Financial Statements, infra.) In short, as a psychological matter Adams, and to a certain extent those who deal with her, are likely to regard Acme Shoe Company as an enterprise or firm that has a certain degree of separateness from Adams herself, with a certain amount of capital. As a matter of law, however, a sole proprietorship has no separate identity from its owner. If Adams takes no special legal step, like incorporating the enterprise, all of her wealth will be committed to the enterprise, because an individual who owns a

1

sole proprietorship has unlimited personal liability for obligations incurred in the conduct of the business.

The second reason for calling a sole proprietorship an organization is that a sole proprietor typically will not conduct the business by herself, but will engage various people—salespersons, mechanics, managers—to act on her behalf in conducting the business. The employment by one person of another to act on her behalf brings us to the most elementary form of organizational law, known as the law of agency. An *agent* is a person who by mutual assent acts on behalf of another and subject to the other's control. Restatement, Second, Agency § 1. The person for whom the agent acts is a *principal.* Id. Agency law governs the relationship between agents and principals, and among agents, principals, and third parties with whom the agent deals on the principal's behalf. Although agency is a consensual relationship, whether an agency relationship has been created does not turn on whether the parties think of themselves as agent and principal. "Agency is a legal concept which depends upon the existence of required factual elements: the manifestation by the principal that the agent shall act for him, the agent's acceptance of the undertaking and the understanding of the parties that the principal is to be in control of the undertaking. The relation which the law calls agency does not depend upon the intent of the parties to create it, nor their belief that they have done so. To constitute the relation, there must be an agreement, but not necessarily a contract, between the parties; if the agreement results in the factual relation between them to which are attached the legal consequences of agency, an agency exists although the parties did not call it agency and did not intend the legal consequences of the relation to follow. Thus, when one ... asks a friend to do a slight service for him, such as to return for credit goods recently purchased from a store, [an agency relationship may be created although] neither one may have any realization that they are creating an agency relation or be aware of the legal obligations which would result from performance of the service." Restatement (Second) of Agency § 1, Comment b.

SECTION 2.   AUTHORITY

CROISANT v. WATRUD

Oregon Supreme Court, 1967.
248 Or. 234, 432 P.2d 799.

Before PERRY, Chief Justice, and McALLISTER, O'CONNELL, GOODWIN and DENECKE, Justices.

Reversed and Remanded.

O'CONNELL, J.

This is a suit in equity for an accounting brought against co-partners in a firm of certified public accountants and the executrix of a deceased partner, LaVern Watrud. Plaintiff appeals from a decree in favor of defendants.

We shall refer to the deceased partner, Watrud, as one of the defendants. The defendants engaged in the accounting practice with their principal office in Klamath Falls and their branch office in Medford. Watrud was in charge of the Medford office.

Plaintiff was the owner of a sawmill, timberlands, and other property over which she exercised general control, delegating the details of management of the business to others.

In 1955 plaintiff employed the defendant partnership to advise her on tax matters and to prepare income tax returns for her business enterprises. All of these services were performed by Watrud, who was in charge of the Medford office.

In 1956 plaintiff sold her sawmill. Thereafter her business activities consisted almost entirely of making collections under the contract for the sale of the mill, collections on the sale of timber, collections of rents, and various disbursements from the moneys so collected.

In 1957 plaintiff moved to California. She made arrangements with Watrud to make the collections referred to above, to make certain disbursements, to keep her financial books and records, and to prepare her financial statements and tax returns. The moneys collected by Watrud were deposited in the account of the Lloyd Timber Company (plaintiff's business name in Oregon) in a Grants Pass bank.

In 1957 plaintiff learned that her husband, Glenn Lloyd, had induced Watrud to make unauthorized payments out of the Lloyd Timber Company account to him. Plaintiff instructed Watrud not to make any further payments to her husband, but Watrud violated her instructions. Plaintiff was informed of these subsequent misappropriations by Watrud on behalf of Glenn Lloyd in 1958. She also learned that her husband was unfaithful to her. Plaintiff again excused Watrud's breach of trust and her husband's infidelity. After their reconciliation, plaintiff and her husband took a trip to Europe. When they returned, plaintiff discovered that her husband had forged checks on her California bank account and had also forged her signature upon a $75,000 note and negotiated it. Plaintiff also

became aware of the fact that Watrud had continued to pay money
to Glenn Lloyd out of plaintiff's Oregon account. In addition, she
learned that Watrud, without authorization, had drawn a check
payable to himself. When Watrud was confronted with this evidence he finally acknowledged his abuse of his trust. Soon thereafter Watrud died from gunshot wounds while hunting. Plaintiff then
filed this suit for an accounting against the surviving partners.

The trial court held that the trust assumed by Watrud in
handling plaintiff's business affairs was an "independent trustee
employment," separate and distinct from the activities in which the
partnership itself was engaged.

It is undisputed that plaintiff's initial business arrangements for
tax advice and the preparation of tax returns were with the partnership and not simply with Watrud individually. After the partnership
was employed, Watrud individually performed all of the services
sought by plaintiff. As time went on plaintiff called upon Watrud to
perform additional services in connection with her business including the collection and disbursements of funds. The initial question
is whether these subsequent services performed by Watrud are to be
regarded as having been performed as a part of the partnership
business or under a separate arrangement calling only for the
services of Watrud personally.

The record suggests that plaintiff, Watrud, and defendants
considered all of Watrud's services to the plaintiff as services performed by a member of a partnership on behalf of that firm. The
partnership received a check each month for all of Watrud's services
including the services involved in handling plaintiff's business affairs. Had the parties viewed the services in making collections and
disbursements for plaintiff as independent activities separate compensation would have been in order. Although the partnership's
Medford office was geographically separated from the Klamath Falls
office, both operations constituted one autonomous business enterprise and consequently defendants cannot insulate themselves from
liability on the ground that the Medford office was a separate
business operation. Defendants are liable, therefore, if Watrud can
be regarded as the agent of the partnership in performing the fund-
handling services for plaintiff.

It is clear that Watrud had no express authority from defendants to perform these services. And there was no evidence from
which an authority implied in fact could be derived. If it were
common knowledge that accountants frequently act as trustees in
the collection and disbursement of funds, we would be in a position
to take judicial notice of the common practice and thus find an
implied authority or an apparent authority. But we have no basis
for saying that accountants commonly or frequently perform fund-

handling services. Thus we conclude that liability cannot be rested upon a manifestation by defendants that they assented to be bound for such services. However, an agent can impose liability upon his principal even where there is no actual or apparent authority or estoppel. An agent may have an "inherent agency power" to bind his principal. Such power is defined in Restatement (Second), Agency § 8A as "the power of an agent which is derived not from authority, apparent authority or estoppel, but solely from the agency relation and exists for the protection of persons harmed by or dealing with a servant or other agent." When an agent has acted improperly in entering into a contract the inherent agency power "is based neither upon the consent of the principal nor upon his manifestations."[1] The scope of the principal's liability under an inherent agency power is stated in Section 161:

> "A general agent for a disclosed or partially disclosed principal subjects his principal to liability for acts done on his account which usually accompany or are incidental to transactions which the agent is authorized to conduct if, although they are forbidden by the principal, the other party reasonably believes that the agent is authorized to do them and has no notice that he is not so authorized." Restatement (Second), Agency § 161, p. 378 (1958).

It will be noted that Section 161 states that the principal is liable only for his agent's acts "which *usually accompany* or are *incidental* to transactions which the agent is authorized to conduct...." (Emphasis added.) As we have previously observed, we have neither evidence nor judicial knowledge of the practice of accountancy from which to decide whether the collection and disbursement of accounts is commonly undertaken by accountants. We cannot say, therefore, that the fund-handling services performed by Watrud in this case were the type which "usually accompany" the transactions which accountants ordinarily conduct viewed from the standpoint of those engaged in accountancy. Upon similar reasoning we are unable to say that the services here were "incidental" to the transactions Watrud was authorized to conduct.

But this does not conclude the matter. Assuming that accountants do not regard the collection and disbursement of funds as a part of the services usually offered by members of their profession, what significance should this have if, in the particular circumstances, a person dealing with a member of an accounting partnership reasonably believes that accountants perform the kind of service which he seeks to have performed? If the phrase "acts ... which usually accompany ... transactions which the agent is authorized to conduct" is to be tested solely from the viewpoint of accountants in

1. Comment to § 8A, p. 37.

describing the kind of services they usually perform then, of course, Section 161 of the Restatement (Second) of Agency would not be applicable even though a client of an accounting firm mistakenly but reasonably believed that the services he requested were not alien to the work of accountants. The basis for the principal's liability under these circumstances is best explained by the comments appended to Section 8A and related sections of the Restatement; whether the theory is categorized as one of apparent authority (treating the circumstances as a manifestation of authority by principal), or as arising out of an inherent agency power is immaterial. The rationale begins with the idea that:

"The principles of agency have made it possible for persons to utilize the services of others in accomplishing far more than could be done by their unaided efforts.... [The] primary function [of agency] in modern life is to make possible the commercial enterprises which could not exist otherwise.... Partnerships and corporations, through which most of the work of the world is done today, depend for their existence upon agency principles. The rules designed to promote the interests of these enterprises are necessarily accompanied by rules to police them. It is inevitable that in doing their work, either through negligence or excess of zeal, agents will harm third persons or will deal with them in unauthorized ways. It would be unfair for an enterprise to have the benefit of the work of its agents without making it responsible to some extent for their excesses and failures to act carefully. The answer of the common law has been the creation of special agency powers or, to phrase it otherwise, the imposition of liability upon the principal because of unauthorized or negligent acts of his servants and other agents...." Restatement (Second) Agency, § 8A, comment *a* (1958).

The basis for [a] principal's liability under this section is further explained in the comment as follows:

"... His liability exists solely because of his relation to the agent. It is based primarily upon the theory that, if one appoints an agent to conduct a series of transactions over a period of time, it is fair that he should bear losses which are incurred when such an agent, although without authority to do so, does something which is usually done in connection with the transactions he is employed to conduct. Such agents can properly be regarded as part of the principal's organization in much the same way as a servant is normally part of the master's business enterprise.* In fact most general agents are also

---

* The terms "master" and "servant" have technical meanings in agency law. See the Note on Authority following this case. (Footnote by ed.)

servants, such as managers and other persons continuously employed and subject to physical supervision by the employer. The basis of the extended liability stated in this Section is comparable to the liability of a master for the torts of his servant. See Comment *a* on § 219. In the case of the master, it is thought fair that one who benefits from the enterprise and has a right to control the physical activities of those who make the enterprise profitable, should pay for the physical harm resulting from the errors and derelictions of the servants while doing the kind of thing which makes the enterprise successful. The rules imposing liability upon the principal for some of the contracts and conveyances of a general agent, whether or not a servant, which he is neither authorized nor apparently authorized to make, are based upon a similar public policy. Commercial convenience requires that the principal should not escape liability where there have been deviations from the usually granted authority by persons who are such essential parts of his business enterprise. In the long run it is of advantage to business, and hence to employers as a class, that third persons should not be required to scrutinize too carefully the mandates of permanent or semi-permanent agents who do no more than what is usually done by agents in similar positions." Restatement (Second), Agency § 161 at p. 379–380.

If a third person reasonably believes that the services he has requested of a member of an accounting partnership [are] undertaken as a part of the partnership business, the partnership should be bound for a breach of trust incident to that employment even though those engaged in the practice of accountancy would regard as unusual the performance of such service by an accounting firm.

The reasonableness of a third person's belief in assuming that a partner is acting within the scope of the partnership should not be tested by the profession's own description of the function of its members. Those who seek accounting services may not understand the refinements made by accountants in defining the services they offer to the public. Whether a third person's belief is reasonable in assuming that the service he seeks is within the domain of the profession is a question which must be answered upon the basis of the facts in the particular case.

We are of the opinion that the facts in the present case are sufficient to establish a reasonable belief on the part of plaintiff that Watrud had undertaken all of the work assigned to him by plaintiff as a continuation of the original employment of the partnership firm. The initial work for which defendants were engaged was the preparation of income tax returns. Thereafter plaintiff sought Watrud's advice on tax matters and continued to have him prepare income tax returns for her business ventures. Watrud did not do the actual bookkeeping for plaintiff's business activities when the partnership was first employed, but eventually he prepared and kept in his own custody the financial books and records of plaintiff's enterprises. This service was assumed by Watrud when plaintiff decided to move to California permanently. When plaintiff left Grants Pass she also arranged with Watrud to have him receive all the income from her Oregon and California properties and to make disbursements from the money so collected. Before she employed him to handle her funds she asked him if he was bonded and he assured her that he was. We think it is important to note that the increased responsibilities directed to Watrud coincided with plaintiff's departure for California. Thereafter, Watrud was the only person who drew checks on the account set up pursuant to the arrangement with plaintiff, although the bank signature card included the names of plaintiff and others. Watrud handled a very substantial amount of plaintiff's money during the course of his employment, drawing as many as 1500 checks per year. The bank statements and cancelled checks were sent directly to Watrud; he collected her business mail at her post office box in Grants Pass and in other respects acted in her behalf after her departure for California. As we have already mentioned, the partnership received compensation for these services at the rate of $800 per month.

As plaintiff testified, nothing was ever said or done by Watrud which might have indicated to her that he was acting on his account as distinguished from acting for the partnership. It was reasonable for plaintiff to assume that the added assignment of collecting and disbursing funds delegated to Watrud was an integral part of the function of one employed to keep the accounts reflecting the income and disbursement of those funds. This assumption, we think, is even more likely in circumstances such as we have here where there is trust and confidence reposed in the person employed. This is not a case in which a person deals with an ordinary commercial partnership. Accountants stand in a fiduciary relation to their clients and out of that relationship there is generated a trust and confidence which invites the client to rely upon the advice and guidance of the one she employs. . . .

The trial court also held that since plaintiff, after learning that Watrud was violating his trust continued to allow him to handle her funds [, she] is estopped as against defendants to assert a claim for subsequent breaches of duty by Watrud in paying out money to plaintiff's husband and himself. After a careful reading of the record we are of the opinion that plaintiff did not act unreasonably in further trusting Watrud after the disclosure of his unauthorized payment of funds to plaintiff's husband.

The decree of the trial court is reversed and the cause is remanded for further proceedings not inconsistent with this opinion.[6]

———

Contra: Rouse v. Pollard, 130 N.J.Eq. 204, 21 A.2d 801 (E. & A. 1941).

———

NOTE ON AUTHORITY

An *agent* is a person who acts on behalf of, and subject to the control of, another. For some purposes, agents are classified as general or special. A *general agent* is an agent who is authorized to conduct a series of transactions involving continuity of service. A *special agent* is an agent authorized to conduct a single transaction or a series of transactions not involving continuity of service.

A *principal* is a person on whose behalf, and subject to whose control, an agent acts. Principals are conventionally divided into three classes: disclosed, partially disclosed, and undisclosed.

A principal is *disclosed* if at the time of the relevant transaction the third party knows that the agent is acting on behalf of a principal and knows the principal's identity.

A principal is *partially disclosed* if at the time of the transaction the third party knows that the agent is acting on behalf of a principal, but does not know the principal's identity.

A principal is *undisclosed* if the agent, in dealing with the third party, purports to be acting on his own behalf. An undisclosed principal is liable for her agent's authorized activities, even though, because the agent does not disclose his agency, the third party believes the agent is acting strictly on his own behalf. One reason the undisclosed principal is liable is that she set the transaction in motion and stood to gain from it. A second reason is this: Even if the undisclosed principal was not directly liable to the third party, the agent would be. Therefore, the third party could sue the agent, and the agent could then sue the principal for indemnification of the damages he had to pay the third party. See Section 5 of this Note, infra. Accordingly, allowing the third party to sue the undisclosed principal does not materially enlarge the principal's liability, and collapses two lawsuits into one.

---

6. By stipulation the parties agreed to try initially only the issue of defendants' liability and defer the trial of the issue of the extent of defendants' liability, if any.

A *master* is a principal who controls or has the right to control the physical conduct of an agent in the performance of the agent's services. A *servant* is an agent whose physical conduct in the performance of services for the principal is controlled by or subject to the control of the principal. Restatement (Second) Agency § 2. The terms master and servant are customarily (although not exclusively) used in connection with a principal's liability for the torts of an agent. Both terms are purely technical, and "do not denote menial or manual service. Many servants perform exacting work requiring intelligence rather than muscle. Thus the officers of a corporation or a ship, the [intern] in a hospital ... are servants...." Id., Comment c.

A variety of problems can arise out of an actual or alleged principal-agency relationship. Perhaps the most common problem is that considered in *Croisant*—what liabilities arose out of a certain transaction between the agent and a third party? Most of the issues implicated by that question are addressed by the legal rules governing *authority*. This Note will emphasize the liability of the principal to the third party (Section 1), but will also consider the liability of the third party to the principal (Section 2), the liability of the agent to the third party (Section 3), and the liabilities of the agent and the principal to each other (Sections 4 and 5). Although the law of agency encompasses liabilities in tort as well as in contract, for the most part this Note will address only issues that relate to contractual transactions.

1. *Liability of Principal to Third Party.* Under the law of agency, a principal becomes liable to a third party as a result of an act or transaction by another, A, on the principal's behalf if A had actual or apparent authority, was an agent by estoppel, or had inherent authority, or if the principal ratified the act or transaction.

a. *Actual authority.* An agent has *actual authority* to act in a given way on a principal's behalf if the principal's words or conduct would lead a reasonable person in the agent's position to believe that the principal had authorized him to so act.

> *Restatement (Second) of Agency § 26, Illustration 2:* P goes to an office where, as he knows, several brokers have desks, and leaves upon the desk of A, thinking it to be the desk of X, a note signed by him, which states: "I authorize you to contract in my name for the purchase of 100 shares of Western Union stock at today's market." A comes in, finds the note and, not knowing of the mistake, immediately makes a contract with T in P's name for the purchase of the shares. A had [actual] authority to make the contract.[1]

---

1. Restatement (Second) of Agency uses the term "authority" to mean what is conventionally called "actual authority." The latter terminology is easier to work with,

Actual authority may be either *implied* or *express:* "It is possible for a principal to specify minutely what the agent is to do. To the extent that he does this, the agent may be said to have express authority. But most authority is created by implication. Thus, in the authorization to 'sell my automobile', the only fully expressed power is to transfer title in exchange for money or a promise to give money. In fact, under some circumstances ... there may ... be power to take or give possession of the automobile or to extend credit or to accept something in partial exchange. These powers are all implied or inferred from the words used, from customs and from the relations of the parties. They are described as 'implied authority.'" Restatement (Second) of Agency § 7, Comment c.[2]

A common type of implied actual authority is *incidental authority,* which is the authority to do incidental acts that are reasonably necessary to accomplish an authorized transaction or that usually accompany it.

> *Restatement (Second) of Agency § 35, Illustration 4:* P directs A to sell goods by auction at a time and place at which, as P and A know, a statute forbids anyone but a licensed auctioneer to conduct sales by auction. Nothing to the contrary appearing, A's authority includes authority to employ a licensed auctioneer.

> *Restatement (Second) of Agency § 26, Illustration 5:* P authorizes A, a local broker, to sell and convey land. At the time and place it is the custom to make such sales with a warranty of title. A has implied authority to execute and deliver a proper deed to the purchaser and to insert in the deed the usual covenants as to title.

Incidental authority is a type of implied actual authority, because if the principal has authorized the agent to engage in a given transaction, and certain acts are reasonably necessary to accomplish the transaction, or usually accompany it, a reasonable person in the agent's position would interpret the authority to engage in the transaction as also conferring authority to engage in the incidental acts.

Note that if an agent has actual authority, the principal is bound even if the third party did not know that the agent had actual authority, and indeed even if the third party thought the agent was herself the principal, not merely an agent.

See Restatement (Second) of Agency §§ 26, 32, 33, 35, 39, 43, 144 in the Appendix.

---

because it sets up a clear opposition between authority of various types.

2. Occasionally, courts use the term "implied authority" to mean apparent authority, but this is bad usage and is not often encountered.

   b.   *Apparent authority.*   An agent has *apparent authority* to
act in a given way on a principal's behalf in relation to a third party,
T, if the words or conduct of the principal would lead a reasonable
person in T's position to believe that the principal had authorized
the agent to so act.

   Restatement (Second) of Agency § 8, Illustration 1:   P
writes to A directing him to act as his agent for the sale of
Blackacre.   P sends a copy of this letter to T, a prospective
purchaser.   A has [actual] authority to sell Blackacre and, as to
T, apparent authority.

   Illustration 2:   Same facts as in Illustration 1, except that in
the letter to A, P adds a postscript, not included in the copy to
T, telling A to make no sale until after communication with P.
A has no [actual] authority to sell Blackacre but, as to T, he has
apparent authority.

   Illustration 3:   Same facts as in Illustration 1, except that
after A and T have received the letters, P telegraphs a revocation
to A.   A has no [actual] authority but, as to T, he has apparent
authority to sell Blackacre.

   In most cases, actual and apparent authority go hand in hand,
as Restatement (Second) of Agency § 8, Illustration 1, supra, suggests.   For example, if P Bank appoints A as cashier, and nothing
more is said, A will reasonably believe she has the authority that
cashiers normally have, and third parties who deal with A will
reasonably believe the same thing.   Apparent authority becomes
salient in such a case if P Bank does not actually give A all the
authority that cashiers usually have, and T deals with A knowing that
A is a cashier, but not knowing that P Bank has placed special limits
on A's authority.

   The apparent authority of A in the cashier hypothetical is a
special type of apparent authority known as *power of position.*
"... [A]pparent authority can be created by appointing a person to
a position, such as that of manager or treasurer, which carries with
it generally recognized duties; to those who know of the appointment there is apparent authority to do the things ordinarily entrusted to one occupying such a position, regardless of unknown
limitations which are imposed upon the particular agent. . . .   If a
principal puts an agent into, or knowingly permits him to occupy, a
position in which according to the ordinary habits of persons in the
locality, trade or profession, it is usual for such an agent to have a
particular kind of authority, anyone dealing with him is justified in
inferring that he has such authority, in the absence of reason to
know otherwise."   Restatement (Second) of Agency § 27, Comment
a, § 49, Comment c.

Restatement (Second) of Agency § 49, Illustration 4: The P bank appoints A as an information clerk, with authority only to answer questions of depositors. During alterations, however, the bank directs A to occupy the space normally occupied by one of the receiving tellers, a sign indicating that it is the "information" window. The sign becomes displaced and T, a depositor in the bank, makes a cash deposit with A, believing that he is a teller. P is bound by this transaction.

See Restatement (Second) of Agency §§ 27, 49, 159 in the Appendix.

c. *Agency by estoppel.* Still another type of authority is known as "agency by estoppel." The core of agency by estoppel is described as follows in Restatement (Second) of Agency § 8B:

(1) A person who is not otherwise liable as a party to a transaction purported to be done on his account, is nevertheless subject to liability to persons who have changed their positions because of their belief that the transaction was entered into by or for him, if

(a) he intentionally or carelessly caused such belief, or

(b) knowing of such belief and that others might change their positions because of it, he did not take reasonable steps to notify them of the facts.

The concept of agency by estoppel is so close to the concept of apparent authority that for most practical purposes the former concept can be subsumed in the latter.

d. *Inherent authority.* As *Croisant* indicates, under the doctrine of inherent authority an agent may bind a principal even when the agent had neither actual nor apparent authority. Indeed, under this doctrine an agent may bind her principal even when she has no apparent authority and disobeys the principal's instructions.

Although the doctrine of inherent authority is relatively well established, its exact contours are not always clear. Restatement (Second) of Agency § 8A provides that "Inherent agency power is a term used in the restatement of this subject to indicate the power of an agent which is derived not from [actual] authority, apparent authority or estoppel, but solely from the agency relation and exists for the protection of persons harmed by or dealing with a servant or other agent." Section 8A purports to be a definition, but isn't. It states that inherent authority is an agency power that is not derived from actual authority, apparent authority, or estoppel. It states the reason why inherent authority should be recognized. But it doesn't state what inherent authority *is*.

Section 161 of the Restatement concerns the inherent authority of general agents of disclosed or partially disclosed principals.

Under Section 161, a disclosed or partially disclosed principal is liable for an act done on his behalf by a general agent, even if the principal had forbidden the agent to do the act, if (i) the act usually accompanies or is incidental to transactions that the agent is authorized to conduct, and (ii) the third party reasonably believes the agent is authorized to do the act. But this leaves open the issue, under what circumstances is a third party reasonable in believing that an agent has authority that by hypothesis is beyond the agent's apparent authority?

Section 194 of the Restatement concerns the inherent authority of agents for undisclosed principals. It provides that "A general agent for an undisclosed principal authorized to conduct transactions subjects his principal to liability for acts done on his account, if usual or necessary in such transactions, although forbidden by the principal to do them." Unlike Section 161, Section 194 does not require that the third party reasonably believes the agent is authorized to act. Indeed, such a requirement could not be imposed, because in the case of an undisclosed principal the third party will not know he is dealing with an agent.

See Restatement (Second) of Agency §§ 3, 8A, 159–161A, 194, 195A in the Appendix.

Why should a principal be bound when an agent has neither actual nor apparent authority? One rationale for inherent authority, stated in the Comments to Restatement (Second) of Agency as quoted in *Croisant,* is comparable to the rationale of the doctrine of respondeat superior—that is, the doctrine that a principal (a "master") is liable for torts of an agent (a "servant") if the servant's physical conduct in the performance of services for the master is controlled by the master or is subject to the master's control, and the tort is committed while the servant is acting within the scope of her employment. The latter rationale has been aptly summarized by Professor Fishman:

> The adoption of enterprise liability under respondeat superior is justified on several policy grounds. First, the ability of the enterprise to spread the risk from losses is important. The enterprise is in a better position than ... the injured third party to spread the risk of loss, either through insurance or the ability to factor the potential losses into the price for the goods produced. A second reason suggests that proper allocation of resources is promoted by requiring an enterprise to include in the price of its goods the costs of the accidents which are closely associated with the enterprise's operations. A third reason ... is that the [principal] is in a position to control the employee and placing the risk of loss here could lead to greater safety. A fourth reason is that it is considered more equitable

to place the liability on the [principal], because it provides greater assurance that the accident victim will be paid, or because there is a societal preference to make certain losses costs of doing business rather than losses to be borne by individual households.

Fishman, Inherent Agency Power—Should Enterprise Liability Apply to Agents' Unauthorized Contracts?, 19 Rutgers L.J. 1, 48–49 (1987). Under the Restatement's comparable rationale for inherent authority, that doctrine operates as to contracts in much the same way that the doctrine of respondeat superior operates as to torts, so that the liability of principals for an agent's torts and contracts is treated in a unified way. See Restatement (Second) of Agency §§ 219, 220, 228–231 in the Statutory Supplement.

An alternative rationale of inherent authority is based on the principal's reasonable expectations. In a world with perfect information, faithful agents will follow all instructions impeccably. In the real world, however, agents acting in good faith will not infrequently deviate from their instructions. Agents, like everyone else, will make mistakes, which may take the form of misinterpreting their instructions or forgetting one of numerous instructions. Furthermore, an agent may reasonably believe that her principal's objective is best served by violating a particular instruction. A principal's instructions to his agents are necessarily given in the present to govern the future. The future, however, may develop in such a way that the agents reasonably believe that if the principal knew all the facts, he would not want the agent to follow a given instruction. Of course, the agent could go back to the principal for further instructions, but often it is infeasible to take that course of action—for example, because a valuable opportunity must be taken immediately or not at all. These real-world facts are reflected in a passage in the Comment to Restatement § 8A: "It is inevitable that in doing their work, either through negligence or excess of zeal, agents will harm third persons or will deal with them in unauthorized ways. It would be unfair for an enterprise to have the benefit of the work of its agents without making it responsible to some extent for their excesses and failures to act carefully."

Given these realities, the doctrine of inherent authority can be justified on the ground that it is or should be foreseeable to a principal, when he appoints an agent, that as a practical matter the agent is likely to deviate occasionally from instructions. As between the principal, who appointed the agent, who benefits from the agent's activities, and who could or should have foreseen a certain range of deviations from instructions, on the one hand, and the third party who contracts with the agent, on the other, a loss that results from such deviations is better placed on the principal.

This reasonable-foreseeability rationale leads to a definition of inherent authority: Inherent authority is authority to take an action that a person in the principal's position reasonably should have foreseen the agent would be likely to take, even though the action would be in violation of the agent's instructions. The reasonable foreseeability rationale also leads to a test for inherent authority: Would a reasonable person in the *principal's* position have foreseen that, despite his instructions, there was a significant likelihood that the agent would act as he did? This test complements the test of actual authority, which is based on the *agent's* reasonable expectations, and the test for apparent authority, which is based on the *third party's* reasonable expectations.

Unlike the Restatement provisions, a definition and test of inherent authority based on reasonable foreseeability does not limit such authority to general agents. It is true that as a practical matter the application of the doctrine may partly depend on whether an agent is general or special, because it may be reasonably foreseeable that a general agent will be especially likely to deviate occasionally from instructions, due to the expansive grant of actual authority that is usually conferred upon such agents. As a matter of principle, however, even under the Restatement's rationale there is no reason why inherent authority should turn on whether the agent is general or special. To put this differently, in applying the principle of inherent authority it is relevant but not dispositive that a general agent is involved.

A much narrower view of the concept of inherent authority has been advocated by Professor Fishman in the article cited above. Fishman argues that the principle of inherent authority merely serves as a minor expansion of the principle of apparent authority. Under his view, the role of inherent authority is to impose liability on a principal where the principal expressly prohibited an agent from conducting class T transactions, but authorized the agent to engage in Conduct C, and authority to engage in Class T transactions usually accompanies authority to engage in Conduct C. A third party, observing that the agent is engaging in Conduct C, would reasonably believe that the agent was also authorized to engage in a Class T transaction. Fishman defends this very narrow view of inherent authority by arguing that the reasons for enterprise liability in tort don't apply in the contract context. When a third party is tortiously injured by an agent, normally the third party is entirely innocent. In contrast, Fishman argues, when a third party deals with an agent who exceeded her authority to enter into contractual transactions, the third party may be deemed at fault for failing to investigate the agent's authority.

This argument for distinguishing between a principal's contract and tort liability lacks explanatory power. To begin with, the argument is inconsistent not only with the rules set out in the Restatement, but with what the cases say and do. For example, under this view an agent's inherent authority binds a principal only if the third party has observed that the agent had engaged in Conduct C. The cases have not imposed such a requirement.

Furthermore, this argument has no force in the case of undisclosed or partially disclosed principals. A third party who deals with an agent of an undisclosed principal cannot be deemed at fault for failing to investigate the agent's authority, because the third party does not know he is dealing with an agent. Similarly, although a third party who deals with the agent of a partially disclosed principal does know he is dealing with an agent, as a practical matter it is difficult or impossible for a third party to investigate the authority of an agent when he does not even know the principal's name.

Even in the case of disclosed principals, the force of the argument is very limited. It seems unlikely that the interests of principals as a class would be served by a rule that gives third parties a powerful incentive to contact the principal every time they consider doing business with agents. It's not easy to see how much benefit there would be to principals in using agents to contract on their behalf, under such a rule, because the principal would end up dealing with every third party himself.

e. *Ratification.* Even if an agent has neither actual, apparent, nor inherent authority, the principal will be bound to the third party if the agent purported to act on the principal's behalf and the principal, with knowledge of the material facts, either (1) affirmed the agent's conduct by manifesting an intention to treat the agent's conduct as authorized, or (2) engaged in conduct that was justifiable only if he had such an intention.

Manifesting an intention to treat the agent's conduct as authorized is sometimes known as *express ratification.*

> *Restatement (Second) of Agency § 84, Illustration 1:* Without power to bind P, A purports to represent him in buying a horse from T. P affirms. P is now a party to the transaction.

Engaging in conduct that is justifiable only if the principal intends to treat the agent's conduct as authorized is sometimes known as *implied ratification.* The most common example is the case where, as a result of the purported agent's transaction, the principal, with knowledge of the facts, receives or retains something to which he would otherwise not be entitled.

> *Restatement (Second) of Agency § 98, Illustration 1:* P authorizes A to sell a refrigerator at a specified price without a warranty. A, purporting to have authority to do so, contracts

with T for the sale of the refrigerator at a lower price than that specified and with a warranty of performance for two years, T paying part of the purchase price. P receives the check given by T, knowing all the facts. The contract as made between A and T is affirmed.

> *Restatement (Second) of Agency § 98, Illustration 2:* P authorizes A to sell a typewriter for $50 in cash. A, purporting to have authority to do so, contracts to sell it to T for $25 and T's old typewriter, which T delivers to A. P receives T's old typewriter, knowing the facts. The transaction between T and A is affirmed.

Ratification need not be communicated to the third party to be effective, although it must be objectively manifested. Restatement (Second) of Agency § 95. However, to be effective a ratification must occur before either the third party has withdrawn, the agreement has otherwise terminated, or the situation has so materially changed that it would be inequitable to bind the third party and the third party elects not to be bound. See Restatement (Second) of Agency §§ 88, 89.

Ratification should be distinguished from a related concept: the creation of actual or apparent authority by *acquiescence.* "[I]f the agent performs a series of acts of a similar nature, the failure of the principal to object to them is an indication that he consents to the performance of similar acts in the future under similar conditions." Restatement (Second) of Agency § 43, Comment b. Suppose, for example, an agent engages in a series of comparable purchases on the principal's behalf. Prior to the first purchase, a reasonable person in the agent's position would not have thought she had authority to enter into such a transaction. Nevertheless, the principal did not object either to that purchase or to a later such purchase when he learned of them. At that point, a reasonable person in the agent's position would assume that the principal approved the agent's engaging in such purchases. Accordingly, the principal's acquiescence gives rise both to actual authority and, as to third persons who know of the acquiescence, apparent authority.

See Restatement (Second) of Agency §§ 82–85, 87–90, 93, 94, 97–100A, 143 in the Appendix.

f. *Termination of agent's authority.* A principal normally has the *power* to terminate an agent's authority even if doing so violates a contract between the principal and the agent, and even if the authority is stated to be irrevocable. Accordingly, a contractual provision that an agent's authority cannot be terminated by either party is normally effective only to create *liability* for wrongful termination. This rule rests largely on the ground that contracts relating to personal services will not be specifically enforced.

Restatement (Second) of Agency § 118, Illustration 1: In consideration of A's agreement to advertise and give his best energies to the sale of Blackacre, its owner, P, grants to A "a power of attorney, irrevocable for one year" to sell it. A advertises and spends time trying to sell Blackacre. At the end of three months P informs A that he revokes. A's authority is terminated.

See Restatement (Second) of Agency § 118 in the Appendix.

2. *Liability of Third Party to Principal.* Section 1 considered the liability of a principal to a third party. What is the liability of the third party to the principal? The general rule is that if an agent and a third party enter into a contract under which the agent's principal is liable to the third party, then the third party is liable to the principal. Restatement (Second) of Agency § 292. The major exception is that the third party is not liable to an undisclosed principal if the agent or the principal knew that the third party would not have dealt with the principal. Id., Comment c.

3. *Liability of Agent to Third Party.* The liability of an agent to a third party depends in part on whether the principal was disclosed, partially disclosed, or undisclosed.

a. *Undisclosed principal.* If the principal is undisclosed (that is, if at the time of the transaction the agent purported to act on her own behalf), the general rule is that the agent is bound even though the principal is bound too. Restatement (Second) of Agency § 322. The theory is that the third party must have expected the agent to be a party to the contract, because that is how the agent presented the transaction. However, there is a quirk in the law here. Under the majority rule, if the third party, after learning of an undisclosed principal's identity, obtains a judgment against the principal, the agent is discharged from liability even if the judgment is not satisfied. (A counterpart rule discharges the undisclosed principal if the third party obtains a judgment against the agent.) Under the minority rule, which is sounder, neither the agent nor the principal is discharged by a judgment against the other, but only by satisfaction of the judgment.

b. *Partially disclosed principal.* If the principal is partially disclosed (that is, if at the time of the transaction the third party knows that the agent is acting on behalf of a principal, but does not know the principal's identity), the general rule is that both the principal and the agent are bound to the third party. Restatement (Second) of Agency § 321. The theory is that if the third party did not know the identity of the principal, and therefore could not investigate the principal's credit or reliability, he probably expected that the agent would be liable, either solely or as a co-promisor or surety. Id., Comment a.

c. *Disclosed principal.* Assume now that the principal was disclosed (that is, at the time of the transaction the third party knew that the agent was acting on behalf of a principal and knew the principal's identity). If the principal is bound by the agent's act, because the agent had actual, apparent, or inherent authority or because the principal ratified the act, the general rule is that the agent is not bound to the third party. Restatement (Second) of Agency § 320. The theory is that in such a case the third party does not expect the agent to be bound, does expect the principal to be bound, and gets just what he expects.

If the principal is *not* bound by the agent's act, because the agent did not have actual, apparent, or inherent authority, the general rule is that the agent is liable to the third party, either for breach of an implied warranty of authority, Restatement (Second) of Agency § 329, or, under some cases, in tort for misrepresentation or on the contract itself. In principle, the difference between the two theories might lead to a difference in the measure of damages. Under the liability-on-the-contract theory, the third party will recover gains that would have been derived under the contract—essentially, expectation damages. In contrast, under the implied-warranty theory it might seem that the third party would recover only losses suffered by having entered into the transaction—essentially, reliance damages. However, Restatement (Second) of Agency § 329, while adopting the implied-warranty theory, provides for an expectation measure of damages, just as if it had adopted the contract theory: "The third person can recover in damages not only for the harm caused to him by the fact that the agent was unauthorized, but also for the amount by which he would have benefitted had the authority existed." Id., Comment j.

See Restatement (Second) of Agency §§ 320–322, 328–330 in the Appendix.

4. *Liability of Agent to Principal.* If an agent takes an action that she has no actual authority to perform, but the principal is nevertheless bound because the agent had apparent authority, the agent is liable to the principal for any resulting damages. Restatement (Second) of Agency § 383, Comment e. Whether an agent is liable to the principal for an act that binds the principal by virtue of the agent's inherent but not actual authority is an unsettled point.

5. *Liability of Principal to Agent.* If an agent has acted within her actual authority, the principal is under a duty to indemnify the agent for payments authorized or made necessary in executing the principal's affairs. This includes authorized payments made by the agent on the principal's behalf, payments made by the agent to a third party on contracts upon which the agent was authorized to make herself liable (as where the agent acted on behalf of a partially

disclosed or undisclosed principal), payments of damages to third parties that the agent incurs because of an authorized act that constituted a breach of contract, and expenses in defending actions brought against the agent by third parties because of the agent's authorized conduct.

See Restatement (Second) of Agency §§ 438–440 in the Appendix.

SECTION 3. THE AGENT'S DUTY OF LOYALTY

TARNOWSKI v. RESOP

Supreme Court of Minnesota, 1952.
236 Minn. 33, 51 N.W.2d 801.

KNUTSON, Justice.

Plaintiff desired to make a business investment. He engaged defendant as his agent to investigate and negotiate for the purchase of a route of coin-operated music machines. On June 2, 1947, relying upon the advice of defendant and the investigation he had made, plaintiff purchased such a business from Phillip Loechler and Lyle Mayer of Rochester, Minnesota, who will be referred to hereinafter as the sellers. The business was located at LaCrosse, Wisconsin, and throughout the surrounding territory. Plaintiff alleges that defendant represented to him that he had made a thorough investigation of the route; that it had 75 locations in operation; that one or more machines were at each location; that the equipment at each location was not more than six months old; and that the gross income from all locations amounted to more than $3,000 per month. As a matter of fact, defendant had made only a superficial investigation and had investigated only five of the locations. Other than that, he had adopted false representations of the sellers as to the other locations and had passed them on to plaintiff as his own. Plaintiff was to pay $30,620 for the business. He paid $11,000 down. About six weeks after the purchase, plaintiff discovered that the representations made to him by defendant were false, in that there were not more than 47 locations; that at some of the locations there were no machines and at others there were machines more than six months old, some of them being seven years old; and that the gross income was far less than $3,000 per month. Upon discovering the falsity of defendant's representations and those of the sellers, plaintiff rescinded the sale. He offered to return what he had received, and he demanded the return of his money. The sellers refused to comply, and he brought suit against them in the district court of Olmsted county. The action was tried, resulting in a verdict of $10,000 for plaintiff. Thereafter, the sellers paid plaintiff $9,500, after which the action was dismissed with prejudice pursuant to a stipulation of the parties.

In this action, brought in Hennepin county, plaintiff alleges that defendant, while acting as agent for him, collected a secret commission from the sellers for consummating the sale, which plaintiff seeks to recover under his first cause of action. In his second cause of action, he seeks to recover damages for (1) losses suffered in operating the route prior to rescission; (2) loss of time devoted to operation; (3) expenses in connection with rescission of the sale and his investigation in connection therewith; (4) nontaxable expenses in connection with prosecution of the suit against the sellers; and (5) attorneys' fees in connection with the suit. The case was tried to a jury, and plaintiff recovered a verdict of $5,200. This appeal is from the judgment entered pursuant thereto. . . .

1. With respect to plaintiff's first cause of action, the principle that all profits made by an agent in the course of an agency belonging to the principal, whether they are the fruits of performance or the violation of an agent's duty, is firmly established and universally recognized. Smitz v. Leopold, 51 Minn. 455, 53 N.W. 719; Crump v. Ingersoll, 44 Minn. 84, 46 N.W. 141; Kingsley v. Wheeler, 95 Minn. 360, 104 N.W. 543; Goodhue Farmers' Warehouse Co. v. Davis, 81 Minn. 210, 83 N.W. 531; Snell v. Goodlander, 90 Minn. 533, 97 N.W. 421; City of Minneapolis v. Canterbury, 122 Minn. 301, 142 N.W. 812, 48 L.R.A.N.S., 842; Doyen v. Bauer, 211 Minn. 140, 300 N.W. 451; Magee v. Odden, 220 Minn. 498, 20 N.W.2d 87.

It matters not that the principal has suffered no damage or even that the transaction has been profitable to him. Raymond Farmers Elevator Co. v. American Surety Co., 207 Minn. 117, 290 N.W. 231, 126 A.L.R. 1351.

The rule and the basis therefor are well stated in Lum v. Clark, 56 Minn. 278, 282, 57 N.W. 662, where, speaking through Mr. Justice Mitchell, we said: "Actual injury is not the principle the law proceeds on, in holding such transactions void. Fidelity in the agent is what is aimed at, and, as a means of securing it, the law will not permit him to place himself in a position in which he may be tempted by his own private interests to disregard those of his principal. . . . It is not material that no actual injury to the company [principal] resulted, or that the policy recommended may have been for its best interest. Courts will not inquire into these matters. It is enough to know that the agent in fact placed himself in such relations that he might be tempted by his own interests to disregard those of his principal. The transaction was nothing more or less than the acceptance by the agent of a bribe to perform his duties in the manner desired by the person who gave the bribe. Such a contract is void. This doctrine rests on such plain principles of law, as well as common business honesty, that the citation of authorities is unnecessary."

The right to recover profits made by the agent in the course of the agency is not affected by the fact that the principal, upon discovering a fraud, has rescinded the contract and recovered that with which he parted. Restatement, Agency, § 407(2). Comment e on Subsection (2) reads: "If an agent has violated a duty of loyalty to the principal so that the principal is entitled to profits which the agent has thereby made, the fact that the principal has brought an action against a third person and has been made whole by such action does not prevent the principal from recovering from the agent the profits which the agent has made. Thus, if the other contracting party has given a bribe to the agent to make a contract with him on behalf of the principal, the principal can rescind the transaction, recovering from the other party anything received by him, or he can maintain an action for damages against him; in either event the principal may recover from the agent the amount of the bribe."

It follows that, insofar as the secret commission of $2,000 received by the agent is concerned, plaintiff had an absolute right thereto, irrespective of any recovery resulting from the action against the sellers for rescission.

2. Plaintiff's second cause of action is brought to recover damages for (1) losses suffered in the operation of the business prior to rescission; (2) loss of time devoted to operation; (3) expenses in connection with rescission of the sale and investigation therewith; (4) nontaxable expenses in connection with the prosecution of the suit against the sellers; and (5) attorneys' fees in connection with the suit.

The case comes to us on a bill of exceptions. No part of the testimony of the witnesses is included, so we must assume that the evidence establishes the items of damage claimed by plaintiff. Our inquiry is limited to a consideration of the question whether a principal may recover of an agent who has breached his trust the items of damage mentioned after a successful prosecution of an action for rescission against the third parties with whom the agent dealt for his principal.

The general rule is stated in Restatement, Agency, § 407(1), as follows: "If an agent has received a benefit as a result of violating his duty of loyalty, the principal is entitled to recover from him what he has so received, its value, or its proceeds, and also the amount of damage thereby caused, except that if the violation consists of the wrongful disposal of the principal's property, the principal cannot recover its value and also what the agent received in exchange therefor."

In Comment a on Subsection (1) we find the following: "... In either event, whether or not the principal elects to get back the thing improperly dealt with or to recover from the agent its value or the amount of benefit which the agent has improperly received, he is, in addition, entitled to be indemnified by the agent for any loss which has been caused to his interest by the improper transaction. Thus, if the purchasing agent for a restaurant purchases with the principal's money defective food, receiving a bonus therefor, and the use of the food in the restaurant damages the business, the principal can recover from the agent the amount of money improperly expended by him, the bonus which the agent received, and the amount which will compensate for the injury to the business."

The general rule with respect to damages for a tortious act is that "The wrong-doer is answerable for all the injurious consequences of his tortious act, which according to the usual course of events and the general experience were likely to ensue, and which, therefore, when the act was committed, he may reasonably be supposed to have foreseen and anticipated." 1 Sutherland, Damages (4 ed.) § 45, quoted with approval in Sargent v. Mason, 101 Minn. 319, 323, 112 N.W. 255, 257.

The general rule is given in Restatement, Torts, § 910, as follows: "A person injured by the tort of another is entitled to recover damages from him for all harm, past, present and prospective, legally caused by the tort."

Bergquist v. Kreidler, 158 Minn. 127, 196 N.W. 964, involved an action to recover attorneys' fees expended by plaintiffs in an action seeking to enforce and protect their right to the possession of real estate. Defendant, acting as the owner's agent, had falsely represented to plaintiffs that they could have possession on August 1, 1920. It developed after plaintiffs had purchased the premises that a tenant had a lease running to August 1, 1922, on a rental much lower than the actual value of the premises. Defendant (the agent) conceded that plaintiffs were entitled to recover the loss in rent, but contended that attorneys' fees and disbursements expended by plaintiffs in testing the validity of the tenant's lease were not recoverable. In affirming plaintiffs' right to recover we said, 158 Minn. at 132, 196 N.W. at 966: "... the litigation in which plaintiffs became involved was the direct, legitimate, and a to be expected result of appellant's misrepresentation. The loss sustained by plaintiffs in conducting that litigation 'is plainly traceable' to appellant's wrong and he should make compensation accordingly."

So far as the right to recover attorneys' fees is concerned, the same may be said in this case. Plaintiff sought to return what had been received and demanded a return of his down payment. The sellers refused. He thereupon sued to accomplish this purpose, as he had a right to do, and was successful. His attorneys' fees and expenses of suit were directly traceable to the harm caused by defendant's wrongful act. As such, they are recoverable.

. . . The general rule applicable here is stated in 15 Am.Jur., Damages, § 144, as follows: "It is generally held that where the wrongful act of the defendant has involved the plaintiff in litigation with others or placed him in such relation with others as makes it necessary to incur expense to protect his interest, such costs and expenses, including attorneys' fees, should be treated as the legal consequences of the original wrongful act and may be recovered as damages."

The same is true of the other elements of damage involved. See, generally, 15 Am.Jur., Damages, § 138. . . .

Affirmed.

RESTATEMENT (SECOND) OF AGENCY §§ 13, 387–396, 401, 403, 404, 407

[See Appendix]

READING v. ATTORNEY–GENERAL, [1951] App.Cas. 507 (H.L.). Reading was a sergeant in the Royal Army Medical Corps during World War II, stationed in Cairo. In 1943, an unidentified man asked Reading whether he would assist in selling cases of whisky and brandy in Cairo, for which he would be paid a few pounds. About a month later Reading was met by a man named Manole, who told Reading that a truck, which Reading was to board, would come at a specified time and place. Reading, dressed in uniform, boarded the truck and conducted it through Cairo. By arrangement he met Manole later on the same day, and received an envelope which contained £2,000. This process was repeated on a number of occasions. In all, Reading was paid around £20,000. The Crown (that is, the English Government) later seized these amounts, on the ground that they had been paid to Reading "for accompanying . . . a loaded lorry in and about Cairo whilst dressed in uniform and thereby falsely representing himself as acting in the course of his military duties ... in order to avoid police inspection of the said lorry." Reading brought suit to recover the seized amount. Justice Denning, at trial, dismissed Reading's complaint:

> In my judgment, it is a principle of law that if a servant, in violation of his duty of honesty and good faith, takes advantage of his service to make a profit for himself, in this sense, that the assets of which he has control, or the facilities which he enjoys, or the position which he occupies, are the real cause of his obtaining the money, as distinct from being the mere opportunity for getting it, that is to say, if they play the predominant part in his obtaining the money, then he is accountable for it to the master. It matters not that the master has not lost any profit, nor suffered any damage. Nor does it matter that the master could not have done the act himself. It is a case where the servant has unjustly enriched himself by virtue of his service without his master's sanction. It is money which the servant ought not to be allowed to keep, and the law says it shall be taken from him and given to his master, because he got it solely by reason of the position which he occupied as a servant of his master.... [Reading] ... was using his position as a sergeant in His Majesty's Army and the uniform to which his rank entitled him to obtain the money which he received. In my opinion any official position, whether marked by a uniform or not, which enables the holder to earn money by its use gives his master a right to receive the money so earned even though it was earned by a criminal act. "You have earned", the master can say, "money by the use of your position as my servant. It is not for you, who have gained this advantage, to set up your own wrong as a defence to my claim."

The House of Lords affirmed.

JENSEN & MECKLING, THEORY OF THE FIRM: MANAGERIAL BEHAVIOR, AGENCY COSTS AND OWNERSHIP STRUCTURE

3 J. Financial Economics 305, 308 (1976).

We define an agency relationship as a contract under which one or more persons (the principal(s)) engage another person (the agent) to perform some service on their behalf which involves delegating some decision making authority to the agent. If both parties to the relationship are utility maximizers there is good reason to believe that the agent will not always act in the best interests of the principal.   The *principal* can limit divergences from his interest by establishing appropriate incentives for the agent and by incurring monitoring costs designed to limit the aberrant activities of the agent.   In addition in some situations it will pay the *agent* to expend resources (bonding costs) to guarantee that he will not take certain actions which would harm the principal or to ensure that the principal will be compensated if he does take such actions.   However, it is generally impossible for the principal or the agent at zero cost to ensure that the agent will make optimal decisions from the principal's viewpoint.   In most agency relationships the principal and the agent will incur positive monitoring and bonding costs (non-pecuniary as well as pecuniary), and in addition there will be some divergence between the agent's decisions and those decisions which would maximize the welfare of the principal. The dollar equivalent of the reduction in welfare experienced by the principal due to this divergence is also a cost of the agency relationship, and we refer to this latter cost as the "residual loss". We define *agency costs* as the sum of:

(1) the monitoring expenditures by the principal,

(2) the bonding expenditures by the agent,

(3) the residual loss.

Chapter II

PARTNERSHIP

INTRODUCTORY NOTE

Although partnership had a rich history under the common law, it has long been governed by statute. Until recently, the relevant statute was the Uniform Partnership Act ("the UPA"), which was promulgated by the Commissioners on Uniform State Laws in 1914 and was adopted in every state except Louisiana.

In 1994, the Commissioners on Uniform State Laws adopted the Revised Uniform Partnership Act ("RUPA"), which is intended to supersede the UPA. As of early 1995, RUPA had been enacted in several states, and undoubtedly it will be enacted by additional states in the future. Under RUPA § 1006, RUPA normally applies not only to all partnerships formed after RUPA is adopted in any given state, but, after a transition period, to all partnerships, even those formed before RUPA was adopted.

Because RUPA is so new, because it has yet to be adopted in most states, and because RUPA continues many of the rules of the UPA, the cases and materials in this Section will largely concern the UPA. In general, however, where RUPA changes a relevant UPA rule the changes will be set out and discussed in a Note.

SECTION 1.   PARTNERSHIP FORMATION

UNIFORM PARTNERSHIP ACT §§ 6, 7

REVISED UNIFORM PARTNERSHIP ACT § 202

[See Appendix]

MARTIN v. PEYTON

New York Court of Appeals, 1927.
246 N.Y. 213, 158 N.E. 77.

Appeal from Supreme Court, Appellate Division, First Department.

Action by Charles S. Martin against William C. Peyton and others. A judgment of the Special Term, entered on the report of a referee in favor of the defendants was affirmed by the Appellate Division (219 App.Div. 297, 220 N.Y.S. 29), and plaintiff appeals. Affirmed.

ANDREWS, J. Much ancient learning as to partnership is obsolete. Today only those who are partners between themselves may be charged for partnership debts by others. (Partnership Law [Cons. Laws, ch. 39], sec. 11.) There is one exception. Now and then a recovery is allowed where in truth such relationship is absent. This is because the debtor may not deny the claim. (Sec. 27.)

Partnership results from contract, express or implied. If denied it may be proved by the production of some written instrument; by testimony as to some conversation; by circumstantial evidence. If nothing else appears the receipt by the defendant of a share of the profits of the business is enough. (Sec. 11.)

Assuming some written contract between the parties the question may arise whether it creates a partnership. If it be complete; if it expresses in good faith the full understanding and obligation of the parties, then it is for the court to say whether a partnership exists. It may, however, be a mere sham intended to hide the real relationship. Then other results follow. In passing upon it effect is to be given to each provision. Mere words will not blind us to realities. Statements that no partnership is intended are not conclusive. If as a whole a contract contemplates an association of two or more persons to carry on as co-owners a business for profit a partnership there is. (Sec. 10.) On the other hand, if it be less than this no partnership exists. Passing on the contract as a whole, an arrangement for sharing profits is to be considered. It is to be given its due weight. But it is to be weighed in connection with all the rest. It is not decisive. It may be merely the method adopted to pay a debt or wages, as interest on a loan or for other reasons.

An existing contract may be modified later by subsequent agreement, oral or written. A partnership may be so created where there was none before. And again, that the original agreement has been so modified may be proved by circumstantial evidence—by showing the conduct of the parties.

In the case before us the claim that the defendants became partners in the firm of Knauth, Nachod & Kuhne, doing business as bankers and brokers, depends upon the interpretation of certain instruments. There is nothing in their subsequent acts determinative of or indeed material upon this question. And we are relieved of questions that sometimes arise. "The plaintiff's position is not," we are told, "that the agreements of June 4, 1921, were a false expression or incomplete expression of the intention of the parties. We say that they express defendants' intention and that that intention was to create a relationship which as a matter of law constitutes a partnership." Nor may the claim of the plaintiff be rested on any question of estoppel. "The plaintiff's claim," he stipulates, "is a claim of actual partnership, not of partnership by estoppel...."

Remitted then, as we are, to the documents themselves, we refer to circumstances surrounding their execution only so far as is necessary to make them intelligible. And we are to remember that although the intention of the parties to avoid liability as partners is clear, although in language precise and definite they deny any design to then join the firm of K.N. & K.; although they say their interests in profits should be construed merely as a measure of compensation for loans, not an interest in profits as such; although they provide that they shall not be liable for any losses or treated as partners, the question still remains whether in fact they agree to so associate themselves with the firm as to "carry on as co-owners a business for profit."

In the spring of 1921 the firm of K.N. & K. found itself in financial difficulties. John R. Hall was one of the partners. He was a friend of Mr. Peyton. From him he obtained the loan of almost $500,000 of Liberty bonds, which K.N. & K. might use as collateral to secure bank advances. This, however, was not sufficient. The firm and its members had engaged in unwise speculations, and it was deeply involved. Mr. Hall was also intimately acquainted with George W. Perkins, Jr., and with Edward W. Freeman. He also knew Mrs. Peyton and Mrs. Perkins and Mrs. Freeman. All were anxious to help him. He, therefore, representing K.N. & K., entered into negotiations with them. While they were pending a proposition was made that Mr. Peyton, Mr. Perkins and Mr. Freeman or some of them should become partners. It met a decided refusal. Finally an agreement was reached. It is expressed in three documents, executed on the same day, all a part of the one transaction. They were drawn with care and are unambiguous. We shall refer to them as "the agreement," "the indenture" and "the option."

We have no doubt as to their general purpose. The respondents were to loan K.N. & K. $2,500,000 worth of liquid securities, which were to be returned to them on or before April 15, 1923. The firm might hypothecate them to secure loans totalling $2,000,-

000, using the proceeds as its business necessities required. To insure respondents against loss K.N. & K. were to turn over to them a large number of their own securities which may have been valuable, but which were of so speculative a nature that they could not be used as collateral for bank loans. In compensation for the loan the respondents were to receive 40 per cent of the profits of the firm until the return was made, not exceeding, however, $500,-000 and not less than $100,000. Merely because the transaction involved the transfer of securities and not of cash does not prevent its being a loan within the meaning of section 11. The respondents also were given an option to join the firm if they or any of them expressed a desire to do so before June 4, 1923.

Many other detailed agreements are contained in the papers. Are they such as may be properly inserted to protect the lenders? Or do they go further? Whatever their purpose, did they in truth associate the respondents with the firm so that they and it together thereafter carried on as co-owners a business for profit? The answer depends upon an analysis of these various provisions.

As representing the lenders, Mr. Peyton and Mr. Freeman are called "trustees." The loaned securities when used as collateral are not to be mingled with other securities of K.N. & K., and the trustees at all times are to be kept informed of all transactions affecting them. To them shall be paid all dividends and income accruing therefrom. They may also substitute for any of the securities loaned securities of equal value. With their consent the firm may sell any of its securities held by the respondents, the proceeds to go, however, to the trustees. In other similar ways the trustees may deal with these same securities, but the securities loaned shall always be sufficient in value to permit of their hypothecation for $2,000,000. If they rise in price the excess may be withdrawn by the defendants. If they fall they shall make good the deficiency.

So far there is no hint that the transaction is not a loan of securities with a provision for compensation. Later a somewhat closer connection with the firm appears. Until the securities are returned the directing management of the firm is to be in the hands of John R. Hall, and his life is to be insured for $1,000,000, and the policies are to be assigned as further collateral security to the trustees. These requirements are not unnatural. Hall was the one known and trusted by the defendants. Their acquaintance with the other members of the firm was of the slightest. These others had brought an old and established business to the verge of bankruptcy. As the respondents knew, they also had engaged in unsafe speculation. The respondents were about to loan $2,500,000 of good securities. As collateral they were to receive others of problematical value. What they required seems but ordinary caution. Nor does it imply an association in the business.

The trustees are to be kept advised as to the conduct of the business and consulted as to important matters. They may inspect the firm books and are entitled to any information they think important. Finally they may veto any business they think highly speculative or injurious. Again we hold this but a proper precaution to safeguard the loan. The trustees may not initiate any transaction as a partner may do. They may not bind the firm by any action of their own. Under the circumstances the safety of the loan depended upon the business success of K.N. & K. This success was likely to be compromised by the inclination of its members to engage in speculation. No longer, if the respondents were to be protected, should it be allowed. The trustees, therefore, might prohibit it, and that their prohibition might be effective, information was to be furnished them. Not dissimilar agreements have been held proper to guard the interests of the lender.

As further security each member of K.N. & K. is to assign to the trustees their interest in the firm. No loan by the firm to any member is permitted and the amount each may draw is fixed. No other distribution of profits is to be made. So that realized profits may be calculated the existing capital is stated to be $700,000, and profits are to be realized as promptly as good business practice will permit. In case the trustees think this is not done, the question is left to them and to Mr. Hall, and if they differ then to an arbitrator. There is no obligation that the firm shall continue the business. It may dissolve at any time. Again we conclude there is nothing here not properly adapted to secure the interest of the respondents as lenders. If their compensation is dependent on a percentage of the profits still provision must be made to define what these profits shall be.

The "indenture" is substantially a mortgage of the collateral delivered by K.N. & K. to the trustees to secure the performance of the "agreement." It certainly does not strengthen the claim that the respondents were partners.

Finally we have the "option." It permits the respondents or any of them or their assignees or nominees to enter the firm at a later date if they desire to do so by buying 50 per cent or less of the interests therein of all or any of the members at a stated price. Or a corporation may, if the respondents and the members agree, be formed in place of the firm. Meanwhile, apparently with the design of protecting the firm business against improper or ill-judged action which might render the option valueless, each member of the firm is to place his resignation in the hands of Mr. Hall. If at any time he and the trustees agree that such resignation should be accepted, that member shall then retire, receiving the value of his interest calculated as of the date of such retirement.

This last provision is somewhat unusual, yet it is not enough in itself to show that on June 4, 1921, a present partnership was created nor taking these various papers as a whole do we reach such a result.   It is quite true that even if one or two or three like provisions contained in such a contract do not require this conclusion, yet it is also true that when taken together a point may come where stipulations immaterial separately cover so wide a field that we should hold a partnership exists.   As in other branches of the law a question of degree is often the determining factor.   Here that point has not been reached. . . .

The judgment appealed from should be affirmed, with costs.

CARDOZO, Ch. J., POUND, CRANE, LEHMAN, KELLOGG and O'BRIEN, JJ., concur.

Judgment affirmed, etc.

LUPIEN v. MALSBENDEN

Supreme Judicial Court of Maine, 1984.
477 A.2d 746.

Before McKUSICK, C.J., and NICHOLS, ROBERTS, WATHEN, GLASSMAN and SCOLNIK, JJ.

McKUSICK, Chief Justice.

Defendant Frederick Malsbenden appeals a judgment of the Superior Court (York County) holding him to partnership liability on a written contract entered into between plaintiff Robert Lupien and one Stephen Cragin doing business as York Motor Mart.[1]   The sole issue asserted on appeal is whether the Superior Court erred in its finding that Malsbenden and Cragin were partners in the pertinent part of York Motor Mart's business.   We affirm.

On March 5, 1980, plaintiff entered into a written agreement with Stephen Cragin, doing business in the town of York as York Motor Mart, for the construction of a Bradley automobile.[2]   Plaintiff made a deposit of $500 towards the purchase price of $8,020 upon signing the contract, and made a further payment of $3,950 one week later on March 12.   Both the purchase order of March 5, 1980, and a later bill of sale, though signed by Cragin, identified the seller as York Motor Mart.   At the jury-waived trial, plaintiff testified

---

1. Cragin "disappeared" several months before this action was commenced.   Plaintiff Lupien originally named Cragin as a co-defendant.   However, since Cragin was never served with process, the Superior Court at the behest of both Lupien and defendant Malsbenden dismissed the claim against Cragin.

2. A Bradley automobile is a "kit car" constructed on a Volkswagen chassis.

that after he signed the contract he made visits to York Motor Mart on an average of once or twice a week to check on the progress being made on his car. During those visits plaintiff generally dealt with Malsbenden because Cragin was seldom present. On one such visit in April, Malsbenden told plaintiff that it was necessary for the latter to sign over ownership of his pickup truck, which would constitute the balance of the consideration under the contract, so that the proceeds from the sale of the truck could be used to complete construction of the Bradley. When plaintiff complied, Malsbenden provided plaintiff with a rental car, and later with a "demo" model of the Bradley, for his use pending the completion of the vehicle he had ordered. When it was discovered that the "demo" actually belonged to a third party who had entrusted it to York Motor Mart for resale, Malsbenden purchased the vehicle for plaintiff's use. Plaintiff never received the Bradley he had contracted to purchase.

In his trial testimony, defendant Malsbenden asserted that his interest in the Bradley operation of York Motor Mart was only that of a banker. He stated that he had loaned $85,000 to Cragin, without interest, to finance the Bradley portion of York Motor Mart's business.[3] The loan was to be repaid from the proceeds of each car sold. Malsbenden acknowledged that Bradley kits were purchased with his personal checks and that he had also purchased equipment for York Motor Mart. He also stated that after Cragin disappeared sometime late in May 1980, he had physical control of the premises of York Motor Mart and that he continued to dispose of assets there even to the time of trial in 1983.

The Uniform Partnership Act, adopted in Maine at 31 M.R.S.A. §§ 281–323 (1978 & Supp.1983–1984), defines a partnership as "an association of 2 or more persons ... to carry on as co-owners[4] a business for profit." 31 M.R.S.A. § 286 (1978). Whether a partnership exists is an inference of law based on established facts. *See Dalton v. Austin*, 432 A.2d 774, 777 (Me.1981); *Roux v. Lawand*, 131 Me. 215, 219, 160 A. 756, 757 (1932); *James Bailey Co. v. Darling*, 119 Me. 326, 328, 111 A. 410, 411 (1920). A finding that the relationship between two persons constitutes a partnership may be based upon evidence of an agreement, either express or implied,

to place their money, effects, labor, and skill, or some or all of them, in lawful commerce or business with the understanding

---

3. Malsbenden's testimony indicated that Cragin carried on an automotive repair business at the York Motor Mart that was unrelated to the Bradley operation. Malsbenden testified, without contradiction, that he had no involvement with that other business.

4. As we made clear in *Dalton v. Austin*, 432 A.2d 774, 777 (Me.1981), the term "co-owners" as used in the statute does not necessarily mean joint title to all assets. On the contrary, "the right to participate in control of the business is the essence of co-ownership." *Id.*

that a community of profits will be shared. . . . No one factor is alone determinative of the existence of a partnership. . . . *Dalton v. Austin,* 432 A.2d at 777; *Cumberland County Power & Light Co. v. Gordon,* 136 Me. 213, 218, 7 A.2d 619, 622 (1939). *See James Bailey Co. v. Darling,* 119 Me. at 328, 111 A. at 411. If the arrangement between the parties otherwise qualifies as a partnership, it is of no matter that the parties did not expressly agree to form a partnership or did not even intend to form one:

> It is possible for parties to intend no partnership and yet to form one. If they agree upon an arrangement which is a partnership in fact, it is of no importance that they call it something else, or that they even expressly declare that they are not to be partners. The law must declare what is the legal import of their agreements, and names go for nothing when the substance of the arrangement shows them to be inapplicable.

James Bailey Co. v. Darling, 119 Me. at 328, 111 A. at 411 (quoting *Beecher v. Bush,* 45 Mich. 188, 193–94, 7 N.W. 785, 785–86 (1881)).

Here the trial justice concluded that, notwithstanding Malsbenden's assertion that he was only a "banker," his "total involvement" in the Bradley operation was that of a partner. The testimony at trial, both respecting Malsbenden's financial interest in the enterprise and his involvement in day-to-day business operations, amply supported the Superior Court's conclusion. Malsbenden had a financial interest of $85,000 in the Bradley portion of York Motor Mart's operations. Although Malsbenden termed the investment a loan, significantly he conceded that the "loan" carried no interest. His "loan" was not made in the form of a fixed payment or payments, but was made to the business, at least in substantial part, in the form of day-to-day purchases of Bradley kits, other parts and equipment, and in the payment of wages. Furthermore, the "loan" was not to be repaid in fixed amounts or at fixed times, but rather only upon the sale of Bradley automobiles.

The evidence also showed that, unlike a banker, Malsbenden had the right to participate in control of the business and in fact did so on a day-to-day basis.[5] According to Urbin Savaria, who worked at York Motor Mart from late April through June 1980, Malsbenden during that time opened the business establishment each morning, remained present through part of every day, had final say on the ordering of parts, paid for parts and equipment, and paid Savaria's salary. On plaintiff's frequent visits to York Motor Mart, he generally dealt with Malsbenden because Cragin was not present. It was

---

5. Thus its facts clearly distinguish the case at bar from *James Bailey Co. v. Darling,* 119 Me. 326, 332, 111 A. 410, 413 (1920), where although the defendant advanced money for the purchase of automobiles that was to be repaid upon the sale of individual automobiles, the defendant had no control over the business.

Malsbenden who insisted that plaintiff trade in his truck prior to the completion of the Bradley because the proceeds from the sale of the truck were needed to complete the Bradley. When it was discovered that the "demo" Bradley given to plaintiff while he awaited completion of his car actually belonged to a third party, it was Malsbenden who bought the car for plaintiff's use. As of three years after the making of the contract now in litigation, Malsbenden was still doing business at York Motor Mart, "just disposing of property."

Malsbenden and Cragin may well have viewed their relationship to be that of creditor-borrower, rather than a partnership. At trial Malsbenden so asserts, and Cragin's departure from the scene in the spring of 1980 deprives us of the benefit of his view of his business arrangement with Malsbenden. In any event, whatever the intent of these two men as to their respective involvements in the business of making and selling Bradley cars, there is no clear error in the Superior Court's finding that the Bradley car operation represented a pooling of Malsbenden's capital and Cragin's automotive skills, with joint control over the business and intent to share the fruits of the enterprise. As a matter of law, that arrangement amounted to a partnership under 31 M.R.S.A. § 286.

The entry is:

Judgment affirmed.

All concurring.

NOTE ON THE FORMATION OF PARTNERSHIPS

1. Corporations and limited partnerships can be organized (formed) only if certain formalities are complied with and certain filings are made. In contrast, general partnerships can be organized with no formalities and no filings. The absence of a filing requirement reflects in part a conception that partnership status depends on the factual characteristics of a relationship between two or more persons, not on whether the persons think of themselves as having entered into a partnership.

Although no filings are *required* under either the UPA or RUPA, RUPA *permits* certain filings. See, e.g., Note on the Authority of Partners Under RUPA, p. 60, infra.

2. The Comment to RUPA § 105 states that "partnerships [are] ... the default form of business organizations." See also RUPA § 202, Comment. This is a serious misconception. Most business organizations are formal organizations, such as corpora-

tions, general partnerships, limited partnerships, and limited liability companies. However, many less formal relationships are also business organizations. For example, a sole proprietorship that employs 1,000 persons is certainly a business organization, in which the relevant body of organizational law is the law of agency. Indeed, every commercial principal-agent relationship is a type of business organization, however rudimentary. Therefore, partnership is not a default form, but a legal characterization of those business organizations that satisfy the definition of partnership stated in UPA § 6(a) or RUPA § 202.

Another common misconception about partnership law is that a business organization that satisfies the statutory definition of partnership, although the parties do not conceptualize their relationship as a partnership, is an "inadvertent" partnership. This is a misconception because private actors often don't know the law, and focus on the characteristics of their relationship rather than on the legal name of their relationship. Partnership is a legal characterization of a certain type of private relationship. To say that persons who have voluntarily organized their relationship in a way that the law characterizes as a partnership have formed an "inadvertent" partnership is like saying that parties who make a bargain, but don't know the law of contracts, have formed an "inadvertent contract."

3. It is sometimes said that where there is no express partnership agreement among the parties, a relationship will be considered a partnership only if four elements are present—an agreement to share profits, an agreement to share losses, a mutual right of control or management of the business, and a community of interest in the venture. See, e.g., Weingart v. C & W Taylor Partnership, 248 Mont. 76, 809 P.2d 576 (1991); Corpus Christi v. Bayfront Associates, Ltd., 814 S.W.2d 98 (Tex.App.1991). This four-element test departs from the statutory test of both UPA § 6(a) and RUPA § 202, which provide only that, with certain exceptions, a partnership is "an association of two or more persons to carry on as co-owners a business for profit," and say nothing about control or loss-sharing. Although the Comments to both Sections say that "to state that partners are co-owners of a business is to state that they each have the power of ultimate control," in fact even explicit partnership agreements frequently do not involve either mutual control or loss-sharing. For example, many partnership agreements vest all control in one or more managing partners, or create elaborate allocations of voting power in which some partners do not share. Similarly, not every partnership agreement provides for loss sharing by every partner.

If explicit partnership agreements do not always include mutual control and loss-sharing as elements of the partnership relation, why should courts require those elements as a condition to finding an implicit partnership? A better approach is that the presence or absence of the four specified elements, including mutual control and loss-sharing, is evidence, but not a requirement, of a partnership relation. This approach was taken, for example, in Beckman v. Farmer, 579 A.2d 618, 627 (D.C.App.1990), where the court said that "[t]he customary attributes of partnership, such as loss sharing and joint control of decisionmaking are necessary guideposts of inquiry, but none is conclusive." Other cases have held that if profit-sharing is established, it is not essential to show that there was an agreement to share in the losses. See Hansford v. Maplewood Station Business Park, 621 N.E.2d 347 (Ind.App.1993); Endsley v. Game-Show Placements, Ltd., 401 N.E.2d 768 (Ind.App.1980)

SECTION 2. THE LEGAL NATURE OF A PARTNERSHIP

UNIFORM PARTNERSHIP ACT § 6

REVISED UNIFORM PARTNERSHIP ACT §§ 101(4), 201

[See Appendix]

NOTE ON THE LEGAL NATURE OF A PARTNERSHIP: ENTITY OR AGGREGATE STATUS

1.   Individuals may associate in a wide variety of forms, and the issue often arises whether a given form of association has a legal status separate from that of its members. Frequently, this issue is stated in terms of whether or not a form of association is a "separate entity" or a "legal person" (as opposed to a natural person, that is, an individual). A variety of issues may turn on the answer to this question—for example, whether the association can sue and be sued in its own name, and whether it can hold property in its own right.

In the history of English and American law this issue arose in the context of many different kinds of associations, such as universities, charitable institutions, and even municipalities. In most cases the issue was eventually resolved in a straightforward way, but in the case of partnerships it continued to be vexing. The predominant although not exclusive view under the common law was that a partnership was not an entity, but merely an aggregate of its members, so that a partnership was no more a legal person than was a friendship.

In 1902, when the Conference of Commissioners on Uniform State Laws determined to promulgate a Uniform Partnership Act, Dean James Barr Ames of Harvard Law School was appointed to draft the Act. Subsequently, the Commissioners instructed Dean Ames, at his own urging, to draft the Act on the theory that a partnership is a legal entity. Accordingly, in the drafts submitted by Dean Ames a partnership was defined as "a legal person formed by the association of two or more individuals for the purpose of carrying on business with a view to profit," and various provisions of the drafts reflected the entity theory. Dean Ames died before the work was completed, however, and his successor, Dean William Draper Lewis of the University of Pennsylvania Law School, was distinctly unfriendly to the entity view. Ultimately, Dean Lewis convinced the Commissioners to instruct him to draft the Act on the aggregate theory. UPA Section 6 therefore provides that "A partnership is an association of two or more persons to carry on as co-owners a business for profit." Although the language of this provision does not in itself render the issue free from doubt, it is clear that the Act was intended to adopt the aggregate theory.

That is not, however, the end of the story. Having adopted the aggregate theory, the UPA nevertheless deals with a number of issues *as if* the partnership were an entity. This may seem to be a pragmatic solution, and for many purposes the UPA does work pretty well. On the whole, however, the use of an aggregate theory in the UPA was unfortunate. Generally speaking, the entity theory of a partnership is much more functional than the aggregate theory. In those cases where the UPA does not treat the partnership as if it were an entity, the result tends to be bad, and in need of legislative revision. In those cases where the UPA does treat the partnership as if it were an entity, the result is good, but the statutory approach is often made needlessly complex by the mechanics of reconciling the entity result with the aggregate theory.[1]

2. The question often arises whether a partnership is to be treated as an aggregate or an entity for the purpose of some statute other than the UPA. This question is a matter of legislative intent

---

1. On the common law background and the statutory history of the entity/aggregate debate, see Commissioners' Prefatory Note to the Uniform Partnership Act, 6 Uniform Laws Ann. 5 (1969); Lewis, The Uniform Partnership Act, 24 Yale L.J. 617 (1915); Crane, The Uniform Partnership Act—A Criticism, 28 Harv.L.Rev. 762 (1915); Crane, The Uniform Partnership Act and Legal Persons, 29 Harv.L.Rev. 838 (1916); Jensen, Is a Partnership Under the Uniform Partnership Act an Aggregate or an Entity?, 16 Vand.L.Rev. 377 (1963).

under the particular statute. As in all such matters, the answer will depend on the language employed and the purposes manifested in the statute at hand. The fact that the UPA adopted the aggregate theory will be relevant, but not dispositive, in answering that question. A legislature may choose to treat a partnership as an entity for purposes of another statute even though a partnership is defined as an association under the U.P.A. See, e.g., United States v. A & P Trucking Co., 358 U.S. 121, 79 S.Ct. 203, 3 L.Ed.2d 165 (1958).

3. In contrast to the UPA, RUPA confers entity status on partnerships. RUPA § 101 (Definitions) defines a partnership as "an association of two or more persons to carry on as co-owners a business for profit." RUPA § 201 then squarely provides that "A partnership is an entity." The Comment to § 201 adds:

> Giving clear expression to the entity nature of a partnership is intended to allay previous concerns stemming from the aggregate theory, such as the necessity of a deed to convey title from the "old" partnership to the "new" partnership every time there is a change of cast among the partners. Under RUPA, there is no "new" partnership just because of membership changes. That will avoid the result in cases such as *Fairway Development Co. v. Title Insurance Co.*, 621 F.Supp. 120 (N.D.Ohio 1985), which held that the "new" partnership resulting from a partner's death did not have standing to enforce a title insurance policy issued to the "old" partnership.

The use of the term "association" in § 101 might lead to some confusion, because it may seem to suggest non-entity status. However, a distinction must be drawn between an "association" and an "aggregation." Any form of business that involves two or more owners can be deemed an association of owners. The question whether the law should treat any given kind of association of owners as an entity with a legal identity separate from its owners, or as an aggregation with no separate legal identity, is a policy issue, or perhaps more accurately, a series of policy issues.

The UPA withheld entity status from partnerships, but then created complex rules to arrive at entity-like results. RUPA, by conferring entity status on partnerships, is able to drastically simplify many partnership rules, such as those dealing with partnership property and partnership litigation. Nevertheless, entity status does not inherently resolve every issue to which it is relevant. Just as the drafters of the UPA, having denied entity status to partnerships, remained free to (and did) craft rules to reach entity-like results in certain areas, so the drafters of RUPA, having conferred entity status on partnerships, remained free to (and did) craft rules to reach aggregation-like results in certain areas.

To put this differently, no result on any specific partnership-law issue can be "derived" or follows "logically" or "by necessity" from a partnership's entity status under RUPA, any more than any result on any specific issue can be derived, or follows "logically" or "by necessity" from the UPA's denial of that status. Having declared that a partnership is an entity, the drafters of RUPA still had to make policy choices on such issues as whether the partnership could hold property, could sue and be sued in its own name, and so forth. It is true that generally speaking the best rule in many of these areas is one that is consistent with entity status, but it is important not to forget that an independent policy choice must still be made on each issue. The adoption of entity status for partnerships at most simplified the drafting of RUPA and gave a slight push toward certain results.

Thus in one or two areas RUPA itself reaches an aggregate-like result. Most notably, under RUPA, as under the UPA, a partner is individually liable for partnership debts. Although individual liability is consistent with entity status, it is usually associated with an aggregate conception. Similarly, under RUPA § 404(b) a partner has a duty of loyalty and care not only to the partnership but to the other partners, and under RUPA § 404(d) a partner's duty of good faith and fair dealing extends both to the partnership and to the other partners.

———

SECTION 3. THE ONGOING OPERATION OF PARTNERSHIPS

———

(a) MANAGEMENT

———

UNIFORM PARTNERSHIP ACT §§ 18(a), (e), (g), (h), 19, 20

REVISED UNIFORM PARTNERSHIP ACT §§ 401(f), (i), (j), 403

[See Appendix]

———

SUMMERS v. DOOLEY

Supreme Court of Idaho, 1971.
94 Idaho 87, 481 P.2d 318.

DONALDSON, Justice.

This lawsuit, tried in the district court, involves a claim by one partner against the other for $6,000. The complaining partner asserts that he has been required to pay out more than $11,000 in expenses without any reimbursement from either the partnership funds or his partner. The expenditure in question was incurred by the complaining partner (John Summers, plaintiff-appellant) for the purpose of hiring an additional employee. The trial court denied him any relief except for ordering that he be entitled to one half $966.72 which it found to be a legitimate partnership expense.

The pertinent facts leading to this lawsuit are as follows. Summers entered a partnership agreement with Dooley (defendant-respondent) in 1958 for the purpose of operating a trash collection business. The business was operated by the two men and when either was unable to work, the non-working partner provided a replacement at his own expense. In 1962, Dooley became unable to work and, at his own expense, hired an employee to take his place. In July, 1966, Summers approached his partner Dooley regarding the hiring of an additional employee but Dooley refused. Nevertheless, on his own initiative, Summers hired the man and paid him out of his own pocket. Dooley, upon discovering that Summers had hired an additional man, objected, stating that he did not feel additional labor was necessary and refused to pay for the new employee out of the partnership funds. Summers continued to operate the business using the third man and in October of 1967 instituted suit in the district court for $6,000 against his partner, the gravamen of the complaint being that Summers has been required to pay out more than $11,000 in expenses, incurred in the hiring of the additional man, without any reimbursement from either the partnership funds or his partner. After trial before the court, sitting without a jury, Summers was granted only partial relief[1] and he has appealed. He urges in essence that the trial court erred by failing to conclude that he should be reimbursed for expenses and costs connected in the employment of extra help in the partnership business.

The principal thrust of appellant's contention is that in spite of the fact that one of the two partners refused to consent to the hiring

---

1. The trial court did award Summers one half of $966.72 which it found to be a legitimate partnership expense.

of additional help, nonetheless, the non-consenting partner retained profits earned by the labors of the third man and therefore the non-consenting partner should be estopped from denying the need and value of the employee, and has by his behavior ratified the act of the other partner who hired the additional man.

The issue presented for decision by this appeal is whether an equal partner in a two man partnership has the authority to hire a new employee in disregard of the objection of the other partner and then attempt to charge the dissenting partner with the costs incurred as a result of his unilateral decision.

The State of Idaho has enacted specific statutes with respect to the legal concept known as "partnership." Therefore any solution of partnership problems should logically begin with an application of the relevant code provision.

In the instant case the record indicates that although Summers requested his partner Dooley to agree to the hiring of a third man, such requests were not honored. In fact Dooley made it clear that he was "voting no" with regard to the hiring of an additional employee.

An application of the relevant statutory provisions and pertinent case law to the factual situation presented by the instant case indicates that the trial court was correct in its disposal of the issue since a majority of the partners did not consent to the hiring of the third man. I.C. § 53–318(8) provides:

"Any difference arising as to ordinary matters connected with the partnership business may be decided by a *majority of the partners....*" (emphasis supplied)

It is the opinion of this Court that the preceding statute is of a mandatory rather than permissive nature. This conclusion is based upon the following reasoning. Whether a statute is mandatory or directory does not depend upon its form, but upon the intention of the legislature, to be ascertained from a consideration of the entire act, its nature, its object, and the consequences that would result from construing it one way or the other. In re McQuiston's Adoption, 238 Pa. 304, 86 A. 205 (1913).

The intent of the legislature may be implied from the language used, or inferred on grounds of policy or reasonableness. See Barnett v. Prairie Oil & Gas Co. et al., 19 F.2d 504 (8th Cir.1927); Motorcoach Operators Ass'n v. Board of Street Railway Commissioners of the City of Detroit, 267 Mich. 568, 255 N.W. 391 (1934); 3 Sutherland, Statutory Construction, § 5803, p. 79. A careful reading of the statutory provision indicates that subsection 5 bestows *equal rights in the management and conduct of the partnership business* upon all of the partners. The concept of equality between partners with respect to management of business affairs is a central theme and recurs throughout the Uniform Partnership law, I.C. § 53–301 et seq., which has been enacted in this jurisdiction. Thus the only reasonable interpretation of I.C. § 53–318(8) is that business differences must be decided by a majority of the partners provided no other agreement between the partners speaks to the issues.

A noted scholar has dealt precisely with the issue to be decided.

"... if the partners are equally divided, those who forbid a change must have their way." Walter B. Lindley, A Treatise on the Law of Partnership, Ch. II, § III, ¶ 24–8, p. 403 (1924). See also, W. Shumaker, A Treatise on the Law of Partnership, § 97, p. 266.

See also, Clark et al. v. Slate Valley R. Co., 136 Pa. 408, 20 A. 562 (1890) for a discussion of this rule.

In the case at bar one of the partners continually voiced objection to the hiring of the third man. He did not sit idly by and acquiesce in the actions of his partner. Under these circumstances it is manifestly unjust to permit recovery of an expense which was incurred individually and not for the benefit of the partnership but rather for the benefit of one partner.

Judgment affirmed. Costs to respondent.

McQUADE, C.J., and McFADDEN, SHEPARD and SPEAR, JJ., concur.

QUESTION

Suppose that A, B, and C form a partnership. A contributes 90% of the capital, and by agreement is entitled to 90% of any profits and is responsible for 90% of any losses. B and C each contribute 5% of the capital and by agreement are each entitled to 5% of any profits and are responsible for 5% of any losses. Nothing is said in the agreement concerning how decisions will be made. If, on an ordinary matter connected with the partnership, A votes one way, and B and C another, who prevails?

NOTE ON THE MANAGEMENT OF PARTNERSHIPS

1. The cases and authorities are divided on the issue raised in Summers v. Dooley. In accord with *Summers* is Covalt v. High, 100

N.M. 700, 675 P.2d 999 (App.1983). But see National Biscuit Co. v. Stroud, 249 N.C. 467, 106 S.E.2d 692 (1959), noted, 1960 Duke L.J. 150 (where one of two partners transacts with a third party on a matter that is otherwise within the ordinary business of the partnership, the other partner is liable even though he had put the third party on notice that the partners were divided on the matter).

2. The rule of UPA Section 18(h), that any difference arising as to ordinary matters connected with the partnership business may be decided by a majority of the partners, is "subject to any agreement between them." Partnership agreements often contain provisions vesting management in a managing partner, a managing committee, "senior partners," or some other group composed of less than all the partners, and such agreements override Section 18(h). The same result may be reached even without explicit agreement, for example on the basis of a course of conduct:

> [I]t is ... well settled, as we think the Oklahoma Uniform Partnership Act recognizes, that partners may agree that, as among themselves, one or more of them shall have exclusive control over the management of the partnership business, and that an agreement for exclusive control of the management of the business by one partner may be implied from the course of conduct of the parties. Here, it was fairly [inferable] from the course of conduct of Parks and Patterson that there was an implied agreement that Parks should be the managing partner.

Parks v. Riverside Ins. Co. of Am., 308 F.2d 175, 180 (10th Cir. 1962). Such an implied agreement, if found, would pretty clearly block the nonmanaging partners from objecting to a decision of the managing partners relating to ordinary matters connected with the partnership business, solely on the ground that the decision was not arrived at by a majority vote. Cf. Hillman, The Dissatisfied Participant in the Solvent Business Venture: A Consideration of the Relative Permanence of Partnerships and Close Corporations, 67 Minn.L.Rev. 1, 18 (1982): "One of the more ironic features of the U.P.A. is that while it shows great deference to an agreement among the partners it at no time defines what it means by 'agreement.' Naturally, the ideal situation is one in which the parties, with the assistance of legal counsel, have developed a comprehensive written document embodying the series of agreements which will govern their relationship. Between the comprehensive written agreement and the unplanned partnership governed by U.P.A. rules lie a variety of relations among partners based to some degree on unwritten understandings."

3. Because UPA Section 18(h) provides that partnership action requires a majority vote, what is added by UPA Section 18(e), which provides that all partners have equal rights in the management and

conduct of the partnership business? Presumably, the effect of this Section is to require that, absent contrary agreement, every partner be provided on an ongoing basis with information concerning the partnership business and be consulted in partnership decisions. See Hillman, Power Shared and Power Denied: A Look at Participatory Rights in the Management of General Partnerships, 1984 U.Ill. L.Rev. 865 (1984); E. Scamell & R. Banks, Lindley on the Law of Partnership, 427 (14th ed. 1979).

> For a majority of partners to say; We do not care what one partner may say, we, being the majority, will do what we please, is, I apprehend what this Court will not allow. So, again, with respect to making Mr. *Robertson* the treasurer, Mr. *Const* had a right to be consulted; his opinion might be overruled, and honestly over-ruled, but he ought to have had the question put to him and discussed: In all partnerships . . . the partners are bound to be true and faithful to each other: They are to act upon the joint opinion of all, and the discretion and judgment of anyone cannot be excluded: What weight is to be given to it is another question. . . .

Const v. Harris, 37 Eng.Rep. 1191, 1202 (Ch.1824) (Lord Chancellor Eldon). Thus a majority of partners who made decisions without consulting a minority partner would violate § 18(e), absent contrary agreement.

4. RUPA § 401(f) continues the rule of UPA § 18(e), conferring on each partner the right to participate in management. The Comment to § 401(f) notes that UPA § 18(e) "has been interpreted broadly to mean that, absent contrary agreement, each partner has a continuing right to participate in the management of the partnership and to be informed about the partnership business, even if his assent . . . is not required."

RUPA § 401(j) generally follows the voting rules of UPA § 18(h), although there are several differences between the sections. Under UPA § 18(h):

> Any difference arising as to ordinary matters connected with the partnership business may be decided by a majority of the partners; but no act in contravention of any agreement between the partners may be done rightfully without the consent of all the partners.

Under RUPA § 401(j):

> A difference arising as to a matter in the ordinary course of business of a partnership may be decided by a majority of the partners. An act outside the ordinary course of business of a partnership and an amendment to the partnership agreement may be undertaken only with the consent of all of the partners.

RUPA § 401(j) must be read in conjunction with RUPA § 101(5), which defines the term "partnership agreement" to mean "the agreement, written or oral, among the partners concerning the partnership." The Comment to § 101(5) adds:

> The definition of "partnership agreement".... is intended to include any agreement among the partners ... concerning either the affairs of the partnership or the conduct of its business.... [T]he agreement may be inferred from the conduct of the parties.

In many partnerships, there is no single document—or no document at all—called a "Partnership Agreement," either because the partnership is itself implicit rather than explicit, or because the partners lack either the inclination or the funds to make a formal agreement. In such cases, under RUPA § 101(5) the "partnership agreement" consists of the fragmentary explicit and implicit agreements that are made from time to time as the partnership relation evolves. Furthermore, even when a partnership does have an explicit and formal "Partnership Agreement," under RUPA § 401(j) unanimity is required not only to depart from this formal agreement, but to depart from any further fragmentary agreement or course of conduct that gives rise to an implied agreement. Thus changes in the way the partnership is actually conducted, not just changes in the way in which it has been explicitly agreed that the partnership will be conducted, may constitute amendments of the partnership agreement for purposes of § 401(j).

Although the term "amendment" in RUPA § 401(j) is not well chosen, it presumably includes acts in violation of the partnership agreement as well as changes in the agreement.

––––––

NOTE ON WHAT LAW GOVERNS THE INTERNAL AFFAIRS OF PARTNERSHIPS

Legal rules concerning business associations—such as corporations, limited partnerships, and general partnerships—fall into two general categories: (i) rules dealing with the powers, rights, and duties of the owners, managers, agents, and organs of the association as among themselves; and (ii) rules dealing with the powers, rights, and duties of the owners, managers, organs, and agents of the association, and of the association itself, as to third persons. The rules in the first category are often collectively referred to as the rules that govern an association's internal affairs.

Often, the laws of two or more different states might in theory be applied to determine what rules govern an association's internal affairs. In such cases, the body of law known as conflict of laws or choice of law determines which state's law governs. In the case of corporations and limited partnerships, which are formed by filing organizational documents in a given state, the general choice-of-law rule is that internal affairs are governed by the state in which the corporation is incorporated or the limited partnership is organized. In contrast, the formation of a general partnership does not require the filing of organizational documents. Accordingly, the choice-of-law rule to determine what law governs the internal affairs of general partnerships must depend on other factors. The UPA does not include any provision governing the choice of law for the internal affairs of a general partnership. However, RUPA § 106 provides that a general partnership's internal affairs are governed by the law of the state in which the partnership has its chief executive office.

(b) DISTRIBUTIONS, REMUNERATION, INDEMNIFICATION, AND CONTRIBUTION

UNIFORM PARTNERSHIP ACT §§ 18(b), (c), (d), (f)

REVISED UNIFORM PARTNERSHIP ACT § 401(a)–(e), (h)

[See Appendix]

QUESTION

Suppose A, B, and C form a partnership. A contributes 90% of the capital, and B and C each contribute 5%. All work full-time in the partnership business, with roughly equal responsibilities. Nothing is said in the partnership agreement concerning how partnership profits will be divided. If the partnership makes a profit in a given year, how is it to be divided?

NOTE ON "SERVICES PARTNERS"

1. UPA § 18(f) provides that unless otherwise agreed, no partner is entitled to remuneration for services for acting in an ongoing partnership business. Where one partner is to contribute only capital and another only services, this rule, if literally applied, can yield results that the partners probably would not have agreed to if they had addressed the issue at the time of partnership formation.

For example, UPA § 40(b) sets out the rules for distribution after a partnership is dissolved. The first priority, not surprisingly, is to pay off creditors other than partners. The second priority is to pay off partners for obligations other than capital or profits (for example, where a partner has made an advance to the partnership). The third priority is to pay off partners in respect of capital. The fourth priority is to pay off partners in respect of profits. All of these priorities, even those in respect of partnership capital and profits, are defined as "liabilities"—an unusual meaning of that term, which usually refers to debts, not to ownership or equity claims.

Suppose C and S form Partnership P. By agreement, C contributes $100,000 capital but will not be actively engaged in running the business, while S contributes no capital and will spend his full time running the business. Profits are to be shared 50–50, but nothing is said about sharing losses. S performs services of a value of $100,000, which augment the value of P's assets by that amount. After three years, the partnership is dissolved. During these three years, no distribution had been made to either partner. On dissolution, the partnership's assets are worth $200,000 and the partnership owes $100,000 to creditors. C's capital account remains $100,000. If the value of S's services do not augment S's capital account, on liquidation the creditors will get $100,000, C will get $100,000, and S will get nothing, although if not for S's services the assets would have been worth only $100,000, which would all have gone to the creditors.

Where the value of P's assets directly reflects the value of S's services, this result seems inappropriate. In Schymanski v. Conventz, 674 P.2d 281, 284 (Alaska 1983), the court said, in such a case, that although "[t]he general rule is that, in the absence of an agreement to such effect, a partner contributing only personal services is ordinarily *not* entitled to any share of partnership capital pursuant to dissolution," nevertheless "[p]ersonal services may qualify as capital contributions to a partnership where an express or implied agreement to such effect exists." (Emphasis in original.) This exception makes it easy for a court to get around the general rule, by finding an implied agreement when necessary to avoid a particularly unfair result. See also Parker v. Northern Mixing Co., 756 P.2d 881 (Alaska 1988).

Similarly, in Thompson v. Beth, 14 Wis.2d 271, 111 N.W.2d 171, 175 (1961), the court distinguished between cases in which a partner contributes services only on a "day-to-day" basis, and cases in which "the skill and labor of the partner are his contribution to the capital assets of the partnership." In the former type of case, the court said, the partner's services would not augment his capital account. In the latter type of case, however, the partner's services would augment his capital account. This distinction also leaves a lot of room for a court to get around the general rule by finding that a partner's services were in the latter category rather than the former.

2. UPA § 40(a) defines the pool out of which the priorities on dissolution will be satisfied. This pool has two components. The first component is the partnership's property. The second component is the contributions that partners must make for payment of the "liabilities" described in § 40(b).

What are these required contributions? Under § 40(d), the partners must contribute the amount necessary to satisfy "liabilities," as provided in § 18(a). Section 18(a), in turn, provides that each partner shall contribute toward the "losses" sustained by the partnership according to his share in the profits. "Losses" in § 18(a) is defined, like "liabilities" in § 40(b), to include losses to capital.

These provisions have a special bite where the partnership has losses in the ordinary sense of that term—that is, if expenses have exceeded revenues. In such a case, it might be expected that in paying off the losses the partnership would first exhaust partnership property and would then exhaust partnership capital. Instead, under §§ 18 and 40 all partners must pay off the losses according to their share in the profits. If the partners' profit shares are equal (which is the default rule under § 18), then a partner who has contributed a lot of capital and a partner who has contributed services but no capital must contribute equally to paying off the losses. The effect is to preserve, as far as possible, the right of partners who have contributed capital to the return of that capital, at the expense of partners who have not contributed capital.

This effect may lead to results that the partners probably did not contemplate. To take the extreme (but not terribly unusual) case, suppose that in the Partnership P hypothetical discussed above, after all debts to creditors are paid the partnership is worth only $50,000. If UPA Section 18(a) is read in a relatively straightforward way, so that S must contribute toward losses of capital according to his share in the profits, S must contribute $25,000 to equalize the capital loss—in effect, to reduce C's capital loss. See Richert v. Handly, 53 Wash.2d 121, 330 P.2d 1079 (1958). This result has often been criticized, and despite the language of UPA Section 18(a) the cases do not uniformly require a services-only partner, like S, to contribute toward reducing a capital-partner's capital loss. Some cases hold that a special rule applies to joint ventures, and then conclude that the relationship in question was a joint venture rather than a partnership. In Kovacik v. Reed, 49 Cal.2d 166, 169–70, 315 P.2d 314, 315–16 (1957), the court drew a different distinction:

> It is the general rule that in the absence of an agreement to the contrary the law presumes that partners and joint adventurers intended to participate equally in the profits and losses of the common enterprise, irrespective of any inequality in the amounts each contributed to the capital employed in the venture, with the losses being shared by them in the same proportions as they share the profits. . . .

> However, it appears that in the cases in which the above stated general rule has been applied, each of the parties had contributed capital . . . or else was to receive compensation for services rendered to the common undertaking which was to be paid before computation of the profits or losses. Where, however, as in the present case, one partner or joint adventurer contributes the money capital as against the other's skill and labor, all the cases cited, and which our research has discovered, hold that neither party is liable to the other for contribution for any loss sustained. Thus, upon loss of the money the party who contributed it is not entitled to recover any part of it from the party who contributed only services. . . . The rationale of this rule . . . is that where one party contributes money and the other contributes services, then in the event of a loss each would lose his own capital—the one his money and the other his labor. Another view would be that in such a situation the parties have, by their agreement to share equally in profits, agreed that the values of their contributions—the money on the one hand and the labor on the other—were likewise equal; it would follow that upon the loss, as here, of both money and labor, the parties have shared equally in the losses.

Accord; Becker v. Killarney, 177 Ill.App.3d 793, 127 Ill.Dec. 102, 532 N.E.2d 931 (1988); Snellbaker v. Herrmann, 315 Pa.Super. 520, 462 A.2d 713 (1983). (*Kovacik* has been distinguished where the services partner received compensation for his services. See Century Universal Enterprises, Inc. v. Triana Development Corp., 158 Ill.App.3d 182, 110 Ill.Dec. 229, 510 N.E.2d 1260 (1987).)

The line taken in *Kovacik* is sound. If a services-only partner has been fully compensated for his services, it is hard to see why he should not be required to contribute toward making up a capital loss. Otherwise, a capital partner would bear all the partnership's loss and the services-only partner would bear none. But if a services-only partner has not been compensated for his services, then if he must contribute toward the capital loss he would lose all the value of his services while the capital partner would lose only part of the value of his capital. It is unlikely that the parties would have agreed to this result if they had negotiated on the issue when the partnership was formed. As *Kovacik* suggests, therefore, where a services-only partner has not been compensated for his services, the partners should normally be deemed to have impliedly agreed that he need not contribute to a capital loss.

3. RUPA § 401(h) continues the rule of UPA § 18. The Comment to § 401(h) makes clear that the rule is intended to apply in the capital-loss context, and provides the following justification for applying the rule to services partners:

> The default rules [of § 401(h)] apply, as does UPA Section 18(a), where one or more of the partners contribute no capital, although there is case law to the contrary. See, e.g., Kovacik v. Reed, 49 Cal.2d 166, 315 P.2d 314 (1957); Becker v. Killarney, 177 Ill.App.3d 793, 127 Ill.Dec. 102, 532 N.E.2d 931 (1988). It may seem unfair that the contributor of services, who contributes little or no capital, should be obligated to contribute toward the capital loss of the large contributor who contributed no services. In entering a partnership with such a capital structure, the partners should foresee that application of the default rule may bring about unusual results and take advantage of their power to vary by agreement the allocation of capital losses.

This attempt at justification does more to show why RUPA § 401(h) is wrong than why it is right. The Comment begins by frankly recognizing that the result "may seem unfair." It then states that even if the rule is unfair the partners can contract around it. Of course, any rule of partnership law, no matter how bad, could always be "justified" by the argument that it can be contracted around. The point of partnership law, however, should be to make good rules that the parties probably would have agreed to if they had addressed the issue, not to make bad rules that the partners can contract around. Furthermore, many partners don't know partnership law and therefore won't realize they need to contract around the rule. Indeed, because persons can be partners without an intention to form a partnership, many partners don't even know they are partners, let alone know that they need to worry about contracting around partnership law.

————

NOTE ON INDEMNIFICATION AND CONTRIBUTION

As shown in Section 5, infra, each partner is individually liable to a partnership creditor for partnership obligations. As between the partners, however, each partner is liable only for his share of a partnership obligation. Thus if one partner pays off a partnership obligation in full (or, for that matter, if he simply pays more than his share), he is entitled to indemnification from the partnership for the difference between what he paid and his share of the liability.

Indemnification should be distinguished from contribution. A *partner* has a right to be indemnified in a proper case by the partnership. Correspondingly, the obligation to indemnify a partner is a partnership liability. In contrast, the *partnership* has a right to require contribution in a proper case from one or more partners. Correspondingly, the obligation to make contribution is a liability of a partner. Contribution may be required to fund indemnification, so that all partners share a burden initially placed on only one. Contribution may also be required for other purposes—in particular, paying off partnership creditors and equalizing capital losses.

————

NOTE ON JOINT VENTURES

As pointed out in the Note on "Services Partners," supra, some courts have held that a services partner need not contribute toward a capital loss where the enterprise is a "joint venture" rather than a partnership. The line between a joint venture and a partnership is exceedingly thin. "[M]ost courts have [distinguished] between isolated transactions and continuing enterprises by classifying the former as joint ventures." 1 A. Bromberg & L. Ribstein, Partnership 2:42–2:43 (1994).

Some authorities take the position that joint ventures are generally governed by partnership law. See, e.g., id. at 192 ("Whether a [joint venture] is considered a partnership or merely analogized to one, the venturers are governed by the rules applicable to partners"); Comment, The Joint Venture: Problem Child of

Partnership, 38 Calif.L.Rev. 860 (1950). In contrast, other commentators argue that joint ventures are not merely a form of partnership, and not entirely subject to partnership rules. See, e.g., Jaeger, Partnership or Joint Venture?, 37 Notre Dame Law. 138 (1961). The same split is found in the cases. Some cases suggest that it makes no legal difference whether an enterprise is characterized as a partnership or a joint venture, while others suggest that special rules apply to joint ventures.

As a realistic matter, what seems to be involved is this: Certain rules of the UPA, such as Section 18(a), produce unsatisfactory results in certain kinds of cases. Courts that want to avoid these results will sometimes do so, if they plausibly can, by holding that a "special rule" applies to joint ventures, and that the enterprise in the case at hand falls within the special rule. In many or most such cases, the desired result could probably be reached, without applying special rules to joint ventures, by finding that the parties had an implied agreement that overrides the relevant rule of the UPA.

(c) CAPITAL ACCOUNTS AND DRAWS

W. KLEIN & J. COFFEE, BUSINESS ORGANIZATION AND FINANCE 79–84

Fifth ed., 1993.

... CONTRIBUTIONS, ACCOUNTS, AND RETURNS

A.   CAPITAL ACCOUNTS

Suppose that Abe, Bill, Pamela and Morris have formed a partnership for the acquisition and operation of a grocery store. Abe and Bill each are to contribute $15,000 and Pamela $20,000, in cash or in property to be used in the business. Morris will contribute neither cash nor property but will agree to manage the store for five years and will receive a salary slightly lower than what he might earn elsewhere. If the partnership follows customary bookkeeping patterns, its books will show the following information under a heading that is likely to be called "Capital Accounts":

Abe	$15,000
Bill	15,000
Pamela	20,000
Morris	0
Total	$50,000

... In the absence of an agreement to the contrary, if the business were sold for cash, each partner would be entitled to receive an amount equal to his or her capital account, if available. Any excess or deficit would be shared in accordance with each partner's share of gain and loss (a point to be illustrated below).

Capital contribution does not necessarily control the sharing of gain and loss, and shares of gain may differ from shares of loss. For example, our four partners could agree that each will be entitled to an equal 25 percent share of any profits, despite the difference in initial contribution. Indeed, this is the result that will be provided by the Uniform Partnership Act (Sec. 18(a)) in the absence of an agreement to the contrary. At the same time, and again in the absence of an agreement to the contrary, no partner will be entitled to interest on his or her capital account. Losses might be allocated equally among the partners (again, the result in the absence of express agreement) or might be allocated first pro rata among the contributors of initial capital, to the extent of such capital, and then, perhaps, equally among all partners. ...

Suppose that all profits and losses are to be shared equally, and suppose that at the end of the first year of operation the profit (after the payment of Morris's salary) is $20,000, or $5,000 per partner. One way of recording this outcome would be to adjust the capital accounts, which would then appear as follows:

Abe	$20,000 *
Bill	20,000
Pamela	25,000
Morris	5,000
Total	$70,000

*$15,000 initial capital plus $5,000 profit share.

If, on the other hand, the firm experienced a loss of $20,000 in its first year of operations, the capital accounts would be:

Abe	$10,000
Bill	10,000
Pamela	15,000
Morris	(5,000)
Total	$30,000

(Parentheses around a number indicate that it is a negative amount.) If, at this point, the business were sold for exactly the amount of the total capital accounts, $30,000, Morris would be required to contribute $5,000 and the resulting total, $35,000, would then be distributed $10,000 each to Abe and Bill and $15,000 to Pamela. This result may seem to be hard on Morris, and there is some legal authority for relieving him of the debt, at least to the extent that he contributed services without adequate compensation. The issue is one that the partners should think about at the outset. They might well agree that losses are to be shared by the partners in accordance with their initial capital contributions.   ...

B.   DRAW

Thus far we have referred to profits and losses, which are bookkeeping concepts.   It is vital to note that profit does not necessarily generate any spare cash.   For example, a new retail store may be highly profitable but may need all its profits to expand its inventory.   And even if a firm has had profits and does have spare cash, the partners are not automatically entitled to receive a cash payment.   There is a separate term—called "draw"—that is used to describe cash distributions to partners.   The amount of the draw of each partner is determined by majority vote of the partners (again, in the absence of some other express agreement) and may be more or less than the profit.   ...

Returning now to the bookkeeping effects of a draw, suppose that our grocery store partnership generates an accounting profit of $20,000 in the first year of its operations.   ... We have just seen how this net profit figure can be translated into adjustments to partner capital accounts.   Now suppose that there is a draw. Suppose, for example, that the partners agree that each is to be paid $3,000 from partnership funds.   The $3,000 would reduce the capital accounts, so they would then be:

Abe	$17,000 *
Bill	17,000
Pamela	22,000
Morris	2,000
Total	$58,000

*$15,000 initial capital account, plus $5,000 profit share, minus $3,000 draw.

Next, assume that there is a loss of $20,000 in the first year, instead of a profit; that the partnership agreement allocates this loss equally among all the partners; and that despite the loss, there is a cash distribution (draw) of $3,000 to each partner.   The partnership capital accounts would then be as follows:

Abe	$ 7,000*
Bill	7,000
Pamela	12,000
Morris	(8,000)
Total	$18,000

* $15,000 initial capital account, minus $5,000 loss share, minus $3,000 draw.

All of this makes sense if you think about it for a few moments. Bear in mind that the capital accounts are not expected to correspond to values in the firm but instead are merely intended to reflect the relative claims of the partners to the assets of the partnership, which is of importance mostly in the case of withdrawal of a partner or liquidation of the partnership. A partner's share of profit can be thought of as something that he or she has earned and reinvested in the firm. The draw can be thought of as earnings or capital taken out of the firm. The capital account allows us to keep track of relative claims where initial contributions and profit shares differ. The same function is served where, for one reason or another, partners do not draw from the firm amounts strictly in proportion to their profit shares.

C.   CAPITAL ACCOUNTS AND VALUE OF A PARTNER'S INTEREST

To illustrate the difference between capital account and value, and the role of the capital account, suppose that the partnership capital accounts stand as follows:

Abe	$17,000
Bill	17,000
Pamela	22,000
Morris	2,000
Total	$58,000

Suppose that the business has increased in value because of the construction of a large housing development nearby. This is the kind of gain that [under the principles of accounting] ordinarily would not be reflected on the partnership books as long as the firm continues to operate with the same owners. Now suppose that the business is sold for $78,000 cash, net of all debts or other obligations. There is a surplus of $20,000 above the amount in the capital accounts (that is, above the amount of the initial contributions increased by profits and decreased by distributions to the partners). This $20,000 can be thought of as previously unrecorded profit; it would be allocated equally among the partners ($5,000 apiece), so that each partner would receive the following amount:

Abe	$22,000 *
Bill	22,000
Pamela	27,000
Morris	7,000
Total	$78,000

*$17,000 current capital account, plus $5,000 share of profit on sale of business.

Finally, assume that the store is sold for less than the amount in the capital accounts—for example, for $38,000. Here there is a previously unrecognized loss of $20,000. In the absence of an agreement to the contrary, the loss would be borne equally by all the partners (again, $5,000 apiece). The relative claims of the partners would therefore be as follows:

Abe	$12,000
Bill	12,000
Pamela	17,000
Morris	(3,000)
Total	$38,000

————

SECTION 4. THE AUTHORITY OF A PARTNER

————

UNIFORM PARTNERSHIP ACT §§ 3, 4(3), 9, 10, 11, 12, 13, 14

REVISED UNIFORM PARTNERSHIP ACT §§ 301, 302, 303, 304, 305, 306, 308

[See Appendix]

————

CROISANT v. WATRUD

See p. 2, supra.

————

CRANE, THE UNIFORM PARTNERSHIP ACT—A CRITICISM, 28 Harv.L.Rev. 762, 779–80 (1915). "The partner has under this Act authority to bind the partnership by any act 'for apparently carrying on in the usual way the business of the partnership of which he is a member.' This may be taken to mean an act within the apparent course of business as carried on by his particular firm. It has been generally held that not only the course of business of his firm may be relied on as evidence of his authority, but the course of business of other firms in the same locality engaged in the same general line of business. It is submitted that a narrower rule imposes an undue burden on the third person to learn the habits of the particular firm, and because this Act is susceptible of a narrow interpretation the language of the English Act, 'any act for the carrying on in the usual way business of the kind carried on by the firm,' should be substituted."

———

LEWIS, THE UNIFORM PARTNERSHIP ACT—A REPLY TO MR. CRANE'S CRITICISM [pt. 2], 29 Harv.L.Rev. 291, 299–300 (1916). "[In the drafting of the U.P.A., it was argued] as Mr. Crane has argued, that to declare that the inquiry should be: 'How is this partnership apparently carried on?' imposes an undue burden on the third person to learn the habits of this particular firm. On the other hand, it was contended that the wording of the English Act was susceptible of the interpretation that a partnership was bound, if the act was a usual act in the business of the kind carried on by the partnership, even though it was apparent that this particular partnership did not carry on the business in that manner. The argument which finally led the Commissioners to adopt the present wording was that it emphasizes the fundamental reason why a partnership is ever bound by an act of a partner not authorized by his co-partners, namely, that partners are bound because they have held him out to do that class of acts. The question therefore which should be determined in each case is, was it an act for apparently carrying on in the usual way the business of the partnership of which he is a member? Again, even if the contract was not one for carrying on in the usual way the business of the kind carried on by the firm, the partnership should be held, if it was a contract for apparently carrying on in the usual way that particular partnership; a matter which would be more than doubtful if the wording suggested by Mr. Crane had been adopted."

———

BURNS v. GONZALEZ, 439 S.W.2d 128 (Tex.Civ.App.1969). Bosquez and Gonzalez were partners in a business that sold broadcast time on a radio station located in Mexico. The station was owned and operated by a Mexican corporation, Radiodifusora. Bosquez and Gonzalez each owned 50% of Radiodifusora's stock, and Bosquez was its president. In 1957, Radiodifusora made a contract with Burns, which it failed to perform. Subsequently, Bosquez, purporting to act on his own behalf and on behalf of the partnership, executed a $40,000 promissory note payable to Burns, partly in exchange for Burns's promise not to sue Radiodifusora. Burns sued Bosquez and Gonzalez on the note, as partners, and Gonzalez argued that Bosquez had no authority to execute the note on the partnership's behalf. In reviewing a jury verdict in favor of defendants, the court stated:

> [Because the] express limitation on the authority of Bosquez was unknown to Burns, then, under the language of Sec. 9(1), his act in executing the note would bind the partnership if such act can be classified as an act "for apparently carrying on in the usual way the business of the partnership."
>
> As we interpret Sec. 9(1), the act of a partner binds the firm, absent an express limitation of authority known to the party dealing with such partner, if such act is for the purpose of "apparently carrying on" the business of the partnership in the way in which other firms engaged in the same business in the locality usually transact business, or in the way in which the particular partnership usually transacts its business. In this case, [however,] there is no evidence relating to the manner in which firms engaged in the sale of advertising time on radio stations usually transact business.

NOTE ON THE AUTHORITY OF PARTNERS UNDER RUPA

For most practical purposes, the major difference between the UPA and RUPA concerning a partner's authority is that RUPA § 301(1) makes clear, as the UPA did not, that a partnership is bound by an act of the partner for apparently carrying on in the usual way the partnership business or business *of the kind* carried on by the partnership. The Comment to § 301(1) states:

> Section 301(1) . . . . clarifies that a partner's apparent authority includes acts for carrying on in the ordinary course "business of the kind carried on by the partnership," not just the business of the particular partnership in question. The UPA is ambiguous on this point, but there is some authority for an expanded construction. . . . See, e.g., Burns v. Gonzalez, 439 S.W.2d 128, 131 (Tex.Civ.App. 1969) (dictum) . . . .

Although RUPA § 301(1) has the look and feel of apparent authority, essentially it involves a kind of inherent authority. Under § 301(1), a partnership is bound by an act of a partner that would be in the ordinary course of the kind of business the partnership carries on, even though the partner has no actual authority to engage in the act, the third person does not know the kind of business the partnership carries on, and the third person does not know that the party with whom he deals is a partner.

The treatment of authority under RUPA also differs from the UPA in certain other respects. For example, RUPA § 302 provides elaborate rules concerning when a transfer of partnership property is binding. In addition:

1. RUPA § 301 makes subtle shifts in determining when a third person's knowledge or notice of a restriction on a partner's authority will be effective to prevent partnership liability from arising. "Under UPA section 9(1), the partnership was not bound by the unauthorized actions of a partner if the third party had 'knowledge' of the partner's lack of authority. Under UPA section 9(1), a third party had knowledge when he or she had actual knowledge or 'when he [or she] has knowledge of such other facts as in the circumstances shows bad faith.' This latter language creates an implied or inquiry notice, the exact parameters of which are ill-defined. Under RUPA, the third party will not be placed under a duty of inquiry or be deemed to have notice from the facts and circumstances. Only actual knowledge or receipt of a notification of a partner's lack of authority will meet the standard." Merrill, Partnership Property and Partnership Authority Under the Revised Uniform Partnership Act, 49 Bus.Law. 83, 88–89 (1993).

2. RUPA § 303 enables a partnership to file a "Statement of Partnership Authority." Under § 303, a *grant* of authority set forth in such a Statement is normally conclusive in favor of third persons, even if they have no actual knowledge of the Statement, unless they have actual knowledge that the partner has no such authority. However, a *limitation* on a partner's authority that is contained in such a Statement, other than a limitation on the partner's authority to transfer real property, will not be effective unless the third party knows of the limitation or the Statement has been delivered to him. The Comment states:

> Under Section 301, only a third party who knows or has *received* a notification of a partner's lack of authority in an ordinary course transaction is bound [by a limitation in the notification]. Thus, a limitation on a partner's authority to transfer personal property or to enter into other non-real property transactions on behalf of the partnership, contained in a filed statement of partnership authority, is effective only

against a third party who knows or has received a notification of it. The fact of the statement being filed has no legal significance in those transactions, although the filed statement is a potential source of actual knowledge to third parties. (Emphasis added.)

Why would a partnership want to file a Statement that had such an effect? One answer is that persons who deal with a partnership may require such a Statement to ensure themselves that the partnership will be bound. Furthermore, "it is expected that third parties will wish to avail themselves of the benefit of the conclusive presumption of authority for most significant personal property transactions. [Also, in] the process of searching for the grant of authority, the third party will acquire actual knowledge of any restriction on authority in a filed statement. [And] the ... partners may protect themselves by delivering the statement to all known creditors, actual or potential." Merrill, supra, at 89.

In contrast to other types of limitations, a limitation in a Statement of Partnership Authority of a partner's authority to transfer real property held in the name of the partnership is effective against all third persons if a certified copy of the Statement is filed in the real-property recording office.

SECTION 5. LIABILITY FOR PARTNERSHIP OBLIGATIONS

UNIFORM PARTNERSHIP ACT §§ 9, 13, 14, 15, 16, 17, 36

REVISED UNIFORM PARTNERSHIP ACT §§ 305, 306, 307, 308

[See Appendix]

NOTE ON LIABILITY FOR PARTNERSHIP OBLIGATIONS

1. The provisions of the Uniform Partnership Act governing liability for partnership obligations reflect an amalgam of the entity and aggregate theories. On the one hand, UPA §§ 9, 13, and 14 make "the partnership" liable for defined acts of the partners. It might seem to follow that this liability could be enforced by a suit against the partnership. However, the UPA does not authorize such a suit, since it does not recognize a partnership as an entity, and

unless authorized by statute, suit normally cannot be brought against an association that is not an entity. Indeed, the UPA goes to the opposite extreme. Under UPA § 15(a), partners are *jointly and severally* liable for wrongful acts and omissions of the partnership (such as torts) and breaches of trust. Under UPA § 15(b), however, partners are only *jointly* liable "for all other debts and obligations of the partnership." At common law, if an obligation is "joint and several" the obligors can be sued either jointly or separately. If, however, an obligation is only "joint" the obligee must join all the obligors, subject to a few exceptions where jurisdiction over all the obligors cannot be obtained. See C. Clark, Handbook of the Law of Code Pleading 373–74 (2d ed. 1947). Thus under the UPA, not only must an action on a partnership's contractual obligation be brought against all the partners, but if one partner is not joined the action can be dismissed on motion by the partners who were joined. (If the partners who were joined don't move to dismiss, the defense is waived. However, the plaintiff's cause of action is usually considered to be merged into the judgment, thereby extinguishing his claim against unjoined partners.)

2. The inability of a partnership creditor to sue a partnership in its own name under the UPA is obviously undesirable, and many states have statutorily patched up the UPA rule by adopting Common Name Statutes, which explicitly allow a partnership to be sued in its own name. An example is N.Y.Civ.Prac.L. & R. § 1025: "Two or more persons conducting a business as a partnership may sue or be sued in the partnership name. . . ."

3. The need of a partnership contract creditor to join all the partners in a suit to establish individual liability on a contract claim is also undesirable. Some states address this issue by making all partnership liabilities joint and several. Other states have adopted Joint Debtor Statutes, which provide that a suit against joint obligors can proceed even if some of the obligors are not joined. An example is Cal.Civ.Proc.Code § 410.70: "In an action against two or more persons who are jointly, jointly and severally, or severally liable on a contract, the court in which the action is pending has jurisdiction to proceed against such of the defendants as are served as if they were the only defendants."

4. Unlike the UPA, RUPA § 307(a) specifically provides that a partnership may both sue and be sued in its own name. Furthermore, RUPA § 306 provides that partners are jointly and severally *liable* for *all* obligations of the partnership. However, RUPA adds a new barrier to *collecting* against an individual partner on such a liability. RUPA § 307 provides that a judgment against a partner based on a claim against the partnership normally cannot be satisfied against the partner's individual assets unless and until a judgment on the same claim has been rendered against the partnership

and a writ of execution on the judgment has been returned unsatisfied. To put this differently, RUPA § 307 adopts an exhaustion rule, under which partnership assets must be exhausted before a partner's individual assets can be reached. (The exhaustion rule is made subject to certain exceptions, one of which is that the rule does not apply if the partnership is in bankruptcy.) Thus as the Comment to RUPA § 306 points out:

> Joint and several liability under RUPA differs ... from the classic model [of joint and several liability outside partnership law], which permits a judgment creditor to proceed immediately against any of the joint and several judgment debtors.

In effect, RUPA takes an aggregate-like approach to a partner's liability, but an entity-like approach to collecting judgments based on that liability.

Even in the absence of an exhaustion rule, a partner who was required to pay more than her share of a partnership liability could make a claim for indemnification. Professor Bromberg comments:

> The cost to partners of apportioning [among the remaining partners by indemnification or contribution] any liabilities they have to pay personally is probably lower than the cost to third parties of complying with the exhaustion requirement. From this perspective the exhaustion rule is not efficient. The exhaustion rule is efficient in one respect: it can be easily contracted around at a cost which may be relatively low (*e.g.,* if simple guarantee forms are used). However, there is rarely a way to contract around exhaustion in tort cases and it does not provide efficiency there. Equitable considerations plus the lack of efficiency make the exhaustion rule even less justified for torts.

Bromberg, Enforcement of Partnership Obligations—Who Is Sued For The Partnership? 71 Neb.L.Rev. 143, 150 (1992).

Since RUPA § 307 provides that a creditor normally cannot satisfy a judgment against a partnership by collecting from a partner unless the creditor sues the partnership, wins, and is unable to collect his judgment against the partnership, why would a creditor bother suing the partner at all? One answer is that the creditor may believe he can come within an exception to § 307. Another answer is that § 307 provides that a judgment against a partnership is not by itself a judgment against a partner, and cannot be satisfied from a partner's assets unless there is also a judgment against the partner.

SECTION 6. PARTNERSHIP INTERESTS AND PARTNERSHIP PROPERTY

———

UNIFORM PARTNERSHIP ACT §§ 8, 18, 24, 25, 26, 27, 28

REVISED UNIFORM PARTNERSHIP ACT §§ 203, 204, 501, 502, 503, 504

[See Appendix]

———

RAPOPORT v. 55 PERRY CO.

New York Supreme Court, Appellate Division, 1975.
50 A.D.2d 54, 376 N.Y.S.2d 147.

Cross appeals from an order of the Supreme Court (HILDA G. SCHWARTZ, J.), entered July 16, 1975 in New York County, which denied a motion by plaintiffs for summary judgment and a cross motion by defendants for summary judgment dismissing the complaint....

TILZER, J. In 1969, Simon, Genia and Ury Rapoport entered into a partnership agreement with Morton, Jerome and Burton Parnes, forming the partnership known as 55 Perry Company. Pursuant to the agreement, each of the families owned 50% of the partnership interests. In December of 1974 Simon and Genia Rapoport assigned a 10% interest of their share in the partnership to their adult children, Daniel and Kalia. The Parnes defendants were advised of the assignment and an amended partnership certificate was filed in the County Clerk's office indicating the addition of Daniel and Kalia as partners. However, when the plaintiffs, thereafter, requested the Parnes defendants to execute an amended partnership agreement to reflect the above changes in the partnership, the Parnes refused, taking the position that the partnership agreement did not permit the introduction of new partners without consent of all the existing partners. Thereafter, the plaintiffs Rapoport brought this action seeking a declaration that Simon and Genia Rapoport had an absolute right to assign their interests to their adult children without consent of the defendants and that such assignment was authorized pursuant to paragraph 12 of the partnership agreement. The plaintiffs further sought to have Daniel and Kalia be declared partners in 55 Perry Company and have their names entered upon the books of the partnership as partners. The defendants Parnes interposed an answer, taking the position that the partnership agreement did not permit admission of additional partners without consent of all the existing partners and that the filing of the amended certificate of partnership was unauthorized. After joinder of issue plaintiffs moved for summary judgment and although the defendants did not cross-move for similar relief, such was, nevertheless, requested in their answering papers.

On the motion for summary judgment both parties agreed that there were no issues of fact and that there was only a question of the interpretation of the written documents which should be disposed of as a matter of law by the court. Nevertheless, the court below found that the agreement was ambiguous and that there was a triable issue with respect to the intent of the parties. We disagree and conclude that the agreement is without ambiguity and that pursuant to the terms of the agreement and of the Partnership Law, consent of the Parnes defendants was required in order to admit Daniel Rapoport and Kalia Shalleck to the partnership.

Plaintiffs, in support of their contention that they have an absolute right to assign their interests in the partnership to their adult children and that the children must be admitted to the partnership as partners rely on paragraph 12 of the partnership agreement which provides as follows: "No partner or partners shall have the authority to transfer, sell . . . assign or in any way dispose of the partnership realty and/or personalty and shall not have the authority to sell, transfer, assign . . . his or their share in this firm, nor enter into any agreement as a result of which any person shall become interested with him in this firm, unless the same is agreed to in writing by a majority of the partners as determined by the percentage of ownership . . . except for members of his immediate family who have attained majority, in which case no such consent shall be required." As indicated, plaintiffs argue that the above provision expressly authorizes entry of their adult children into the partnership. Defendants, on the other hand, maintain that paragraph 12 provides only for the right of a partner to assign or transfer a share of the profits in the partnership. We agree with that construction of the agreement.

A reading of the partnership agreement indicates that the parties intended to observe the differences, as set forth in the Partnership Law, between assignees of a partnership interest and the admission into the partnership itself of new partners. The Partnership Law provides that subject to any contrary agreement between the partners, "[n]o person can become a member of a partnership without the consent of all the partners." (Partnership Law, § 40, subd 7.) Subdivision 1 of section 53 of the Partnership Law provides that an assignee of an interest in the partnership is not entitled "to interfere in the management or administration of the partnership business" but is merely entitled to receive "the profits to which the assigning partner would otherwise be entitled." Additionally, section 50 of the Partnership Law indicates the differences between the rights of an assignee and a new partner. That section states that the "property rights of a partner are (a) his rights in specific partnership property, (b) his interest in the partnership, and (c) his right to participate in the management." On the other hand, as already indicated above, an assignee is excluded in the absence of agreement from interfering in the management of the partnership business and from access to the partnership books and information about partnership transactions. (Partnership Law, § 53.)

The effect, therefore, of the various provisions of the Partnership Law, above discussed, is that unless the parties have agreed otherwise, a person cannot become a member of a partnership without consent of all the partners whereas an assignment of a partnership interest may be made without consent, but the assignee is entitled only to receive the profits of the assigning partner. And, as already stated, the partnership agreement herein clearly took cognizance of the differences between an assignment of an interest in the partnership as compared to the full rights of a partner as set forth in section 50 of the Partnership Law. Paragraph 12 of the agreement by its language has reference to section 53 of the Partnership Law dealing with an "assignment of partner's interest." It (par 12) refers to assignments, encumbrances and agreements "as a result of which any person shall become interested with (the assignor) in this firm." That paragraph does not contain language with respect to admitting a partner to the partnership with all rights to participate in the management of its affairs. Moreover, interpretation of paragraph 12 in this manner is consistent with other provisions of the partnership agreement. For example, in paragraph 15 of the agreement, the following is provided:

"In the event of the death of any partner the business of this firm shall continue with the heir, or distributee providing he has reached majority, or fiduciary of the deceased partner having the right to succeed the deceased partner with the same rights and privileges and the same obligations, pursuant to all of the terms hereof." In that paragraph, therefore, there is specific provision to succeed to all the privileges and obligations of a partner—language which is completely absent from paragraph 12.

Accordingly, it appears that contrary to plaintiffs' contention that paragraph 12 was intended to give the parties the right to transfer a full partnership interest to adult children, without consent of all other partners (an agreement which would vary the rights otherwise existing pursuant to Partnership Law, § 40, subd 7) that paragraph was instead intended to limit a partner with respect to his right to assign a partnership interest as provided for under section 53 of the Partnership Law (i.e., the right to profits)—to the extent of prohibiting such assignments without consent of other partners except to children of the existing partners who have reached majority. Therefore, it must be concluded that pursuant to the terms of the partnership agreement, the plaintiffs could not transfer a full partnership interest to their children and that the children only have the rights as assignees to receive a share of the partnership income and profits of their assignors.

Accordingly, the order entered July 16, 1975 should be modified on the law to grant summary judgment in favor of the defendants to the extent of declaring that the partnership agreement does not permit entry into the partnership of new partners, including adult children of the partners who have reached their majority, without consent of all the partners; [and] that the plaintiffs, pursuant to the terms of the agreement, had the right to assign their interests to their adult children but that such children, i.e., Daniel Rapoport and Kalia Shalleck, have not become partners but only have the rights of assignees to receive a share of the partnership income and profits of their assignors. . . .

NUNEZ, J. (dissenting). I agree with Special Term that the written partnership agreement providing for the assignment of partners' shares to members of their immediate families without the consent of the other partners is ambiguous and that there is a triable issue as to intent. The agreement being ambiguous, construction is a mixed question of law and fact and resolution thereof to determine the parties' intent should await a trial. . . .

STEVENS, P.J., KUPFERMAN and MURPHY, JJ., concur with TILZER, J.; NUNEZ, J., dissents in an opinion. . . .

NOTE ON PARTNERSHIP PROPERTY

1. Whether property that is used by a partnership is partnership property or the property of the individual partners may be important for several different reasons. The issue may be important to determine who has the power to use and transfer the property. The issue may be important if creditors of the partnership are competing with creditors of an individual partner. The issue may also be important if the partnership is dissolved. If property used by the partnership is partnership property, on dissolution the property must be sold for cash, along with other partnership assets, and the proceeds of the sale must be distributed among the partners. In contrast, if property used by the partnership is the individual property of a partner, on dissolution the property must

normally be returned directly to that partner, rather than sold for the account of all the partners.[1] This third issue may be especially important if the property is crucial to the partnership's business, so that as a practical matter whoever owns the property has the ability to continue the business.

If the aggregate theory of the UPA were strictly applied, a partnership could not own property. Rather, the property that the partners think of as partnership property would as a matter of law be held by the individual partners as joint tenants or tenants in common. For a variety of reasons, such a regime would be wholly impracticable. Accordingly, in the matter of partnership property, as in several other matters, the UPA lays down rules that effectively treat the partnership *as if* it were an entity. This objective is accomplished largely with mirrors. UPA Section 8 recognizes the concept of "partnership property," and explicitly permits real property to be held in the partnership's name. (Even before the UPA it was well settled that personal property could be so held.) However, UPA Section 25(1) provides that "partnership property" is owned by the *partners,* under the ingenuous nomenclature, "tenan[cy] in partnership." UPA Section 25(2) then systematically strips from the individual partners every incident normally associated with ownership. Under Section 25(2)(a), a partner has no right to possess partnership property as an individual. Under Section 25(2)(b), a partner cannot individually assign his rights in specific partnership property. Under Section 25(2)(c), a partner's rights in specific partnership property cannot be subject to attachment or execution by a creditor of the partner in the latter's individual capacity. Under Section 25(2)(d), when the partner dies his right in specific partnership property does not devolve on his heirs or legatees. Under Section 25(2)(e), widows, heirs, and next of kin cannot claim dower, curtesy, or allowances in the partner's right to specific partnership property.

In short, under the UPA individual partners own the partnership property in theory, but all the incidents of ownership are vested in the partnership, so that the "tenan[cy] in partnership" rule of the UPA has no real-world significance.

2. RUPA, which confers entity status on partnerships, drops the elaborate tenancy-in-partnership apparatus of the UPA. RUPA § 203 provides that "Property acquired by a partnership is property of the partnership and not the partners individually." RUPA § 204 then sets out a series of rules and presumptions concerning whether any given property is partnership property or the separate

---

1. But see Pav-Saver Corp. v. Vasso Corp., 143 Ill.App.3d 1013, 97 Ill.Dec. 760, 493 N.E.2d 423 (1986) (wrongfully dissolving partner held not entitled to return of property).

property of a partner. These provisions are supplemented by § 501, which provides that "A partner is not a co-owner of partnership property and has no interest in partnership property which can be transferred, either voluntarily or involuntarily." The purpose of § 501 is to explicitly abolish the UPA concept of tenancy-in-partnership.

NOTE ON PARTNERSHIP INTERESTS

1. Although a partner does not own partnership property under the UPA, except in some metaphysical sense, he does own his interest in the partnership, that is, his share of the partnership. The net result is a functional two-level ownership structure somewhat comparable to the legal two-level ownership structure in a corporation. A corporation is the owner of corporate property and a shareholder is the owner of his shares in the corporation. A partnership is the functional owner of partnership property and a partner is the owner of his interest in the partnership.

As compared to ordinary property interests, a partnership interest is conditioned in one very important respect. Normally, the owner of a property interest can freely sell it, and a creditor can freely levy on it. Under UPA § 18(g), however, no person can become a partner without the consent of all the partners. It follows that unless the partnership agreement otherwise provides, a partner cannot make a transfer of his partnership interest that would substitute the transferee as a partner in the transferor's place. Correspondingly, a creditor can neither levy on a partnership interest in such a way as to be substituted as a partner, nor recover his debt by selling the interest to a third party who will be substituted as a partner. Nevertheless, a partnership interest is assignable. As pointed out in *Rapoport,* the assignee does not become a partner (unless all the other partners consent), and has no right to information about the partnership and no right to inspect the partnership books. However, while the partnership continues the assignee has a right to receive the profits to which the assigning partner would otherwise be entitled, and on dissolution the assignee has a right to receive the assigning partner's interest. According to A. Bromberg, supra, at 240, partnership interests have a fairly high degree of assignability despite the limitations on the rights of an assignee.

2. The creditor of a partner in the partner's individual capacity is in a position very similar to the assignee of a partnership interest. Under UPA § 28, if such a creditor obtains a judgment, he can get a "charging order" on the partner's partnership interest. Such an order will effectively permit him to get the share of profits to which

the indebted partner would be otherwise entitled. If the creditor forecloses on the partnership interest under § 28, and thereby causes its sale, the buyer of the interest will have the right to compel dissolution if the term of the partnership has expired or the partnership is at will. Alternatively, the creditor may put the individual partner into bankruptcy, which results in dissolution of the partnership under UPA § 31(5).

RUPA § 504 continues UPA § 28 largely unchanged in substance. RUPA § 504 does add some details that are not found in UPA § 28, but for the most part these details are consistent with the case law under § 28. RUPA § 801(a), like the UPA, provides that a transferee of a partner's transferable interest is entitled to judicial dissolution on the partnership (i) at any time, in a partnership at will, and (ii) after the expiration of the partnership's term or completion of the undertaking, in a partnership for a definite term or particular undertaking.

3. A major problem in partnership law concerns the relative priorities of creditors of the partnership ("partnership creditors") and creditors of a partner in the partner's individual capacity ("separate creditors"). UPA § 40(h), (i) provides that partnership creditors have priority over separate creditors as to partnership assets, and separate creditors have priority over partnership creditors as to the individual assets of the partners. See also UPA § 36(4). This rule, which was also in the Bankruptcy Act prior to 1978, is known as the "dual priorities" or "jingle" rule. The rule was widely criticized on the ground that partnership creditors did not get the full benefit of personal liability of the individual partners. The Bankruptcy Reform Act of 1978 responded to that criticism. Under Chapter 7 of that Act, in the case of bankruptcy partnership creditors have priority over separate creditors as to partnership assets, but if their debts remain unpaid after partnership assets are exhausted, partnership creditors are put on a parity with separate creditors in dividing up the partner's individual assets. 11 U.S.C. § 723(c). See Hanley, Partnership Bankruptcy under the New Act, 31 Hastings L.J. 149, 173–80 (1979). "While the application of the 'jingle' rule to other bankruptcy proceedings has not been conclusively resolved, Professor Kennedy states that the result follows by compelling implication. [Kennedy, Partnerships and Partners Under the Bankruptcy Code: Claims and Distribution, 40 Wash. & Lee L.Rev. 55, 59 and nn. 14, 63 (1983).] Thus in the usual case the UPA jingle rule will be preempted ... by the Bankruptcy Code." Should the Uniform Partnership Act be Revised?—Report of the ABA Subcommittee on the Revision of the UPA, 43 Bus.Law. 121, 177 (1987). RUPA drops the "dual priority"

rule of the UPA, to reflect the abolition of the jingle rule in the Bankruptcy Act.

WILLS v. WILLS, 750 S.W.2d 567, 573–74 (Mo.App.1988). "Prior to the enactment of § 25 of the Uniform Law ... there was great confusion as to the right of one partner's separate creditor to attach or levy execution on an individual partner's interest in the business or firm property.... Under the common law:

> When a creditor obtained a judgment against the partner and he wanted to obtain the benefit of that judgment against the share of that partner in the firm, the first thing was to issue a *fi. fa.*,* and the sheriff went down to the partnership place of business, seized everything, stopped the business, drove the solvent partners wild, and caused the execution creditor to bring an action in Chancery in order to get an injunction to take an account and pay on that which was due by the execution debtor. A more clumsy method of providing could hardly have grown up.

Lord Justice Lindley in Brown, Janson & Co. v. Hutchinson & Co., 1 Q.B. 737 (1895) quoted in Gose, supra, 28 Wash.L.Rev. at 1.

"The need for a solution to the common law approach which would protect partners and the separate creditors of individual partners was evident. The solution came in the form of §§ 25 and 28 of the Uniform Partnership Act.... Section 25 of the Uniform Law ... prohibits any attachment or execution of specific partnership property by a judgment creditor of an individual debtor-partner.... The primary purpose of the Uniform Law is to prevent disruption of partnership affairs by a creditor of an individual partner. Willamette Production Credit Ass'n v. Morley, 248 Or. 183, 433 P.2d 239, 244 (1967).

"In lieu of authorizing attachment or execution upon the partnership property for a debt of one of the partners, the judgment creditor of an individual partner-debtor is given a more circuitous remedy to enforce the judgment in the form of a 'charging order' on the individual partner's interest and his share of the profits and surplus in the partnership. [UPA § 28] This judicial procedure under [UPA § 28] leads to a 'sort of lien' on the interest the individual partner has in the firm and is subject to foreclosure.

---

* *"Fi. fa."* is an abbreviation for the writ of "fieri facias" ("that you cause to be made"). This was a writ of execution com- manding the sheriff to levy on a judgment from the goods of a judgment debtor. (Footnote by ed.)

While this 'charge' is in effect, the debtor-partner continues to be a partner except for distributions from the partnership. . . .

"This 'charging' procedure is the exclusive remedy for a partner's individual creditor, and it has been held to be a proper procedure not only for judgment creditors but for spouses seeking alimony or child support. . . . [T]he charging order on partnership interests has replaced levies of execution as a remedy for reaching such interests.

"Under the Uniform Partnership Law, therefore, the proper method to 'seize' the interest of an individual partner in a partnership is to apply to the proper court for a charging order, and to charge the individual partner's share of the profits and surplus in the partnership with the unsatisfied amount of the judgment . . . and to foreclose on the partner's 'interest' in the partnership. [UPA § 28]; see Tupper v. Kroc, 88 Nev. 146, 494 P.2d 1275 (1972)."

————

FARMERS STATE BANK & TRUST CO. v. MIKESELL, 51 Ohio App.3d 69, 554 N.E.2d 900, 909 (1988). "The rule we derive from [the] cases is that a partner's interest in the partnership, his right to share in profits and surplus, is assignable. However, a partner may not assign his interest in particular assets of the partnership. If the creditor of an individual partner has obtained a judgment against a partner, his sole means of attaching the partner's interest in the partnership is the charging order. . . ."

————

SECTION 7. THE PARTNER'S DUTY OF LOYALTY

————

UNIFORM PARTNERSHIP ACT §§ 20, 21

REVISED UNIFORM PARTNERSHIP ACT §§ 103, 104, 403, 404, 405

[See Appendix]

————

MEINHARD v. SALMON

New York Court of Appeals, 1928.
249 N.Y. 458, 164 N.E. 545.

Appeal from a judgment of the Appellate Division of the Supreme Court in the first judicial department, entered June 28, 1928, modifying and affirming as modified a judgment in favor of plaintiff entered upon the report of a referee.

CARDOZO, Ch. J. On April 10, 1902, Louisa M. Gerry leased to the defendant Walter J. Salmon the premises known as the Hotel Bristol at the northwest corner of Forty-second street and Fifth avenue in the city of New York. The lease was for a term of twenty years, commencing May 1, 1902, and ending April 30, 1922. The lessee undertook to change the hotel building for use as shops and offices at a cost of $200,000. Alterations and additions were to be accretions to the land.

Salmon, while in course of treaty with the lessor as to the execution of the lease, was in course of treaty with Meinhard, the plaintiff, for the necessary funds. The result was a joint venture with terms embodied in a writing. Meinhard was to pay to Salmon half of the moneys requisite to reconstruct, alter, manage and operate the property. Salmon was to pay to Meinhard 40 per cent of the net profits for the first five years of the lease and 50 per cent for the years thereafter. If there were losses, each party was to bear them equally. Salmon, however, was to have sole power to "manage, lease, underlet and operate" the building. There were to be certain pre-emptive rights for each in the contingency of death.

The two were coadventurers, subject to fiduciary duties akin to those of partners (King v. Barnes, 109 N.Y. 267). As to this we are all agreed. The heavier weight of duty rested, however, upon Salmon. He was a coadventurer with Meinhard, but he was manager as well. During the early years of the enterprise, the building, reconstructed, was operated at a loss. If the relation had then ended, Meinhard as well as Salmon would have carried a heavy burden. Later the profits became large with the result that for each of the investors there came a rich return. For each, the venture had its phases of fair weather and of foul. The two were in it jointly, for better or for worse.

When the lease was near its end, Elbridge T. Gerry had become the owner of the reversion. He owned much other property in the neighborhood, one lot adjoining the Bristol Building on Fifth avenue and four lots on Forty-second street. He had a plan to lease the entire tract for a long term to some one who would destroy the buildings then existing, and put up another in their place. In the latter part of 1921, he submitted such a project to several capitalists and dealers. He was unable to carry it through with any of them. Then, in January, 1922, with less than four months of the lease to run, he approached the defendant Salmon. The result was a new lease to the Midpoint Realty Company, which is owned and controlled by Salmon, a lease covering the whole tract, and involving a huge outlay. The term is to be twenty years, but successive covenants for renewal will extend it to a maximum of eighty years at the will of either party. The existing buildings may remain unchanged for seven years. They are then to be torn down, and a new building to cost $3,000,000 is to be placed upon the site. The rental, which under the Bristol lease was only $55,000, is to be from $350,000 to $475,000 for the properties so combined. Salmon personally guaranteed the performance by the lessee of the covenants of the new lease until such time as the new building had been completed and fully paid for.

The lease between Gerry and the Midpoint Realty Company was signed and delivered on January 25, 1922. Salmon had not told Meinhard anything about it. Whatever his motive may have been, he had kept the negotiations to himself. Meinhard was not informed even of the bare existence of a project. The first that he knew of it was in February when the lease was an accomplished fact. He then made demand on the defendants that the lease be held in trust as an asset of the venture, making offer upon the trial to share the personal obligations incidental to the guaranty. The demand was followed by refusal, and later by this suit. A referee gave judgment for the plaintiff, limiting the plaintiff's interest in the lease, however, to 25 per cent. The limitation was on the theory that the plaintiff's equity was to be restricted to one-half of so much of the value of the lease as was contributed or represented by the occupation of the Bristol site. Upon cross-appeals to the Appellate Division, the judgment was modified so as to enlarge the equitable interest to one-half of the whole lease. With this enlargement of plaintiff's interest, there went, of course, a corresponding enlargement of his attendant obligations. The case is now here on an appeal by the defendants.

Joint adventurers, like copartners, owe to one another, while the enterprise continues, the duty of the finest loyalty. Many forms of conduct permissible in a workaday world for those acting at arm's length, are forbidden to those bound by fiduciary ties. A trustee is held to something stricter than the morals of the market place. Not honesty alone, but the punctilio of an honor the most sensitive, is then the standard of behavior. As to this there has developed a tradition that is unbending and inveterate. Uncompromising rigidity has been the attitude of courts of equity when petitioned to undermine the rule of undivided loyalty by the "disintegrating erosion" of particular exceptions (Wendt v. Fischer, 243 N.Y. 439, 444). Only thus has the level of conduct for fiduciaries been kept at a level higher than that trodden by the crowd. It will not consciously be lowered by any judgment of this court.

The owner of the reversion, Mr. Gerry, had vainly striven to find a tenant who would favor his ambitious scheme of demolition and construction. Baffled in the search, he turned to the defendant Salmon in possession of the Bristol, the keystone of the project. He figured to himself beyond a doubt that the man in possession would prove a likely customer. To the eye of an observer, Salmon held the lease as owner in his own right, for himself and no one else. In fact he held it as a fiduciary, for himself and another, sharers in a common venture. If this fact had been proclaimed, if the lease by its terms had run in favor of a partnership, Mr. Gerry, we may fairly assume, would have laid before the partners, and not merely before one of them, his plan of reconstruction. The pre-emptive privilege, or, better, the pre-emptive opportunity, that was thus an incident of the enterprise, Salmon appropriated to himself in secrecy and silence. He might have warned Meinhard that the plan had been submitted, and that either would be free to compete for the award. If he had done this, we do not need to say whether he would have been under a duty, if successful in the competition, to hold the lease so acquired for the benefit of a venture then about to end, and thus prolong by indirection its responsibilities and duties. The trouble about his conduct is that he excluded his coadventurer from any chance to compete, from any chance to enjoy the opportunity for benefit that had come to him alone by virtue of his agency. This chance, if nothing more, he was under a duty to concede. The price of its denial is an extension of the trust at the option and for the benefit of the one whom he excluded.

No answer is it to say that the chance would have been of little value even if seasonably offered. Such a calculus of probabilities is beyond the science of the chancery. Salmon, the real estate operator, might have been preferred to Meinhard, the woolen merchant. On the other hand, Meinhard might have offered better terms, or reinforced his offer by alliance with the wealth of others. Perhaps he might even have persuaded the lessor to renew the Bristol lease alone, postponing for a time, in return for higher rentals, the improvement of adjoining lots. We know that even under the lease as made the time for the enlargement of the building was delayed for seven years. All these opportunities were cut away from him through another's intervention. He knew that Salmon was the manager. As the time drew near for the expiration of the lease, he would naturally assume from silence, if from nothing else, that the lessor was willing to extend it for a term of years, or at least to let it stand as a lease from year to year. Not impossibly the lessor would have done so, whatever his protestations of unwillingness, if Salmon had not given assent to a project more attractive. At all events, notice of termination, even if not necessary, might seem, not unreasonably, to be something to be looked for, if the business was over and another tenant was to enter. In the absence of such notice, the matter of an extension was one that would naturally be attended to by the manager of the enterprise, and not neglected altogether. At least, there was nothing in the situation to give warning to any one that while the lease was still in being, there had come to the manager an offer of extension which he had locked within his breast to be utilized by himself alone. The very fact that Salmon was in control with exclusive powers of direction charged him the more obviously with the duty of disclosure, since only through disclosure could opportunity be equalized. If he might cut off renewal by a purchase for his own benefit when four months were to pass before the lease would have an end, he might do so with equal right while there remained as many years (cf. Mitchell v. Reed, 61 N.Y. 123, 127). He might steal a march on his comrade under cover of the darkness, and then hold the captured ground. Loyalty and comradeship are not so easily abjured.

Little profit will come from a dissection of the precedents. None precisely similar is cited in the briefs of counsel. What is similar in many, or so it seems to us, is the animating principle. Authority is, of course, abundant that one partner may not appropriate to his own use a renewal of a lease, though its term is to begin at the expiration of the partnership (Mitchell v. Reed, 61 N.Y. 123; 84 N.Y. 556). The lease at hand with its many changes is not strictly a renewal. Even so, the standard of loyalty for those in trust relations is without the fixed divisions of a graduated scale. There is indeed a dictum in one of our decisions that a partner, though he may not renew a lease, may purchase the reversion if he acts openly and fairly (Anderson v. Lemon, 8 N.Y. 236; cf. White & Tudor, Leading Cases in Equity [9th ed.], vol. 2, p. 642; Bevan v. Webb, 1905, 1 Ch. 620; Griffith v. Owen, 1907, 1 Ch. 195, 204, 205). It is a dictum, and no more, for on the ground that he had acted slyly he was charged as a trustee. The holding is thus in favor of the conclusion that a purchase as well as a lease will succumb to the infection of secrecy and silence. Against the dictum in that case, moreover, may be set the opinion of DWIGHT, C., in Mitchell v. Reed, where there is a dictum to the contrary (61 N.Y. at p. 143). To say that a partner is free without restriction to buy in the reversion of the property where the business is conducted is to say in effect that he may strip the good will of its chief element of value, since good will is largely dependent upon continuity of possession (Matter of Brown, 242 N.Y. 1, 7.) Equity refuses to confine within the bounds of classified transactions its precept of a loyalty that is undivided and unselfish. . . .

We have no thought to hold that Salmon was guilty of a conscious purpose to defraud. Very likely he assumed in all good faith that with the approaching end of the venture he might ignore his coadventurer and take the extension for himself. He had given to the enterprise time and labor as well as money. He had made it a success. Meinhard, who had given money, but neither time nor labor, had already been richly paid. There might seem to be something grasping in his insistence upon more. Such recriminations are not unusual when coadventurers fall out. They are not without their force if conduct is to be judged by the common standards of competitors. That is not to say that they have pertinency here. Salmon had put himself in a position in which thought of self was to be renounced, however hard the abnegation. He was much more than a coadventurer. He was a managing coadventurer (Clegg v. Edmondson, 8 D.M. & G. 787, 807). For him and for those like him, the rule of undivided loyalty is relentless and supreme (Wendt v. Fischer, supra; Munson v. Syracuse, etc., R.R. Co., 103 N.Y. 58, 74). A different question would be here if there were lacking any nexus of relation between the business conducted by the manager and the opportunity brought to him as an incident of management (Dean v. MacDowell, 8 Ch.D. 345, 354; Aas v. Benham, 1891, 2 Ch. 244, 258; Latta v. Kilbourn, 150 U.S. 524). For this problem, as for most, there are distinctions of degree. If Salmon had received from Gerry a proposition to lease a building at a location far removed, he might have held for himself the privilege thus acquired, or so we shall assume. Here the subject-matter of the new lease was an extension and enlargement of the subject-matter of the old one. A managing coadventurer appropriating the benefit of such a lease without warning to his partner might fairly expect to be reproached with conduct that was underhand, or lacking, to say the least, in reasonable candor, if the partner were to surprise him in the act of signing the new instrument. Conduct subject to that reproach does not receive from equity a healing benediction.

A question remains as to the form and extent of the equitable interest to be allotted to the plaintiff. The trust as declared has been held to attach to the lease which was in the name of the defendant corporation. We think it ought to attach at the option of the defendant Salmon to the shares of stock which were owned by him or were under his control. The difference may be important if the lessee shall wish to execute an assignment of the lease, as it ought to be free to do with the consent of the lessor. On the other hand, an equal division of the shares might lead to other hardships. It might take away from Salmon the power of control and management which under the plan of the joint venture he was to have from first to last. The number of shares to be allotted to the plaintiff should, therefore, be reduced to such an extent as may be necessary to preserve to the defendant Salmon the expected measure of dominion. To that end an extra share should be added to his half.

Subject to this adjustment, we agree with the Appellate Division that the plaintiff's equitable interest is to be measured by the value of half of the entire lease, and not merely by half of some undivided part. A single building covers the whole area. Physical division is impracticable along the lines of the Bristol site, the keystone of the whole. Division of interests and burdens is equally impracticable. Salmon, as tenant under the new lease, or as guarantor of the performance of the tenant's obligations, might well protest if Meinhard, claiming an equitable interest, had offered to assume a liability not equal to Salmon's, but only half as great. He might justly insist that the lease must be accepted by his coadventurer in such form as it had been given, and not constructively divided into imaginary fragments. What must be yielded to the one may be demanded by the other. The lease as it has been executed is single and entire. If confusion has resulted from the union of adjoining parcels, the trustee who consented to the union must bear the inconvenience (Hart v. Ten Eyck, 2 Johns. Ch. 62)....

[Three judges dissented. Andrews, J., who wrote the dissenting opinion, agreed that "(w)ere this a general partnership I should have little doubt as to the correctness of this result assuming the new lease to be an offshoot of the old," but concluded that the parties' joint venture "had in view a very limited object and was to end at a limited time."]

NOTE ON SUITS BY A PARTNER AGAINST A PARTNERSHIP

UPA § 13 provides that "[w]here, by any wrongful conduct or omission of any partner acting in the ordinary course of business of the partnership or with the authority of his co-partners, loss or injury is caused to any person, *not being a partner in the partnership* ... the partnership is liable therefor...." (Emphasis added.) By reason of the italicized phrase, this section is commonly interpreted not to authorize a suit by a partner against a partnership. As a result, the courts have often limited a partner's remedies against the partnership to suits for dissolution or for an accounting. See Beckman v. Farmer, 579 A.2d 618, 649 (D.C.App.1990); Hubbard, Alternative Remedies in Minority Partners' Suits on Partnership Causes of Action, 39 Sw.L.J. 1022 (1986). In *Beckman,* the court justified the rule on the ground that:

> [P]ractical difficulties commend the settlement of accounts before an action at law between partners can be maintained. The value of partners' respective interests cannot be determined while accounts are in flux, but only after partnership liabilities are satisfied, all assets are marshalled, the partners' capital accounts adjusted, and the amount of any surplus ascertained.

Id. at 649–50. This justification is unconvincing. The complete settlement of accounts may be easier at the termination of the partnership, but a partner who wants to make a claim against the partnership is not asking for a complete settlement of accounts.

Given the weak or nonexistent justification of the traditional rule, it is not surprising that the rule is subject to inconsistent and important exceptions:

> The general rule is subject to several exceptions . . . [For example, an accounting in] equity may not be necessary when breach of the partnership agreement, wrongful dissolution, fraudulent breach of trust, or misappropriation of money clearly belonging to another partner is charged. . . .

Id. at 650.

RUPA § 305, which is the counterpart of UPA § 13, drops the phrase "not being a partner in the partnership." The Comment states that this change "is intended to permit a partner to sue the partnership on a tort or other theory during the term of the partnership, rather than being limited to the remedies of dissolution and accounting."

SECTION 8. DISSOLUTION (I): DISSOLUTION BY RIGHTFUL ELECTION

UNIFORM PARTNERSHIP ACT §§ 29, 30, 31(1), 38(1), 40

REVISED UNIFORM PARTNERSHIP ACT §§ 601, 603, 701, 801, 802, 803, 804, 807

[See Appendix]

DREIFUERST v. DREIFUERST

Wisconsin Court of Appeals, 1979.
90 Wis.2d 566, 280 N.W.2d 335.

Before BROWN, P.J., BODE, J., and ROBERT W. HANSEN, Reserve Judge.

BROWN, P.J. The plaintiffs and the defendant, all brothers, formed a partnership. The partnership operated two feed mills, one located at St. Cloud, Wisconsin and one located at Elkhart Lake, Wisconsin. There were no written Articles of Partnership governing this partnership.

On October 4, 1975, the plaintiffs served the defendant with a notice of dissolution and wind-up of the partnership. The action for dissolution and wind-up was commenced on January 27, 1976. The dissolution complaint alleged that the plaintiffs elected to dissolve the partnership. There was no allegation of fault, expulsion or contravention of an alleged agreement as grounds for dissolution. The parties were unable, however, to agree to a winding-up of the partnership.

Hearings on the dissolution were held on October 18, 1976 and March 4, 1977. Testimony was presented regarding the value of the partnership assets and each partner's equity. At the March 4, 1977 hearing, the defendant requested that the partnership be sold pursuant to sec. 178.33(1), Stats., and that the court allow a sale, at which time the partners would bid on the entire property. By such sale, the plaintiffs could continue to run the business under a new partnership, and the defendant's partnership equity could be satisfied in cash.

On February 20, 1978, the trial court, by written decision, denied the defendant's request for a sale and instead divided the partnership assets in-kind according to the valuation presented by the plaintiffs. The plaintiffs were given the physical assets from the Elkhart Lake mill, and the defendant was given the physical assets from the St. Cloud mill. The defendant appeals this order and judgment dividing the assets in-kind.

Under sec. 178.25(1), Stats., a partnership is dissolved when any partner ceases to be associated in the carrying on of the business. The partnership is not terminated, but continues, until the winding-up of the partnership is complete. Sec. 178.25(2), Stats. The action started by the plaintiffs, in this case, was an action for dissolution and wind-up. The plaintiffs were not continuing the partnership and, therefore, secs. 178.36 and 178.37, Stats.,[3] do not apply. The sole question in this case is whether, in the absence of a written agreement to the contrary, a partner, upon dissolution and wind-up of the partnership, can force a sale of the partnership assets.

At the outset, we note, and the parties agree, that the appellant was not in contravention of the partnership agreement since there was no partnership agreement. The partnership was a partnership at will. They also agree there was no written agreement governing distribution of partnership assets upon dissolution and wind-up. The dispute, in this case, is over the authority of the trial court to order in-kind distribution in the absence of any agreement of the partners.

Section 178.33(1), Stats., provides:

> When dissolution is caused in any way, except in contravention of the partnership agreement, each partner, as against his copartners and all persons claiming through them in respect to their interests in the partnership, *unless otherwise agreed,* may have the partnership property applied to discharge its liabilities, and the surplus applied to pay *in cash* the net amount owing to the respective partners. [Emphasis supplied.]

The appellant contends this statute grants him the right to force a sale of the partnership assets in order to obtain his fair share of the partnership assets in cash upon dissolution. He claims that in the absence of an agreement of the partners to in-kind distribution, the trial court had no authority to distribute the assets in-kind. He is entitled to an in-cash settlement after judicial sale.

The respondents contend the statute does not entitle the appellant to force a sale and grants the trial court the power to distribute the assets in-kind if in-kind distribution is equitably possible and doesn't jeopardize the rights of creditors.

We do not believe that the statute can be read in any way to permit in-kind distribution unless the partners agree to in-kind distribution or unless there is a partnership agreement calling for in-kind distribution at the time of dissolution and wind-up.

A partnership at will is a partnership which has no definite term or particular undertaking and can rightfully be dissolved by the express will of any partner. Sec. 178.26(1)(b), Stats.; J. Crane and A. Bromberg, Law of Partnership § 74(b) (1968) [hereinafter cited as Crane and Bromberg]. In the present case, the respondents

---

3. Sections 178.36 and 178.37 deal with cases where the partnership is not wound up, but continues after one partner leaves.

wanted to dissolve the partnership. This being a partnership at will, they could rightfully dissolve this partnership with or without the consent of the appellant. In addition, the respondents have never claimed the appellant was in violation of any partnership agreement. Therefore, neither the appellant nor the respondents have wrongfully dissolved the partnership.

Unless otherwise agreed, partners who have not wrongfully dissolved a partnership have a right to wind up the partnership. Sec. 178.32, Stats. Winding-up is the process of settling partnership affairs after dissolution. Winding-up is often called liquidation and involves reducing the assets to cash to pay creditors and distribute to partners the value of their respective interests. Crane and Bromberg, supra, §§ 73 and 80(c). Thus, lawful dissolution (or dissolution which is caused in any way except in contravention of the partnership agreement) gives each partner the right to have the business liquidated and his share of the surplus paid *in cash*. Young v. Cooper, 30 Tenn.App. 55, 203 S.W.2d 376 (1947); sec. 178.33(1), Stats.; Crane and Bromberg, supra, § 83A. In-kind distribution is permissible only in very limited circumstances. If the partnership agreement permits in-kind distribution upon dissolution or wind-up or if, at any time prior to wind-up, all partners agree to in-kind distribution, the court may order in-kind distribution. Logoluso v. Logoluso, 233 Cal.App.2d 523, 43 Cal.Rptr. 678 (1965); Gathright v. Fulton, 122 Va. 17, 94 S.E. 191, 194 (1917). While at least one court has permitted in-kind distribution, absent an agreement by all partners, Rinke v. Rinke, 330 Mich. 615, 48 N.W.2d 201 (1951), the court's holding in that case was limited. In *Rinke*, the court stated:

> The decree of the trial court provided for dividing the assets of the partnerships rather than for the sale thereof and the distribution of cash proceeds. Appellants insist that such method of procedure is erroneous and [not] contemplated by the uniform partnership act. Attention is directed to Section 38 of said act, C.L. 1948, § 449.38, Stat.Ann. § 20.38. Construing together pertinent provisions of the statute leads to the conclusion that it was not the intention of the legislature in the enactment of the Uniform Partnership Act to impose a mandatory requirement that, under all circumstances, the assets of a dissolved partnership shall be sold and the money received therefor divided among those entitled to it, particularly so, as in the case at bar, where there are no debts to be paid from the proceeds. *The situation disclosed by the record in the present case is somewhat unusual in that no one other than the former partners is interested in the assets of the businesses. In view of this situation and of the nature of the assets,* we think that the trial court was correct in apportioning them to the

partners. There is no showing that appellants have been prejudiced thereby. [Emphasis supplied.]   330 Mich. at 628, 48 N.W.2d at 207.

The Michigan court's holding was limited to situations where: (1) there were no creditors to be paid from the proceeds, (2) ordering a sale would be senseless since no one other than the partners would be interested in the assets of the business, and (3) an in-kind distribution was fair to all partners.

That is not the case here. There was no showing that there were no creditors who would be paid from the proceeds, nor was there a showing that no one other than the partners would be interested in the assets. These factors are important if an in-kind distribution is to be allowed. Section 178.33(1) and § 38 of the Uniform Partnership Act are intended to protect creditors as well as partners. In-kind distributions may affect a creditor's right to collect the debt owed since the assets of the partnership, as a whole, may be worth more than the assets once divided up. Thus, the creditor's ability to collect from the individual partners may be jeopardized. Secondly, if others are interested in the assets, a sale provides a more accurate means of establishing the market value of the assets and, thus, better assuring each partner his share in the value of the assets. Where only the partners are interested in the assets, a fair value can be determined without the necessity of a sale. The sale would be merely the partners bidding with each other without any competition. This process could be accomplished through negotiations or at trial with the court as a final arbitrator of the value of the assets. With these policy considerations in mind, we think the Michigan court's holding in *Rinke* was limited to the facts of that case. Those facts not being present in this case, we do not feel an in-kind distribution in this case was proper.

However, even assuming the respondents in this case can show that there are no creditors to be paid, no one other than the partners are interested in the assets, and in-kind distribution would be fair to all partners, we cannot read § 38 of the Uniform Partnership Act or sec. 178.33(1), Stats. (the Wisconsin equivalent), as permitting an in-kind distribution under any circumstances, unless all partners agree. The statute and § 38 of the Uniform Partnership Act are quite clear that if a partner may force liquidation, he is entitled to his share of the partnership assets, after creditors are paid *in cash*. To the extent that Rinke v. Rinke, supra, creates an exception to cash distribution, we decline to adopt that exception. We, therefore, must hold the trial court erred in ordering an in-kind distribution of the assets of the partnership.

The last question that arises is whether the appellant can force an actual sale of the assets or whether the trial court can determine the fair market value of the assets and order the respondents to pay the appellant in cash an amount equal to his share in the assets.

As discussed above, a sale is the best means of determining the true fair market value of the assets. Generally, liquidation envisions some form of sale. Since the statutes provide that, unless otherwise agreed, any partner who has not wrongfully dissolved the partnership has the right to wind up the partnership and force liquidation, he likewise has a right to force a sale, unless otherwise agreed. Fortugno v. Hudson Manure Co., 51 N.J.Super. 482, 144 A.2d 207, 218–19 (1958); Young v. Cooper, 30 Tenn.App. 55, 203 S.W.2d 376 (1947). See also Crane and Bromberg, supra, § 83A; 4 Vill.L.Rev. 457 (1959). While judicial sales in some instances may cause economic hardships, these hardships can be avoided by the use of partnership agreements.

By the Court.—Judgment reversed and cause remanded for further proceedings not inconsistent with this opinion.

NOTE ON NICHOLES v. HUNT

Nicholes v. Hunt, 273 Or. 255, 541 P.2d 820 (1975) was a case of rightful dissolution of a partnership between Nicholes and Hunt. Hunt had contributed an operating business to the partnership and Nicholes had contributed cash and services. The trial court refused to order a sale of the partnership's assets, and instead awarded the operating assets to Hunt and ordered that Nicholes be paid the value of his partnership interest in cash. Affirmed. "We conclude, as defendant contends and as the trial court found, that the equities lie with the defendant in this case.... The defendant conceived and designed the machinery and the method of operation, which was successfully operated for a number of years before formation of the partnership at will." The court relied in part on Rinke v. Rinke, which was mentioned but distinguished in *Dreirfurst*. See also Swann v. Mitchell, 435 So.2d 797 (Fla.1983); Wiese v. Wiese, 107 So.2d 208 (Fla.App.1958); Schaefer v. Bork, 413 N.W.2d 873 (Minn. App.1987).

PAGE v. PAGE

Supreme Court of California, 1961.
55 Cal.2d 192, 10 Cal.Rptr. 643, 359 P.2d 41.

TRAYNOR, J.—Plaintiff and defendant are partners in a linen supply business in Santa Maria, California. Plaintiff appeals from a

Eisenberg,Intro.To Agency&Partn.—4

judgment declaring the partnership to be for a term rather than at will.

The partners entered into an oral partnership agreement in 1949. Within the first two years each partner contributed approximately $43,000 for the purchase of land, machinery, and linen needed to begin the business. From 1949 to 1957 the enterprise was unprofitable, losing approximately $62,000. The partnership's major creditor is a corporation, wholly owned by plaintiff, that supplies the linen and machinery necessary for the day-to-day operation of the business. This corporation holds a $47,000 demand note of the partnership. The partnership operations began to improve in 1958. The partnership earned $3,824.41 in that year and $2,282.30 in the first three months of 1959. Despite this improvement plaintiff wishes to terminate the partnership.

The Uniform Partnership Act provides that a partnership may be dissolved "By the express will of any partner when no definite term or particular undertaking is specified." (Corp.Code, § 15031, subd. (1)(b).) The trial court found that the partnership is for a term, namely, "such reasonable time as is necessary to enable said partnership to repay from partnership profits, indebtedness incurred for the purchase of land, buildings, laundry and delivery equipment and linen for the operation of such business...." Plaintiff correctly contends that this finding is without support in the evidence.

Defendant testified that the terms of the partnership were to be similar to former partnerships of plaintiff and defendant, and that the understanding of these partnerships was that "we went into partnership to start the business and let the business operation pay for itself,—put in so much money, and let the business pay itself out." There was also testimony that one of the former partnership agreements provided in writing that the profits were to be retained until all obligations were paid.

Upon cross-examination defendant admitted that the former partnership in which the earnings were to be retained until the obligations were repaid was substantially different from the present partnership. The former partnership was a limited partnership and provided for a definite term of five years and a partnership at will thereafter. Defendant insists, however, that the method of operation of the former partnership showed an understanding that all obligations were to be repaid from profits. He nevertheless concedes that there was no understanding as to the term of the present partnership in the event of losses. He was asked: "[W]as there any discussion with reference to the continuation of the business in the event of losses?" He replied, "Not that I can remember." He was then asked, "Did you have any understanding with Mr. Page, your brother, the plaintiff in this action, as to how the obligations were to be paid if there were losses?" He replied, "Not that I can remember. I can't remember discussing that at all. We never figured on losing, I guess."

Viewing this evidence most [favorably] for defendant, it proves only that the partners expected to meet current expenses from current income and to recoup their investment if the business were successful.

Defendant contends that such an expectation is sufficient to create a partnership for a term under the rule of Owen v. Cohen, 19 Cal.2d 147, 150 [119 P.2d 713]. In that case we held that when a partner advances a sum of money to a partnership with the understanding that the amount contributed was to be a loan to the partnership and was to be repaid as soon as feasible from the prospective profits of the business, the partnership is for the term reasonably required to repay the loan. It is true that Owen v. Cohen, supra, and other cases hold that partners may impliedly agree to continue in business until a certain sum of money is earned (Mervyn Investment Co. v. Biber, 184 Cal. 637, 641–642 [194 P. 1037]), or one or more partners recoup their investments (Vangel v. Vangel, 116 Cal.App.2d 615, 625 [254 P.2d 919]), or until certain debts are paid (Owen v. Cohen, supra, at p. 150), or until certain property could be disposed of on favorable terms (Shannon v. Hudson, 161 Cal.App.2d 44, 48 [325 P.2d 1022]). In each of these cases, however, the implied agreement found support in the evidence.

In Owen v. Cohen, supra, the partners borrowed substantial amounts of money to launch the enterprise and there was an understanding that the loans would be repaid from partnership profits. In Vangel v. Vangel, supra, one partner loaned his copartner money to invest in the partnership with the understanding that the money would be repaid from partnership profits. In Mervyn Investment Co. v. Biber, supra, one partner contributed all the capital, the other contributed his services, and it was understood that upon the repayment of the contributed capital from partnership profits the partner who contributed his services would receive a one-third interest in the partnership assets. In each of these cases the court properly held that the partners impliedly promised to continue the partnership for a term reasonably required to allow the partnership to earn sufficient money to accomplish the understood objective. In Shannon v. Hudson, supra, the parties entered into a joint venture to build and operate a motel until it could be sold upon favorable and mutually satisfactory terms, and the court held that the joint venture was for a reasonable term sufficient to accomplish the purpose of the joint venture.

In the instant case, however, defendant failed to prove any facts from which an agreement to continue the partnership for a term may be implied. The understanding to which defendant testified was no more than a common hope that the partnership earnings would pay for all the necessary expenses. Such a hope does not establish even by implication a "definite term or particular undertaking" as required by section 15031, subdivision (1)(b), of the Corporations Code.

All partnerships are ordinarily entered into with the hope that they will be profitable, but that alone does not make them all partnerships for a term and obligate the partners to continue in the partnerships until all of the losses over a period of many years have been recovered.

Defendant contends that plaintiff is acting in bad faith and is attempting to use his superior financial position to appropriate the now profitable business of the partnership. Defendant has invested $43,000 in the firm, and owing to the long period of losses his interest in the partnership assets is very small. The fact that plaintiff's wholly owned corporation holds a $47,000 demand note of the partnership may make it difficult to sell the business as a going concern. Defendant fears that upon dissolution he will receive very little and that plaintiff, who is the managing partner and knows how to conduct the operations of the partnership, will receive a business that has become very profitable because of the establishment of Vandenberg Air Force Base in its vicinity. Defendant charges that plaintiff has been content to share the losses but now that the business has become profitable he wishes to keep all the gains.

There is no showing in the record of bad faith or that the improved profit situation is more than temporary. In any event these contentions are irrelevant to the issue whether the partnership is for a term or at will. Since, however, this action is for a declaratory judgment and will be the basis for future action by the parties, it is appropriate to point out that defendant is amply protected by the fiduciary duties of copartners.

Even though the Uniform Partnership Act provides that a partnership at will may be dissolved by the express will of any partner (Corp.Code, § 15031, subd. (1)(b)), this power, like any other power held by a fiduciary, must be exercised in good faith.

We have often stated that "Partners are trustees for each other, and in all proceedings connected with the conduct of the partnership every partner is bound to act in the highest good faith to his copartner and may not obtain any advantage over him in the partnership affairs by the slightest misrepresentation, concealment, threat or adverse pressure of any kind." (Llewelyn v. Levi, 157 Cal.

31, 37 [106 P. 219]; Richards v. Fraser, 122 Cal. 456, 460 [55 P. 246]; Yeomans v. Lysfjord, 162 Cal.App.2d 357, 361–362 [327 P.2d 957]; cf. MacIsaac v. Pozzo, 26 Cal.2d 809, 813 [161 P.2d 449]; Corp.Code, § 15021.) Although Civil Code, section 2411, embodying the foregoing language, was repealed upon the adoption of the Uniform Partnership Act, it was not intended by the adoption of that act to diminish the fiduciary duties between partners. (See MacIsaac v. Pozzo, 26 Cal.2d 809, 813 [161 P.2d 449]; Yeomans v. Lysfjord, 162 Cal.App.2d 357, 361–362 [327 P.2d 957].)

A partner at will is not bound to remain in a partnership, regardless of whether the business is profitable or unprofitable. A partner may not, however, by use of adverse pressure "freeze out" a copartner and appropriate the business to his own use. A partner may not dissolve a partnership to gain the benefits of the business for himself, unless he fully compensates his copartner for his share of the prospective business opportunity. In this regard his fiduciary duties are at least as great as those of a shareholder of a corporation.

In the case of In re Security Finance Co., 49 Cal.2d 370, 376–377 [317 P.2d 1], we stated that although shareholders representing 50 per cent of the voting power have a right under Corporations Code, section 4600, to dissolve a corporation, they may not exercise such right in order "to defraud the other shareholders [citation], to 'freeze out' minority shareholders [citation], or to sell the assets of the dissolved corporation at an inadequate price. [Citation.]"

Likewise in the instant case, plaintiff has the power to dissolve the partnership by express notice to defendant. If, however, it is proved that plaintiff acted in bad faith and violated his fiduciary duties by attempting to appropriate to his own use the new prosperity of the partnership without adequate compensation to his copartner, the dissolution would be wrongful and the plaintiff would be liable as provided by subdivision (2)(a) of Corporations Code, section 15038 (rights of partners upon wrongful dissolution) for violation of the implied agreement not to exclude defendant wrongfully from the partnership business opportunity.*

The judgment is reversed.

GIBSON, C.J., McCOMB, J., PETERS, J., WHITE, J., DOOLING, J., and WOOD (PARKER), J. pro tem., concurred.

---

* The consequences of wrongful dissolution are considered in Section 9, infra.   [Footnote by ed.]

LEFF v. GUNTER, 33 Cal.3d 508, 189 Cal.Rptr. 377, 658 P.2d 740 (1983). In this case, the California Supreme Court, citing Page v. Page, held that

> There is an obvious and essential unfairness in one part-ner's attempted exploitation of a partnership opportunity for his own personal benefit and to the resulting detriment of his copartners. It may be assumed, although perhaps not always easily proven, that such competition with one's own partner-ship is greatly facilitated by access to relevant information available only to partners. Moreover, it is equally obvious that a formal disassociation of oneself from a partnership does not change this situation unless the interested parties specifically agree otherwise. It is no less a violation of the trust imposed between partners to permit the exploitation of that partnership information and opportunity to the prejudice of one's former associates by the simple expedient of withdrawal from the partnership.

––––––––

ROSENFELD, MEYER & SUSMAN v. COHEN, 146 Cal.App.3d 200, 194 Cal.Rptr. 180 (1983). In this case, the court, citing Page v. Page and Leff v. Gunter, held that a partnership at will (here, a law partnership) cannot be dissolved in bad faith:

> ... RM&S [the partnership] sought to prove that C [and] R [the partners who withdrew] used their threat to resign and cause RM&S a large loss as a weapon to attempt to change the partnership relationships at the expense of other RM&S part-ners.

> ... [T]he law and motion department's holding that a partner may dissolve a partnership at will in bad faith is not only contrary to *Page v. Page* ... and other cases heretofore cited, but is also contrary to the established principle that even non-fiduciaries must exercise their rights in good faith, deal fairly with each other and refrain from injuring the right of another party to receive the benefits of an agreement or rela-tionship....

> Moreover, the law and motion department's ruling that as a matter of law a partner has the absolute right to dissolve a partnership at will without regard to breach of fiduciary conse-quences is contrary to the principle that a person may be estopped from exercising rights in bad faith.

At the trial of C and R's cross-complaint, however, it was found that

RM&S had been guilty of fraud towards C and R on other partnership matters, and therefore had unclean hands; that RM&S had acted in bad faith; and that C and R had not dissolved the partnership in bad faith. 191 Cal.App.3d 1035, 237 Cal.Rptr. 14, 19, 30 (1987).

In Fraser v. Bogucki, 203 Cal.App.3d 604, 250 Cal.Rptr. 41 (1988), the court drew the questionable conclusion that "[t]he *Rosenfeld* case only provides a remedy where a lawyer violates his fiduciary duty to his partners by attempting to reap personal gain from the unfinished business of a dissolved partnership."

———

PRENTISS v. SHEFFEL, 20 Ariz.App. 411, 513 P.2d 949 (1973). A and B each owned a 42.5% interest in a partnership, and C owned a 15% interest. A and B fell out with C and the parties went to court. The trial court concluded that the partnership had been dissolved by the parties' actions, and ordered a sale of the partnership assets. C asked the trial court to order A and B to refrain from bidding for the assets at the judicial sale. The trial court denied the request. Affirmed.

The principal contention urged by the defendant is that he was *wrongfully* excluded from the management of the partnership, and therefore, because he would in some way be disadvantaged, the plaintiffs should not be allowed to purchase the partnership assets at a judicial sale. The record, however, does not support the defendant's position on two particulars. While the trial court did find that the defendant was excluded from the management of the partnership, there was no indication that such exclusion was done for the wrongful purpose of obtaining the partnership assets in bad faith rather than being merely the result of the inability of the partners to harmoniously function in a partnership relationship.

Moreover, the defendant has failed to demonstrate how he was injured by the participation of the plaintiffs in the judicial sale. To the contrary, from all the evidence it appears that if the plaintiffs had not participated, the sales price would have been considerably lower. Absent the plaintiff's bid, there would have been only two qualified initial bids, which were $2,076,000 and $2,040,000 respectively. However, with the participation of plaintiffs, whose initial bid was $2,100,000, the final sales price was bid to $2,250,000. Thus it appears that defendant's 15% interest in the partnership was considerably *enhanced* by the plaintiffs' participation.

The cases the defendant relies upon to support his contention that the plaintiffs should not have been allowed to bid on the partnership assets all deal with instances where, unlike here, a partner has acted in bad faith, engaged in wrongful or fraudulent conduct, or has attempted to avoid paying an adequate consideration for the minority partner's interest. *See Graham v. Street*, 109 Utah 460, 166 P.2d 524 (1946); *Von Au v. Magenheimer*, 126 App.Div. 257, 110 N.Y.S. 629 (1908) and *Theis v. Spokane Falls Gaslight Co.*, 34 Wash. 23, 74 P. 1004 (1904). The defendant characterizes the sale to plaintiffs as a forced sale of his partnership interest. However, defendant was not forced to sell his interest to the plaintiffs. He had the same right to purchase the partnership assets as they did, by submitting the highest bid at the judicial sale. His argument that the plaintiffs were bidding "paper" dollars due to their 85% partnership interest is without force. He too could have bid "paper" dollars to the extent of his 15% interest. Moreover, the fact that the plaintiffs could bid "paper" dollars made it possible, as defendant recognizes in his brief, for them to bid higher than outsiders. As a consequence of this ability to enter a higher bid, the value of the defendant's 15% interest in the sale proceeds increased proportionately.

GIRARD BANK v. HALEY, 460 Pa. 237, 332 A.2d 443 (1975). Mrs. Reid, a partner in an at-will partnership, had sent the following letter to the other three partners: "I am terminating the partnership which the four of us entered into on the 28th day of September, 1958." The issue was whether this letter caused a dissolution of the partnership. The chancellor, at trial, held that it did not, because neither in the letter nor at trial did Mrs. Reid offer evidence to justify a termination of the partnership. Reversed.

In supposing that justification was necessary the learned court below fell into error. Dissolution of a partnership is caused, under § 31 of the [UPA], "by the express will of any partner." The expression of that will need not be supported by any justification. If no "definite term or particular undertaking [is] specified in the partnership agreement," such an at-will dissolution does not violate the agreement between the partners; indeed, an expression of a will to dissolve is effective as a dissolution even if in contravention of the agreement. Ibid. We have recognized the generality of a dissolution at will. If the dissolution results in breach of contract, the aggrieved partners may recover damages for the breach and, if they meet certain conditions, may continue the firm business for the duration of the agreed term or until the particular undertaking is completed. See § 38 of the Act....

The remaining question is whether or not the unilateral dissolution made by Mrs. Reid violated the partnership agreement. The agreement contains no provision fixing a definite term, and the sole "undertaking" to which it refers is that of maintaining and leasing real property. This statement is merely one of general purpose, however, and cannot be said to set forth a "particular undertaking" within the meaning of that phrase as it is used in the Act. A "particular undertaking" under the statute must be capable of accomplishment at some time, although the exact time may be unknown and unascertainable at the date of the agreement. Leasing property, like many other trades or businesses, involves entering into a business relationship which may continue indefinitely; there is nothing "particular" about it. We thus conclude, on the record before us, that the dissolution of the partnership was not in contravention of the agreement.

NOTE ON PARTNERSHIP BREAKUP UNDER THE UPA

One of the most difficult issues in partnership law is how to treat cases in which a person's status as a partner is terminated, the partnership is to be terminated as a going concern, or both. (The complexity of these issues is illustrated by the fact that they occupy about a third of the text and comment of RUPA.) The difficult substantive issues raised by these issues have been made even more complex by the nomenclature that partnership law has employed. The UPA and RUPA take different strategies toward both the nomenclature and the underlying substantive issues. This Note will focus on dissolution under the UPA. A Note in Section 9, infra, will focus on dissolution under RUPA.

Before getting directly into the legal issues, it is useful to outline the business economics involved.

Assume that a partnership is to be terminated as a going concern. Typically, the termination process will fall into three phases.

(i) The first phase consists of an event—which may be a decision of a partner or a court—that sets the termination in motion.

(ii) Inevitably, some period of time must elapse between the moment at which that event occurs and the time at which termination of the partnership is completed. The second phase consists of the process of actually terminating the partnership's business. For example, if the partnership is in the manufacturing business, to terminate the business the partnership will need to pay off its debts, settle its contracts with employees and suppliers, find a purchaser for the factory, and so forth. All this will take time.

(iii) The final phase consists of the completion of the second phase and an end to the partnership as a going concern.

Under the UPA, the first phase is referred to as "dissolution," the second phase is referred to as "winding up," and the third phase is referred to as "termination." As the Official Comment states, "dissolution designates the point in time when the partners cease to carry on the business together; ... winding up, the process of settling partnership affairs after dissolution [; and termination, the point in time when all the partnership affairs are wound up]." Similarly, the principal draftsman of the UPA explained as follows the manner in which that statute uses the term "dissolution":

[The term "dissolution" is used in the UPA to designate] a change in the relation of the partners caused by any partner ceasing to be associated in the carrying on of the business. As thus used "dissolution" does not terminate the partnership, it merely ends the carrying on of the business in that partnership. The partnership continues until the winding up of partnership affairs is completed.

Lewis, The Uniform Partnership Act, 24 Yale L.J. 617, 626–27 (1915).

To put all of this somewhat differently, "dissolution" is used in the UPA to describe a change in the *legal status* of the partners and the partnership. "Winding-up" is used to describe the *economic* event of liquidation that follows dissolution.

Under the UPA, any termination of a person's status as a partner effects a dissolution of the partnership. It's not easy to see why this should be so when, as often happens, the remaining partners rightfully carry on the partnership's business after one partner has departed. Basically, the UPA's treatment of this issue seems to have been driven by a form of conceptualism. The UPA defines a partnership as an aggregation of persons to carry on business for profit as co-owners, rather than as an entity. Because the UPA treats a partnership as an aggregation, the drafters seemed to have believed that it followed "logically" that any change in the identity of the partners "necessarily" worked a dissolution of the partnership. If a partnership is conceptualized as an aggregation of the partners, and if the partners in Partnership P are A, B, C, and D, then it may have seemed to the drafters of the UPA that if D ceases to be a partner, Partnership P "must be" dissolved, because there is no longer an aggregation of A, B, C, and D. Following this line, UPA § 29 defines dissolution as "the change in the relation of partners caused by any partner ceasing to be associated in the carrying on" of the partnership's business.

The law, however, should not be built on deductive logic, but on policy, morality, and experience. We make rules because they are desirable, not because they are deducible. If a person ceases to be a partner, the law can treat the partnership as either dissolved or not dissolved. Which course the law takes should depend on which treatment better protects the parties' expectations and best reflects social policy. This, in turn, depends on what consequences the law should and does attach to dissolution.

Broadly speaking, the law may attach consequences to dissolution: (1) among the partners themselves; (2) between the partners as a group, and third persons such as individuals or firms with whom the partnership has contracted; and (3) for tax purposes. The remainder of this Note will consider each of these areas.

(1) *Consequences among the partners.* Under the UPA, upon the occurrence of dissolution—which, remember, under the UPA means simply that any partner ceases to be a partner—then unless otherwise agreed, the partnership normally must sell its assets for cash and distribute the proceeds of the sale among all the partners. See Dreifuerst v. Dreifuerst, supra. (If, however, a partner, D, *wrongfully* causes dissolution, UPA § 38(2)(b) provides that notwithstanding the occurrence of dissolution the remaining partners can continue the partnership's business. To do so, however, the remaining partners must either (i) pay D the value of his partnership interest (but without counting the value of the partnership's good will), minus any damages caused by the dissolution, or (ii) put up a bond to secure that payment, and indemnify D against present and future partnership liabilities. See Section 9, infra.)

Furthermore, UPA § 38(1) provides that "[w]hen dissolution is [rightfully] caused ... each partner ... *unless otherwise agreed,* may have the partnership property applied to discharge its liabilities, and the surplus applied to pay in cash the net amount owing to the respective partners." (Emphasis added.) It is well accepted, under the "unless" clause, that the partnership agreement can provide that after the termination of a person's status as a partner (and, therefore, after the dissolution of the partnership under the UPA) the remaining partners can continue the partnership business, even if the partnership has been "dissolved" and the dissolution is rightfully caused. See, e.g., Meehan v. Shaughnessy, 404 Mass. 419, 535 N.E.2d 1255 (1989); Adams v. Jarvis, 23 Wis.2d 453, 127 N.W.2d 400 (1964).

Agreements under which the remaining partners can continue the business after dissolution are common, especially in large partnerships, such as law partnerships. Such agreements are usually known as business-continuation agreements or, more simply, continuation agreements. Typically, continuation agreements include not only the right of the remaining partners to continue the partnership's business, but also the terms on which the partner who causes dissolution (or his estate) will be compensated for his partnership interest.

(2) *Effect of dissolution on the relationship between the partnership and third parties.* As among the partners, it often won't matter very much whether the withdrawal of a partner does or does not cause dissolution, because as among the partners a continuation agreement can override the substantive effects that dissolution would otherwise have. However, dissolution may also affect the relationship of the partnership to third persons.

For example, suppose that Partnership P, consisting of partners A, B, C, and D, is dissolved by the withdrawal of D, but the business of the partnership is continued by A, B, and C under a continuation agreement. Because P has been dissolved, the partnership of A, B, and C may be deemed a "new" partnership for legal purposes, so that P's assets and agreements, such as leases, licenses, or franchises, must be "transferred" to the new partnership. See Report of the ABA Subcommittee on the Revision of the U.P.A., 43 Bus.Law. 121, 160–62 (1987). In a much remarked-on case, Fairway Development Co. v. Title Insurance Co., 621 F.Supp. 120 (N.D.Ohio 1985), Fairway, a partnership, sued Title Insurance Co. under a title guarantee policy. The policy had been issued at a time when the partners in Fairway were B, S, and W. Subsequently, B and S transferred their partnership interests to W and a third party, V. W and V apparently continued Fairway's business under the Fairway name. The court nevertheless held that Title Insurance was not bound under its policy because the partnership to which it had issued the policy had been legally dissolved.

A debated point under the UPA is whether a partnership agreement can provide not only that the partnership business may be continued after dissolution, but also that the withdrawal of a partner will not cause dissolution, so that the partnership's relation with third parties will not be affected by a partner's withdrawal, as happened in the *Fairway* case. The prevailing (but not unanimous) answer is no, on the ground that UPA § 31 expressly states that "[d]issolution is caused" by the withdrawal of a partner.

(3) *Tax consequences.* The tax-law treatment of dissolution is relatively straightforward, and largely unimpeded by conceptualism. Internal Revenue Code § 708 provides that a partnership's existence does not terminate for tax purposes until either "(A) no part of any business, financial operation, or venture of the partnership continues to be carried on by any of [the] partners in a partnership,

or (B) within a twelve-month period there is a sale or exchange of fifty percent or more of the total interest in partnership capital and profits.'' Accordingly, dissolution under partnership law is normally a non-event for federal income tax purposes. (Warning: Despite IRC § 708, dissolution may have tax effects on a partner who does not continue, or on his estate. Even these effects, however, can normally be avoided by a continuation agreement.)

———

SECTION 9. DISSOLUTION (II): DISSOLUTION BY JUDICIAL DECREE AND WRONGFUL DISSOLUTION

———

UNIFORM PARTNERSHIP ACT §§ 31(2), 32, 38

REVISED UNIFORM PARTNERSHIP ACT §§ 601, 602, 603, 701, 802, 803, 804, 807

[See Appendix]

———

DRASHNER v. SORENSON

Supreme Court of South Dakota, 1954.
75 S.D. 247, 63 N.W.2d 255.

SMITH, P.J. In January 1951 the plaintiff, C.H. Drashner, and defendants, A.D. Sorenson and Jacob P. Deis, associated themselves as co-owners in the real estate, loan and insurance business at Rapid City. For a consideration of $7500 they purchased the real estate and insurance agency known as J. Schumacher Co. located in an office room on the ground floor of the Alex Johnson Hotel building. The entire purchase price was advanced for the partnership by the defendants, but at the time of trial $3,000 of that sum had been repaid to them by the partnership. Although, as will appear from facts presently to be outlined, their operations were not unsuccessful, differences arose and on June 15, 1951 plaintiff commenced this action in which he sought an accounting, dissolution and winding up of the partnership. The answer and counterclaim of defendants prayed for like relief.

The cause came on for trial September 4, 1951. The court among others made the following findings. VII. "That thereafter the plaintiff violated the terms of said partnership agreement, in that he demanded a larger share of the income of the said partnership than he was entitled to receive under the terms of said partnership agreement; that the plaintiff was arrested for reckless driving and served a term in jail for said offense; that the plaintiff demanded that the defendants permit him to draw money for his own personal use out of the moneys held in escrow by the partnership; that the plaintiff spent a large amount of time during business hours in the Brass Rail Bar in Rapid City, South Dakota, and other bars, and neglected his duties in connection with the business of the said partnership. ... That the plaintiff, by his actions hereinbefore set forth, has made it impossible to carry on the partnership." The conclusions adopted read as follows: I "That the defendants are entitled to continue the partnership and have the value of the plaintiff's interest in the partnership business determined, upon the filing and approval of a good and sufficient bond, conditioned upon the release of the plaintiff from any liability arising out of the said partnership, and further conditioned upon the payment by the defendants to the plaintiff of the value of plaintiffs' interest in the partnership as determined by the Court." II "That in computing the value of the plaintiff's interest in the said partnership, the value of the good will of the business shall not be considered." III "That the value of the partnership shall be finally determined upon a hearing before this Court, ..." and IV "That the plaintiff shall be entitled to receive one-third of the value of the partnership property owned by the partnership on the 12th day of September, 1951, not including the good will of the business, after the payment of the liabilities of the partnership and the payment to the defendants of the invested capital in the sum of $4,500.00." Judgment was accordingly entered dissolving the partnership as of September 12, 1951.

After hearing at a later date the court found: I "That the value of the said partnership property on the 12th day of September, 1951, was the sum of Four Thousand Four Hundred Ninety-eight and 90/100 Dollars ($4498.90), and on said date there was due and owing by the partnership for accountant's services the sum of Four Hundred Eighty Dollars ($480.00), and that on said date the sum of Four Thousand Five Hundred Dollars ($4500.00) of the capital invested by the defendants had not been returned to the defendants." and II "That there is not sufficient partnership property to reimburse the defendants for their invested capital." Thereupon the court decreed "that the plaintiff had no interest in the property of the said partnership", and that the defendants were the sole owners thereof.

The assignments of error are predicated upon insufficiency of the evidence to support the findings and conclusions. Of these assignments, only those which question whether the court was warranted in finding that (a) the plaintiff caused the dissolution wrongfully, and (b) the value of the partnership property, exclusive of good will, was $4498.90 on the 12th day of September, 1951, merit discussion. A preliminary statement is necessary to place these issues in their framework.

The agreement of the parties contemplated an association which would continue at least until the $7500 advance of defendants had been repaid from the gross earnings of the business. Hence, it was not a partnership at will. Vangel v. Vangel, 116 Cal.App.2d 615, 254 P.2d 919; Zeibak v. Nasser, 12 Cal.2d 1, 82 P.2d 375. In apparent recognition of that fact, both plaintiff and defendants sought dissolution in contravention of the partnership agreement, see SDC 49.0603(2) under SDC 49.0604(1)(d) on the ground that the adverse party had caused the dissolution wrongfully by willfully and persistently committing a breach of the partnership agreement, and by so conducting himself in matters relating to the partnership business as to render impracticable the carrying on of the business in partnership with him.

[The court here quoted U.P.A. Section 38(2)].

From this background we turn to a consideration of the evidence from which the trial court inferred that plaintiff caused the dissolution wrongfully.

The breach between the parties resulted from a continuing controversy over the right of plaintiff to withdraw sufficient money from the partnership to defray his living expenses. Plaintiff was dependent upon his earnings for the support of his family. The defendants had other resources. Plaintiff claimed that he was to be permitted to draw from the earnings of the partnership a sufficient amount to support himself and family. The defendants asserted that there was a definite arrangement for the allocation of the income of the partnership and there was no agreement for withdrawal by plaintiff of more than his allotment under that plan. Defendants' version of the facts was corroborated by a written admission of plaintiff offered in evidence. From evidence thus sharply in conflict, the trial court made a finding, reading as follows: "That the oral partnership agreement between the parties provided that each of the three partners were to draw as compensation one-third of one-half of the commissions earned upon sales made by the partners; that the other one-half of the commissions earned on sales made by the partners and one-half of the commissions earned upon sales made by salesmen employed by the partnership, together with the earnings from the insurance business carried on by the partnership, was to be placed in a fund to be used for the payment of the operating expenses of the partnership, and after the payment of such operating expenses to be used to reimburse the defendants for the capital advanced in the purchase of the Julius Schumacher business and the capital advanced in the sum of Eight Hundred Dollars ($800.00) for the operating expenses of the business."

As an outgrowth of this crucial difference, there was evidence from which a court could reasonably believe that plaintiff neglected the business and spent too much time in a nearby bar during business hours. At a time when plaintiff had overdrawn his partners and was also indebted to one of defendants for personal advances, he requested $100 and his request was refused. In substance he then said, according to the testimony of the defendant Deis, that he would see that he "gets some money to run on", if they "didn't give it to him he was going to dissolve the partnership and see that he got it." Thereafter plaintiff pressed his claims through counsel, and eventually brought this action to dissolve the partnership. The claim so persistently asserted was contrary to the partnership agreement found by the court.

The foregoing picture of the widening breach between the parties is drawn almost entirely from the evidence of defendants. Of course, plaintiff's version of the agreement of the parties, and of the ensuing differences, if believed, would have supported findings of a different order by the trier of the fact. It cannot be said, we think, that the trial court acted unreasonably in believing defendants, and we think it equally clear the court could reasonably conclude that the insistent and continuing demands of the plaintiff and his attendant conduct rendered it reasonably impracticable to carry on the business in partnership with him. It follows, we are of the opinion, the evidence supports the finding that plaintiff caused the dissolution wrongfully. Zeibak v. Nasser, 12 Cal.2d 1, 82 P.2d 375; Owen v. Cohen, 19 Cal.2d 147, 119 P.2d 713; Meherin v. Meherin, 93 Cal.App.2d 459, 209 P.2d 36; and Vangel v. Vangel, 116 Cal.App.2d 615, 254 P.2d 919.

This brings us to a consideration of the sufficiency of the evidence to support the finding of the court that the property of the partnership was of the value of $4498.90 as of the date of dissolution.

Bitter complaint is made because the trial court refused to consider the good will of this business in arriving at its conclusion. The feeling of plaintiff is understandable. These partners must have placed a very high estimate upon the value of the good will of this agency because they paid Mr. Schumacher $7500 to turn over that office with its very moderate fixtures and its listing of property, together with an agreement that he would not engage in the business in Rapid City for at least two years. No doubt they attached some of this good will value to the location of the business which was under only a month to month letting. Cf. 38 C.J.S.,

Good Will, § 3, page 951; In re Brown's Will, 242 N.Y. 1, 150 N.E. 581, 44 A.L.R. 510, at page 513. Their estimate of value was borne out by the subsequent history of the business. Its real estate commissions, earned but only partly received, grossed $21,528.25 and its insurance commissions grossed $661.21 in the period January 15 to August 31, 1951. In that period the received commissions paid all expenses, including the commissions of salesmen, retired $3,000 of the $7500 purchase price advanced by defendants, and all of $800 of working capital so advanced, allowed the parties to withdraw $1453.02 each, and accumulated a cash balance of $2221.43. In addition the partnership has commissions due. . . . Notwithstanding this indication of the great value of the good will of this business, the statute does not require the court to take it into consideration in valuing the property of the business in these circumstances. The statute provides such a sanction for causing the dissolution of a partnership wrongfully. SDC 49.0610(2)(c)(2) quoted supra. The court applied the statute. . . .

That the $1500 value placed on [the assets other than good will] was conservative we do not question. However, after mature study and reflection we have concluded that the court's finding is not against the clear weight of the evidence appearing in this record. Hence we are not at liberty to disturb it.

The brief of plaintiff includes some discussion of his right to a share in the profits from the date of the dissolution until the final judgment. It does not appear from the record that this claim was presented to the trial court, or that the net profit of the business during that period was evidenced. Because that issue was not presented below, it is not before us.

The judgment of the trial court is affirmed.

All the Judges concur.

POTTER v. BROWN, 328 Pa. 554, 560–62, 195 A. 901, 903–04 (1938). "The gravamen of the plaintiffs' complaint is that Henry I. Brown, Sr., by endeavoring first to persuade and subsequently to coerce them into accepting Moore as a partner so affected the harmonious operation of the business that its continuance as now constituted is not feasible from a partnership standpoint. The plaintiffs argue that the measures of compulsion adopted by Mr. Brown in furtherance of his purpose to force Moore as a partner upon them was misconduct of such character as to operate as a repudiation and cancellation of the agreement.

"There seems to be no question that the senior partner did endeavor to compel obedience to his wishes by his copartners, and while his conduct undoubtedly was improper and of a character meriting condemnation, the record is nevertheless devoid of any evidence of acts or threatened acts on his part which would cause serious or permanent injury to the partnership business. The increasing profits clearly indicate that the partnership has not materially suffered. Indeed it is undisputed that by permitting his undrawn profits to be used by the partnership for working capital and 'good will' purposes Mr. Brown has contributed toward the prosperity of the business far beyond his duties as a partner.

"Few, if any, reasons upon which ordinarily the dissolution of a partnership will be decreed are present in this case. There is neither allegation nor proof of fraudulent or dishonest practices and conduct upon which a dissolution would be granted. While it is well settled, as we said in Herman v. Pepper, 311 Pa. 104 (p. 108): that 'the exclusion of one partner by another from the management of the partnership business or possession of the partnership property is undoubtedly ground for dissolution by a court of equity,' we are of opinion that the plaintiffs have failed to show that they were denied their proper share of participation in the management of the business. . . .

"The ill-advised and almost immediately abandoned attempt to reduce the salaries of the plaintiffs does not, in our opinion, under the particular circumstances, constitute such gross misconduct on the part of Brown, Sr., and the two partners who supported him, as to require their expulsion from the business. It is not apparent from the evidence that the occurrence has in any way interfered with the success of the partnership. The contention of the plaintiffs that the continuance of the partnership with the defendants is impractical is so manifestly inconsistent with the success of the business that the absence of merit therein is obvious. Differences and discord should be settled by the partners themselves by the application of mutual forbearance rather than by bills in equity for dissolution. Equity is not a referee of partnership quarrels. A going and prosperous business will not be dissolved merely because of friction among the partners; it will not interfere to determine which contending faction is more at fault."

———

FERRICK v. BARRY, 320 Mass. 217, 222, 68 N.E.2d 690, 694–95 (1946). "The decree dissolving the partnership and liquidating its affairs was right. The conduct of Ferrick had brought about a situation in which the business could no longer be carried on jointly in the manner contemplated by the articles of copartnership. The other partners were not required to submit to Ferrick's domination or to continue in an atmosphere of non-cooperation, suspicion, and distrust, even though Ferrick was not actually dishonest, and even though substantial profits were being made. An enterprise organized on the principle of equality in proprietorship and management cannot be expected to realize its aims under such conditions. Even if the court may think that one partner could carry on successfully, if he were allowed to push aside the others, it ought not to sanction such an alteration in the agreed relations of the partners. See G.L. (Ter.Ed.) c. 108A, § 18(e). The case comes within the provision of the uniform partnership act, G.L. (Ter.Ed.) c. 108A, § 32(1)(d), that on application of a partner the court shall decree a dissolution whenever a partner 'so conducts himself in matters relating to the partnership business that it is not reasonably practicable to carry on the business in partnership with him.' "

————

NOTE ON WRONGFUL DISSOLUTION

Drashner v. Sorenson illustrates that rather drastic consequences can befall a wrongfully dissolving partner in the form of damages, a valuation of his interest that does not reflect its real value because goodwill is not taken into account, and a continuation of the business without him. These consequences may have a special impact in a partnership without a stated term. Suppose one of the partners, A, elects to dissolve such a partnership on the theory that the partnership is at will. If the court finds that as a matter of implication the partnership is for a specified term, A will presumably have dissolved in contravention of the partnership agreement under UPA § 38(2). The penalties for guessing wrong on whether the court will make such a finding "may act as significant disincentives to dissolution [and may therefore] tend to stabilize the partnership." Hillman, The Dissatisfied Participant in the Solvent Business Venture: A Consideration of the Relative Permanence of Partnerships and Close Corporations, 67 Minn.L.Rev. 1, 34 (1982). For comparable reasons, a partner is normally ill-advised to try to dissolve a partnership, based on a claim of wrongful conduct, through some sort of self-help election, as opposed to going to court for a decree under UPA Section 32. (The other side of the coin, of course, is the delay that judicial proceedings normally entail.)

————

NOTE ON THE EXPULSION OF A PARTNER

Ordinarily, the expulsion of a partner prior to the end of the partnership term without good cause would be a wrongful violation of the partnership agreement, and the wrongfully expelled partner would have a right to have the partnership dissolved and liquidated. See UPA §§ 31(1)(d); 32(1)(d), 38(1). However, UPA § 38(1) provides that "if dissolution is caused by the expulsion of a partner, *bona fide under the partnership agreement* and if the expelled partner is discharged from all partnership liabilities, either by payment or agreement . . ., he shall receive in cash only the net amount due him from the partnership." (Emphasis added.) Under this Section, a partnership agreement may lawfully provide that a partner can be expelled without cause upon a designated vote of the remaining partners. See Lawlis v. Kightlinger & Gray, 562 N.E.2d 435 (Ind.App.1990); Miller v. Foulston, Siefkin, Powers & Eberhardt, 246 Kan. 450, 790 P.2d 404 (1990).

Where a partner is expelled under such a provision, the expulsion is not wrongful and the expelled partner does not have a right to have the partnership liquidated. However, under UPA § 31(1)(d) an expulsion under a partnership agreement must be "bona fide." In *Lawlis,* supra, the court stated that "if the power to involuntarily expel partners granted by a partnership agreement is exercised in bad faith or for a 'predatory purpose,' . . . the partnership agreement is violated, giving rise to an action for damages the affected partner has suffered as a result of his expulsion." Id. at 440.

What does "bona fide" or "good faith" mean in this context? It cannot mean that a partner may be expelled only for cause, because under such an interpretation the power to expel a partner under an expulsion provision would be no greater than the power to expel a partner that would exist even in the absence of an expulsion provision. In *Lawlis,* the court said, "the expelling partners act in 'good faith' regardless of motivation if [the expulsion] does not cause a wrongful withholding of money or property legally due the expelled partner at the time he is expelled." Id. at 443.

LEVY v. NASSAU QUEENS MEDICAL GROUP, 102 A.D.2d 845, 476 N.Y.S.2d 613, 614 (1984). "The purpose of the termination clause was to provide a simple, practical and speedy method of separating a partner from the partnership, and in the absence of undue penalty or unjust forfeiture, the court may not frustrate this purpose.... While bad faith may be actionable, there must be some showing that the partnership acted out of a desire to gain a business or property advantage for the remaining partners.... Policy disagreements do not constitute bad faith 'since at the heart of the partnership concept is the principle that partners may choose with whom they wish to be associated.' "

NOTE ON PARTNERSHIP BREAKUP UNDER RUPA

RUPA's provisions on partnership breakup are even more complex than those of the UPA. To begin with nomenclature, RUPA continues to use the terms "dissolution," "winding up," and "termination." However, RUPA adds a new term, "dissociation," to describe the termination of a person's status as a partner.

1. *Events of dissociation.* Although the term "dissociation" is new, the concept is not. Even under the UPA, a variety of events result in the termination of a person's status as a partner, and there is a very substantial overlap between the UPA and RUPA concerning the description of those events. For example, RUPA § 602(a) continues the rule of the UPA that every partner has the right to dissociate (withdraw) from the partnership at any time, rightfully or wrongfully, by express will.[1] RUPA § 602(c) provides that a partner who wrongfully dissociates is liable to the partnership and to the other partners for damages cased by the dissociation. Furthermore, if a partner wrongfully dissociates, the partnership can continue without him.

The events that result in dissociation under RUPA, other than voluntary withdrawal, are set out in RUPA § 601(2)–(10).

2. *Rightful and wrongful dissociation.* RUPA § 602 distinguishes between events of dissociation that involve rightful conduct by the dissociated partner and events of dissociation that involve wrongful conduct. An event of dissociation is rightful unless it is specified as wrongful in § 602(b). The major types of wrongful dissociation are (i) a dissociation that is in breach of an express provision of the partnership agreement; (ii) a withdrawal of a partner by the partner's express will before the expiration of the partnership term or the completion of an undertaking for which the partnership was formed; and (iii) a dissociation that results from an expulsion of the partner by judicial order under § 601(5). The

---

1. RUPA § 103(b)(6) provides that the partnership agreement cannot vary the power of a partner to dissociate under § 602(a), except to require that the notice of dissociation must be in writing. RUPA § 103(b)(8) provides that the partnership agreement may not vary the rights of partners to have the partnership dissolved under specified provisions of RUPA § 801.

grounds for expulsion under § 601(5) are that: the partner engaged in wrongful conduct that adversely and materially affected the partnership business; the partner willfully or persistently committed a material breach of the partnership agreement or of a duty of care, loyalty, good faith, and fair dealing owed to the partnership or the other partners under § 404; or the partner engaged in conduct relating to the partnership business that makes it not reasonably practicable to carry on the business in partnership with the partner.

The Comment to RUPA § 602 states:

> [Under 602(a)] . . . a partner has the power to dissociate at any time by expressing a will to withdraw, even in contravention of the partnership agreement. The phrase "rightfully or wrongfully" reflects the distinction between a partner's *power* to withdraw in contravention of the partnership agreement and a partner's *right* to do so. In this context, although a partner can not be enjoined from exercising the power to dissociate, the dissociation may be wrongful under subsection (b). . . .

> . . . The significance of a wrongful dissociation is that it may give rise to damages under subsection (c) and, if it results in the dissolution of the partnership, the wrongfully dissociating partner is not entitled to participate in winding up the business. . . .

3. *Consequences of dissociation.* Unlike the UPA, the partnership-breakup provisions of RUPA are driven by functional considerations rather than by the "nature" of a partnership (although the Comments occasionally lapse into conceptual justifications based on the entity theory). Along these lines, RUPA, unlike the UPA, does not provide that every termination of a person's status as a partner—every dissociation—causes dissolution. In fact, the breakup provisions of RUPA do not even pivot on whether dissolution occurs. Instead, the key issue is whether *dissociation* has occurred.

Under RUPA, a dissociation normally leads to one of two alternatives: winding up of the partnership or mandatory buyout of the dissociated partner. (Depending on the nature of the dissociation, a mandatory buyout may be required to be made immediately or only at some later date. See p. 106, infra.) Accordingly, although the term "dissolution" is used in RUPA, nothing really turns on whether there is a dissolution, and the term could have been left out. As stated by the Reporters for RUPA:

> The term *dissolution* has no independent operative significance under RUPA. Stated somewhat differently, RUPA's provisions are redundant when they state that "a partnership is dissolved, *and* its business must be wound up." Section 801 simply is a list of those situations in which the business of the partnership must begin to be wound up. The word *dissolu-*

tion is nothing more than a shorthand term for the occurrence of one of those situations.[2]

In short, under RUPA, dissociation leads to two forks in the statutory road: winding up under Article 8, or mandatory buyout under Article 7. Which fork must be taken depends on the nature of the event of dissociation. Thus as stated in the Comment to RUPA § 601:

> RUPA dramatically changes the law governing partnership breakups and dissolution. An entirely new concept, "dissociation," is used in lieu of the UPA term "dissolution" to denote the change in the relationship caused by a partner's ceasing to be associated in the carrying on of the business. . . . The entity theory of partnership [adopted in RUPA] provides a conceptual basis of continuing the firm itself despite a partner's withdrawal from the firm.

> Under RUPA, unlike the UPA, the dissociation of a partner does not necessarily cause a dissolution and winding up of the business of the partnership. Section 801 identifies the situations in which the dissociation of a partner causes a winding up of the business. Section 701 provides that in all other situations there is a buyout of the partner's interest in the partnership, rather than a windup of the partnership business. In those other situations, the partnership entity continues, unaffected by the partner's dissociation.

First Fork: Winding Up. The events of dissociation that require the partnership to be wound up under RUPA are described in § 801. The Official Comment adds:

> . . . Under RUPA, not every partner dissociation causes a dissolution of the partnership. Only certain departures trigger a dissolution. The basic rule is that a partnership is dissolved, and its business must be wound up, only upon the occurrence of one of the events listed in Section 801. All other dissociations result in a buyout of the partner's interest under Article 7

---

2. Earlier, the Reporter had commented:

> Initially, RUPA's new rules on breakups were forged without the use of the term "dissolution." After more than two years of work, the Drafting Committee put the word dissolution back in the statute. Yet an examination of RUPA's breakup provisions indicates that the word as reinstated is surplusage.

> Throughout the project, there have been those who have urged the Drafting Committee to reinstate the word dissolu-

tion. They were asked to defer discussion of this suggestion to give the Committee a chance to draft a statute without "the D word." They finally had a chance to state their case, and the Drafting Committee in the Spring of 1990 decided to reinstate the word without changing either the basic structure we had drafted or the substantive decisions we had hung on that structure. . . .

Weidner, Three Policy Decisions [that] Animate [the] Revision of the Uniform Partnership Act, 46 Bus.Law. 427 (1991).

and a continuation of the partnership entity and business by the remaining partners.

Section 801 continues two basic rules from the UPA. First, it continues the rule that any member of an *at-will* partnership has the right to force a liquidation. Second, by negative implication, it continues the rule that the partners who wish to continue the business of a *term* partnership can not be forced to liquidate the business by a partner who withdraws prematurely in violation of the partnership agreement.

Second Fork: Buyout. If, upon the dissociation of a partner, winding up is not required under § 801, then RUPA § 701 requires a mandatory buyout of the dissociated partner's interest by the partnership. However, if the dissociation was wrongfully caused by the dissociated partner, § 701(c) provides that the buyout price under § 701(b) is to be reduced by damages for the wrongful dissociation. Furthermore, under § 701(h) a partner who wrongfully dissociates before the expiration of a definite term, or the completion of a particular undertaking, is not entitled to payment of any portion of the buyout price until the expiration of the term or completion of the undertaking, unless the partner establishes to the satisfaction of the court that earlier payment will not cause undue hardship to the business of the partnership. A deferred payment must be adequately secured and bear interest. Under § 701(b), the buyout price of a dissociated partner's interest is the amount that would have been distributable to the dissociating partner if, on the date of dissociation, the assets of the partnership were sold at a price equal to the greater of the liquidation value or the value based on a sale of the entire business as a going concern, without the dissociated partner, and the partnership was wound up as of that date.

SECTION 10. LIMITED PARTNERSHIPS

(a) THE UNIFORM LIMITED PARTNERSHIP ACTS

Over the course of time, the Commissioners on Uniform State Laws have promulgated several uniform limited partnership acts.

In 1916, the Commissioners promulgated the original Uniform Limited Partnership Act. It was adopted in every state except Louisiana.

In 1976, the Commissioners promulgated a replacement for the Uniform Limited Partnership Act, called the Revised Uniform Partnership Act. The new Act modernized the prior Act, picked up some modifications of the original Act that had been made in adopting states, and generally reflected the influence of the corporate model. It has been widely but not universally adopted.

In 1985, the Commissioners amended the Revised Uniform Limited Partnership Act in a number of important respects. The states are still in the process of adopting these amendments.

In the balance of this Section, the 1916 Act, and the 1976 Act as amended in 1985, will be referred to as the ULPA and the RULPA, respectively.

(b) FORMATION OF A LIMITED PARTNERSHIP

REVISED UNIFORM LIMITED PARTNERSHIP ACT §§ 101, 201

[See Appendix]

Unlike general partnerships, limited partnerships are basically creatures of statute, although they have nonstatutory historical antecedents. Section 1 of the ULPA defined a limited partnership as "a partnership formed by two or more persons under the provisions of Section 2, having as members one or more general partners and one or more limited partners." Section 2, in turn, provided that persons who desire to form a limited partnership must execute a certificate setting forth the name of the partnership, the names and residences of each member (including the limited partners), the contributions of the partners, and much other information, and must file the certificate in a designated state or county office.

RULPA § 101 carries forward the substance of ULPA Section 1. However, Section 201 drastically reduces the amount of information that must be contained in the certificate. Under Section 201, as amended, the certificate need only state the name of the limited partnership, the name and business address of each general partner, the latest date upon which the limited partnership is to dissolve, and the name and address of the agent for service of process. Thus under the RULPA, as amended, neither the identity of the limited partners nor the partnership's capitalization need be stated in the certificate.

(c) LIABILITY OF LIMITED PARTNERS; CORPORATION AS A SOLE GENERAL PARTNER

Section 1 of the ULPA provided that "[t]he limited partners as such shall not be bound by the obligations of the partnership." Section 7 addressed this issue more specifically: "A limited partner shall not become liable as a general partner unless, in addition to the exercise of his rights and powers as a limited partner, he takes part in the control of the business." The policy considerations and interpretive problems involved in this Section remain relevant both in those states that have not adopted the RULPA and as a backdrop for considering the counterpart provisions of the RULPA.

REVISED UNIFORM LIMITED PARTNERSHIP ACT §§ 302, 303

[See Appendix]

PITMAN v. FLANAGAN LUMBER CO.

Supreme Court of Alabama, 1990.
567 So.2d 1335.

HOUSTON, Justice.

The defendant, Robert Edward Pitman, appeals from a judgment in favor of Flanagan Lumber Company, Inc. ("Flanagan"), in this action to recover a debt incurred by Ramsey Homebuilders, Ltd. ("Ramsey Homebuilders"). We affirm.

Pitman was one of two limited partners in Ramsey Homebuilders, a limited partnership that engaged in the business of residential construction. Michael C. Ramsey was the sole general partner in that partnership. Because Ramsey had a poor credit history, he was unable to borrow the money or obtain the credit that was needed to sustain the partnership's business. Pitman, who had a personal account with Flanagan, contacted Wilburn Moore, Flanagan's credit manager, and secured an account in the partnership's name. After the partnership failed to pay the account, Flanagan sued Pitman, alleging that, although Pitman was a limited partner in Ramsey Homebuilders, he was responsible for the partnership's debt under

Ala.Code 1975, § 10–9A–42, which reads, in pertinent part, as follows:

> "(a) Except as provided in subsection (d), a limited partner is not liable for the obligations of a limited partnership unless he is also a general partner or, in addition to the exercise of his rights and powers as a limited partner, he takes part in the control of the business. However, if the limited partner's participation in the control of the business is not substantially the same as the exercise of the powers of a general partner, he is liable only to persons who, with actual knowledge of his participation in control and in reasonable reliance thereon, transact business with the partnership.
>
> "(b) A limited partner does not participate in the control of the business within the meaning of subsection (a) solely by doing one or more of the following . . .
>
> "(3) Acting as surety or guarantor for any liabilities for the limited partnership. . . .

After hearing *ore tenus* evidence, the trial court found that Pitman had participated in the control of the business by interceding on the partnership's behalf to secure credit; that Flanagan had reasonably relied upon that participation in extending credit; and, therefore, that Pitman was liable to Flanagan for the debt subsequently incurred by the partnership.

Pitman argues that the evidence does not support the trial court's finding that he participated in the control of the partnership's business. He argues instead that, if anything, he was operating within the waters of the "safe harbor" provided by § 10–9A–42(b)(3) when he contacted Flanagan. . . . Flanagan contends, however, that the evidence supports the trial court's finding that Pitman participated in the control of the partnership's business. . . .

Where a trial court has heard *ore tenus* evidence, as in this case, its findings, if supported by the evidence, are presumed correct, and its judgment based upon those findings will be reversed only if, after consideration of the evidence and all reasonable inferences to be drawn therefrom, the judgment is found to be plainly and palpably wrong. *Robinson v. Hamilton,* 496 So.2d 8 (Ala.1986).

"Control" is defined in *Black's Law Dictionary* (5th ed. 1979) as the "[p]ower or authority to manage, direct, superintend, restrict, regulate, govern, administer, or oversee." In the present case, the evidence showed that Pitman interceded on behalf of the partnership in order to secure an account with Flanagan. The trial court could have found from this evidence that Pitman participated in the "control" of the partnership's business by securing one of the things that the partnership needed to survive—a source of building materials that would be provided on credit.[1] Furthermore, the evidence supports the trial court's finding that Flanagan reasonably relied on Pitman's participation in the partnership's business by extending credit to the partnership. The trial court's judgment was not plainly and palpably wrong. . . .

AFFIRMED.

HORNSBY, C.J., and JONES, SHORES and KENNEDY, JJ., concur.

NOTE ON RULPA § 303(a)

Alabama § 10–9A–42 was based on the original version of RULPA § 303(a), although it differed from that version in some respects. As part of the 1985 amendments to RULPA, § 303(a) was significantly amended, as reflected in the Statutory Supplement. However, some states that had adopted the original version of RULPA did not adopt the 1985 amendment of RULPA § 303(a).

––––––––

QUESTION

How would *Pitman* have been decided under the present version of RULPA § 303?

––––––––

FRIGIDAIRE SALES CORP. v. UNION PROPERTIES, INC.

Supreme Court of Washington, 1977.
88 Wash.2d 400, 562 P.2d 244.

HAMILTON, J.—Petitioner, Frigidaire Sales Corporation, sought review of a Court of Appeals decision which held that limited partners do not incur general liability for the limited partnership's obligations simply because they are officers, directors, or shareholders of the corporate general partner. Frigidaire Sales Corp. v. Union Properties, Inc., 14 Wn.App. 634, 544 P.2d 781 (1975). We granted review, and now affirm the decision of the Court of Appeals.

1. Although it does not appear to us that any argument concerning this point was made to the trial court, we note that the evidence does not support a finding that Pitman was "[a]cting as surety or guarantor for any liabilities for the limited partnership," § 10–9A–42(b)(3), when he contacted Flanagan. To the contrary, the only reasonable inference that could have been drawn from the evidence was that Pitman never intended to assume responsibility for the partnership's debt.

The facts of the case are adequately set out in the Court of Appeals opinion, and only a cursory summation need be repeated here. Petitioner entered into a contract with Commercial Investors (Commercial), a limited partnership. Respondents, Leonard Mannon and Raleigh Baxter, were limited partners of Commercial. Respondents were also officers, directors, and shareholders of Union Properties, Inc., the only general partner of Commercial. Respondents controlled Union Properties, and through their control of Union Properties they exercised the day-to-day control and management of Commercial. Commercial breached the contract, and petitioner brought suit against Union Properties and respondents. The trial court concluded that respondents did not incur general liability for Commercial's obligations by reason of their control of Commercial, and the Court of Appeals affirmed.

We first note that petitioner does not contend that respondents acted improperly by setting up the limited partnership with a corporation as the sole general partner. Limited partnerships are a statutory form of business organization, and parties creating a limited partnership must follow the statutory requirements. In Washington, parties may form a limited partnership with a corporation as the sole general partner. *See* RCW 25.04.020 and RCW 25.04.060(3); RCW 25.08.010 and RCW 25.08.070(2)(a).

Petitioner's sole contention is that respondents should incur general liability for the limited partnership's obligations under RCW 25.08.070,[1] because they exercised the day-to-day control and management of Commercial. Respondents, on the other hand, argue

---

1. At the time the parties entered into the contract, RCW 25.08.070 read as follows:

A limited partner shall not become liable as a general partner unless, in addition to the exercise of his rights and powers as limited partner, he takes part in the control of the business.

Laws of 1955, ch. 15, § 25.08.070, p. 140.

In 1972, the legislature amended RCW 25.08.070 by adding two additional sections. Laws of 1972, 1st Ex.Sess., ch. 113, § 2, p. 253. RCW 25.08.070 presently reads:

(1) A limited partner shall not become liable as a general partner unless, in addition to the exercise of his rights and powers as limited partner, he takes part in the control of the business.

(2) A limited partner shall not be deemed to take part in the control of the business by virtue of his possessing or exercising a power, specified in the certificate, to vote upon matters affecting the basic structure of the partnership, including the following matters or others of a similar nature:

(a) Election, removal, or substitution of general partners, including, but not limited to, transfer of a majority of the voting stock of a corporate general partner.

(b) Termination of the partnership.

(c) Amendment of the partnership agreement.

(d) Sale of all or substantially all of the assets of the partnership.

(3) The statement of powers set forth in subsection (2) of this section shall not be construed as exclusive or as indicating that any other powers possessed or exercised by a limited partner shall be sufficient to cause such limited partner to be deemed to take part in the control of the business within the meaning of subsection (1) of this section.

that Commercial was controlled by Union Properties, a separate legal entity, and not by respondents in their individual capacities.

Petitioner cites *Delaney v. Fidelity Lease Ltd.,* 526 S.W.2d 543 (Tex.1975), as support for its contention that respondents should incur general liability under RCW 25.08.070 for the limited partnership's obligations. That case also involved the issue of liability for limited partners who controlled the limited partnership as officers, directors, and shareholders of the corporate general partner. The Texas Supreme Court reversed the decision of the Texas Court of Civil Appeals and found the limited partners had incurred general liability because of their control of the limited partnership. *See Delaney v. Fidelity Lease Ltd.,* 517 S.W.2d 420 (Tex.Civ.App.1974), *rev'd,* 526 S.W.2d 543 (Tex.1975).

We find the Texas Supreme Court's decision distinguishable from the present case. In *Delaney,* the corporation and the limited partnership were set up contemporaneously, and the sole purpose of the corporation was to operate the limited partnership. The Texas Supreme Court found that the limited partners who controlled the corporation were obligated to their other limited partners to operate the corporation for the benefit of the partnership. " 'Each act was done then, not for the corporation, but for the partnership.' " *Delaney v. Fidelity Lease Ltd.,* 526 S.W.2d 543, 545 (Tex.1975), quoting from the dissenting opinion in *Delaney v. Fidelity Lease Ltd.,* 517 S.W.2d 420, 426 (Tex.Civ.App.1974). This is not the case here. The pattern of operation of Union Properties was to investigate and conceive of real estate investment opportunities and, when it found such opportunities, to cause the creation of limited partnerships with Union Properties acting as the general partner. Commercial was only one of several limited partnerships so conceived and created. Respondents did not form Union Properties for the sole purpose of operating Commercial. Hence, their acts on behalf of Union Properties were not performed merely for the benefit of Commercial.

Further, it is apparently still undecided in Texas whether parties may form a limited partnership with a corporation as the sole general partner. *See Delaney v. Fidelity Lease Ltd.,* 526 S.W.2d 543, 546 (Tex.1975). The Texas Supreme Court was concerned with the possibility that limited partners might form the corporate general partner with minimum capitalization:

> In no event should they be permitted to escape the statutory liability which would have devolved upon them if there had been no attempted interposition of the corporate shield against personal liability. Otherwise, the statutory requirement of at least one general partner with general liability in a limited partnership can be circumvented or vitiated by limited partners

operating the partnership through a corporation with minimum capitalization and therefore minimum liability.

Delaney v. Fidelity Lease Ltd., supra at 546.

However, we agree with our Court of Appeals analysis that this concern with minimum capitalization is not peculiar to limited partnerships with corporate general partners, but may arise anytime a creditor deals with a corporation. *See Frigidaire Sales Corp. v. Union Properties, Inc., supra* at 638. Because our limited partnership statutes permit parties to form a limited partnership with a corporation as the sole general partner, this concern about minimal capitalization, standing by itself, does not justify a finding that the limited partners incur general liability for their control of the corporate general partner. *See* A. Bromberg, *Crane and Bromberg on Partnership* § 26, at 146–47 (1968). If a corporate general partner is inadequately capitalized, the rights of a creditor are adequately protected under the "piercing-the-corporate-veil" doctrine of corporation law. *See* 1 W. Fletcher, *Cyclopedia of the Law of Private Corporations* § 44.1 (rev. vol. M. Wolf 1974); H. Henn, *Handbook of the Law of Corporations and other Business Enterprises* § 147 (2d ed. 1970).

Furthermore, petitioner was never led to believe that respondents were acting in any capacity other than in their corporate capacities. The parties stipulated at the trial that respondents never acted in any direct, personal capacity. When the shareholders of a corporation, who are also the corporation's officers and directors, conscientiously keep the affairs of the corporation separate from their personal affairs, and no fraud or manifest injustice is perpetrated upon third persons who deal with the corporation, the corporation's separate entity should be respected. *See J.L. Cooper & Co. v. Anchor Sec. Co.,* 9 Wn.2d 45, 113 P.2d 845 (1941); *Garvin v. Matthews,* 193 Wash. 152, 74 P.2d 990 (1938); *H.E. Briggs & Co. v. Harper Clay Prods. Co.,* 150 Wash. 235, 272 P. 962 (1928); *Nursing Home Bldg. Corp. v. DeHart,* 13 Wn.App. 489, 535 P.2d 137 (1975).

For us to find that respondents incurred general liability for the limited partnership's obligations under RCW 25.08.070 would require us to apply a literal interpretation of the statute and totally ignore the corporate entity of Union Properties, when petitioner knew it was dealing with that corporate entity. There can be no doubt that respondents, in fact, controlled the corporation. However, they did so only in their capacities as agents for their principal, the corporate general partner. Although the corporation was a separate entity, it could act only through its board of directors, officers, and agents. *Beall v. Pacific Nat'l Bank,* 55 Wn.2d 210, 347 P.2d 550 (1959); *see* RCW 23A.08.340 and RCW 23A.08.470. Petitioner entered into the contract with Commercial. Respondents signed the contract in their capacities as president and secretary-treasurer of Union Properties, the general partner of Commercial. In the eyes of the law it was Union Properties, as a separate corporate entity, which entered into the contract with petitioner and controlled the limited partnership.

Further, because respondents scrupulously separated their actions on behalf of the corporation from their personal actions, petitioner never mistakenly assumed that respondents were general partners with general liability. *See Frigidaire Sales Corp. v. Union Properties, Inc.,* 14 Wn.App. 634, 641–42, 544 P.2d 781 (1975); *Delaney v. Fidelity Lease Ltd.,* 517 S.W.2d 420 (Tex.Civ.App.1974); Feld, *The "Control" Test for Limited Partnerships,* 82 Harv.L.Rev. 1471 (1969). Petitioner knew Union Properties was the sole general partner and did not rely on respondents' control by assuming that they were also general partners. If petitioner had not wished to rely on the solvency of Union Properties as the only general partner, it could have insisted that respondents personally guarantee contractual performance. Because petitioner entered into the contract knowing that Union Properties was the only party with general liability, and because in the eyes of the law it was Union Properties, a separate entity, which controlled the limited partnership, there is no reason for us to find that respondents incurred general liability for their acts done as officers of the corporate general partner.

The decision of the Court of Appeals is affirmed.

WRIGHT, C.J., and ROSELLINI, STAFFORD, UTTER, BRACHTENBACH, HOROWITZ, and DOLLIVER, JJ., concur.

———

NOTE ON FRIGIDAIRE SALES CORP.
v. UNION PROPERTIES, INC.

1. As stated in *Frigidaire,* it is clear that a corporation can be a general partner in a partnership. Section 1 of the ULPA provided that "[a] limited partnership is a partnership formed by two or more persons under the provisions of Section 2, having as members one or more general partners and one or more limited partners." The ULPA did not define "person," but Uniform Partnership Act Section 2 provides that the term "person" includes corporations, and Uniform Partnership Act Section 6 provides that "this act shall apply to limited partnerships except insofar as the statutes relating to such partnerships are inconsistent herewith."

Section 101(11) of the RULPA also defines "person" to include corporations. Furthermore, Sections 303(b)(1) and 402(9) of that

Act explicitly recognize that a corporation can be a general partner in a limited partnership.

2. That a corporation can be a general partner of a limited partnership does not answer the questions (i) whether a corporation can be the sole general partner, and (ii) whether a limited partner who controls a corporate general partner thereby becomes individually liable for partnership obligations. However, the second question is explicitly addressed by Section 303(b) of the RULPA, as amended, which provides that "[a] limited partner does not participate in the control of the business ... by ... being an officer, director, or shareholder of a general partner that is a corporation...."

GONZALEZ v. CHAPLIN, 77 N.Y.2d 74, 564 N.Y.S.2d 702, 565 N.E.2d 1253 (1990). "Irrefutably, individual liability should not be imposed on a limited partner merely because that person happens also to be an officer, director and/or shareholder of a corporate general partner (see *Frigidaire Sales Corp. v. Union Props.*). But that is not this case. Moreover and conversely, a limited partner who 'takes part in the control of' the limited partnership's business should not automatically be insulated from individual liability merely by benefit of status as an officer and sole owner of the corporate general partner. That is this case.

"A limited partner who assumes such a dual capacity rightly bears a heavy burden when seeking to elude personal liability. For once a plaintiff meets the threshold burden of proving that a limited partner took an active individual part in effectuating the limited partnership's interests, the fulcrum shifts. The limited partner in such a dual capacity must then, at least, prove that any relevant actions taken were performed solely in the capacity as officer of the general partner."*

(d) NOTE ON LIMITED PARTNERSHIPS

1. Approximately 1,485,000 partnerships filed federal income tax returns for 1992. Of these, approximately 271,000 were limited partnerships. The general partnerships had an average of approximately 4 partners. The limited partnerships had an average of approximately 42 partners. Wheeler, Partnership Returns, 1992, Internal Revenue Service, Statistics of Income Bulletin, Fall 1994, at 75-77.

---

* Gonzalez v. Chaplin was decided under the ULPA rather than under RULPA.

2.   Under Internal Revenue Code § 7701(a)(3), the term "corporation" is defined for income-tax purposes to include "associations."   The latter term is not defined, but can include organizations like limited partnerships.   In Morrissey v. Commissioner, 296 U.S. 344, 56 S.Ct. 289, 80 L.Ed. 263 (1935), the Supreme Court held that whether a given partnership was an "association" within the meaning of the Code depended on how closely the partnership resembled a corporation.   Subsequently, the Internal Revenue Service adopted Regulations—known as the Kintner Regulations—that identify four critical "characteristics of corporations" for tax-law purposes: continuity of life, centralized management, limited liability, and free transferability of interests.   The Kintner Regulations indicate that a limited partnership will be treated as an association (and will therefore be taxed like a corporation) if, but only if, it has more than two of these characteristics.   See Treas.Reg. § 301.7701–2(a).

However, the Kintner Regulations and related Revenue Procedures define the relevant characteristics in such a restrictive manner that a limited partnership will normally not have the characteristics. For example, although in fact limited partnerships always have centralized management, vested in the hands of the general partners, under the Regulations and Procedures a limited partnership is deemed *not* to have centralized management as long as the general partners have a defined minimum interest in the firm—normally, 1%.   Similarly, a limited partnership is treated as if it has unlimited liability even if the only general partner is a corporation with limited liability, as long as the corporation meets certain net worth standards.[1]   Furthermore, although the Kintner Regulations purport to adopt the *Morrissey* resemblance test, in fact the test under the Regulations depends on a by-the-numbers count of the relevant characteristics.

As a result of the artificial nature of the definitions in the Regulations and Procedures, a limited partnership will normally not be deemed to have more than two of the four critical characteristics. As a result of the mechanical nature of the by-the-numbers test, as a practical matter a limited partnership that is not publicly held is unlikely to be taxed as a corporation under § 7701.   For example, in Larson v. Commissioner, 66 T.C. 159 (1976), GHL, a corporation, was the sole general partner of two limited partnerships, Mai–Kai and Somis.   Under Morrissey's resemblance test, Mai–Kai and Somis would almost certainly have qualified as "associations" that were taxable as corporations under § 7701.   Management was centralized in GHL's hands; the limited partnership interests were freely transferable; there was no effective personal liability because GHL

---

1. See Rev.Proc. 92–88, 1992–42 I.R.B. 39 (safe harbor guidelines).

had little capital; and effective continuity of life was assured, because the general partner was a corporation. A majority of the Tax Court nevertheless held that Mai–Kai and Somis did not constitute "associations" under the restrictive tests laid down in the Regulations, because both lacked continuity of life and personal liability, as those terms are artificially defined in the Kintner Regulations. Although the court concluded that Mai–Kai and Somis had centralized management and free transferability of interests, the majority read the Regulations to apply a mechanical test under which a limited partnership would not constitute an association unless at least three of the four critical characteristics were present. Chief Judge Dawson, concurring, stressed that the regulations "virtually rule out the possibility that [a limited partnership formed under the ULPA] will be a taxable association within the meaning of section 7701(a)(3)," id. at 187, and the various opinions in the case made it clear that but for the Regulations a different result would have followed.

3. In the last thirty years, many publicly held limited partnerships have been organized. The limited partnership interests in these limited partnerships were initially offered to the public through underwriters, and in some cases were publicly traded on organized markets. These partnerships are known as "master limited partnerships." That term arose "as a description of the method by which these large publicly traded partnerships were first developed. An independent oil company formed the first master limited partnership in 1981. The company consolidated thirty pre-existing drilling and exploration limited partnerships into one 'master' limited partnership. The partners of the drilling and exploration partnerships contributed their partnership interests to a new limited partnership in return for limited partnership interests in the new entity. This method of forming a master limited partnership is called a 'roll up' and is generally used to combine several smaller limited partnerships into one large partnership. The definition of master limited partnerships [was later expanded, and the term] now refers more generally to large partnerships that are widely held and whose ownership interests are frequently traded." Adler, Master Limited Partnerships, 21 U.Fla.L.Rev. 755, 756–57.

A major incentive for forming master limited partnerships is to combine the economic advantages of publicly traded ownership interests and limited liability, on the one hand (advantages that are normally associated with corporations) with the tax treatment accorded to partnerships, on the other. However, the Internal Revenue Code was amended in 1987 to treat any partnership with interests that are "traded on an established securities market," or that "are readily tradeable on a secondary market (or the substantial equivalent thereof)" as "publicly traded partnerships," and to tax such partnerships as corporations. See IRC § 7704.

This tax treatment is subject to certain exceptions. In particular, a publicly traded limited partnership will not be taxed as a corporation if 90 percent of its income consists of interest, dividends, real property rents, gain from the sale of real property or certain other types of "passive income," or gains derived from the exploration, development, mining or production, processing, refining, transportation, or marketing of any minerals or natural resources. "Because master limited partnerships have most often been used in the oil and gas and real estate industries, these exceptions substantially limit the effect of the recharacterization of publicly traded partnerships. For example, of the existing exchange-traded partnerships listed in [a] statement of the Treasury, 66 percent ... are either involved in the natural resource or real estate industry and would likely fit within the passive-type income exception." Adler, supra at 757.

SECTION 11. LIMITED LIABILITY PARTNERSHIPS

DELAWARE LIMITED LIABILITY PARTNERSHIP ACT

[See Appendix]

TEXAS LIMITED LIABILITY PARTNERSHIP ACT

[See Appendix]

NOTE ON LIMITED LIABILITY PARTNERSHIPS

An important new form of business organization is the limited liability partnership ("LLP"). Essentially, LLPs are general partnerships with one core difference and several ancillary differences. The core difference is that, as the name indicates, the liability of general partners of a limited liability partnership is less extensive than the ordinary liability of a general partner. Although the statutes vary, generally speaking a partner in an LLP is not personally liable for *all* partnership obligations arising from negligence, wrongful acts, and misconduct, but only for obligations arising (1) from the partner's own negligence, wrongful acts; (2) from the negligence, wrongful acts, or misconduct of those under the partner's supervision and control; and, (3) under some statutes, from the negligence, wrongful acts, or misconduct of those engaged in a specific activity (as opposed to the general partnership business) in which the partner was involved. This core idea is articulated differently under different LLP statutes, and the precise liability of a partner in an LLP will depend on the statute.

The LLP statutes apparently are generally not intended to exclude a partner's liability for contractual obligations (although that result could sometimes be achieved by a provision in the relevant contract). Furthermore, under the statutes the liability of a partner in an LLP is "limited" only in the sense that the partner is not personally liable for *all* of the LLP's obligations. A partner in an LLP *is* personally liable for certain obligations, and as to those obligations a partner's liability is unlimited—that is, a partner is personally liable for those obligations to the entire extent of her wealth.

An ancillary difference between ordinary general partnerships and LLPs is that under some LLP statutes there is a tradeoff for limited liability, in the form of a requirement of a minimum amount of liability insurance or segregated funds. Another ancillary difference between LLPs and ordinary general partnerships is that LLPs must be registered.

*

APPENDIX

RESTATEMENT (SECOND) OF AGENCY

(Selected Sections)

Chapter 1

INTRODUCTORY MATTERS

TOPIC 1. DEFINITIONS

TOPIC 3. ESSENTIAL CHARACTERISTICS OF RELATION

TOPIC 4. AGENCY DISTINGUISHED FROM OTHER RELATIONS

Chapter 2

CREATION OF RELATION

TOPIC 1. MUTUAL CONSENT AND CONSIDERATION

TOPIC 3. CAPACITY OF PARTIES TO RELATION

Chapter 3

CREATION AND INTERPRETATION OF AUTHORITY AND APPARENT AUTHORITY

TOPIC 1. METHODS OF MANIFESTING CONSENT

Chapter 7

LIABILITY OF PRINCIPAL TO THIRD PERSON; TORTS

TOPIC 2. LIABILITY FOR AUTHORIZED CONDUCT OR CONDUCT INCIDENTAL THERETO

TITLE B. TORTS OF SERVANTS

TITLE C. AGENTS' TORTS—LIABILITY NOT DEPENDENT UPON RELATION OF MASTER AND SERVANT

IN GENERAL

Chapter 10

LIABILITY OF THIRD PERSON TO PRINCIPAL

TOPIC 1. CONTRACTS; DISCLOSED AGENCY

TOPIC 2. CONTRACTS; UNDISCLOSED AGENCY

TOPIC 5. EFFECT OF RATIFICATION

Chapter 11

LIABILITY OF AGENT TO THIRD PERSONS

TOPIC 1.   CONTRACTS AND CONVEYANCES

TITLE A.   AGENT A PARTY TO A TRANSACTION CONDUCTED BY HIMSELF

TITLE B.   AGENT NOT PARTY TO TRANSACTION CONDUCTED BY HIMSELF

TITLE C.   DEFENSES AND EFFECTS OF SUBSEQUENT EVENTS

Chapter 13

DUTIES AND LIABILITIES OF AGENT TO PRINCIPAL

TOPIC 1.   DUTIES

TITLE B.   DUTIES OF SERVICE AND OBEDIENCE

TITLE C.   DUTIES OF LOYALTY

TOPIC 2. LIABILITIES

Chapter 14

DUTIES AND LIABILITIES OF PRINCIPAL TO AGENT

TOPIC 1. CONTRACTUAL AND RESTITUTIONAL DUTIES AND LIABILITIES

TITLE A. INTERPRETATION OF CONTRACTS AND LIABILITIES THEREUNDER

Chapter 1

INTRODUCTORY MATTERS

TOPIC 1. DEFINITIONS

§ 1. Agency; Principal; Agent

(1) Agency is the fiduciary relation which results from the manifestation of consent by one person to another that the other shall act on his behalf and subject to his control, and consent by the other so to act.

(2) The one for whom action is to be taken is the principal.

(3) The one who is to act is the agent.

§ 2. Master; Servant; Independent Contractor

(1) A master is a principal who employs an agent to perform service in his affairs and who controls or has the right to control the physical conduct of the other in the performance of the service.

(2) A servant is an agent employed by a master to perform service in his affairs whose physical conduct in the performance of the service is controlled or is subject to the right to control by the master.

(3) An independent contractor is a person who contracts with another to do something for him but who is not controlled by the

other nor subject to the other's right to control with respect to his physical conduct in the performance of the undertaking. He may or may not be an agent.

Comment:

a. Servants and non-servant agents. A master is a species of principal, and a servant is a species of agent....

b. Servant contrasted with independent contractor. The word "servant" is used in contrast with "independent contractor". The latter term includes all persons who contract to do something for another but who are not servants in doing the work undertaken. An agent who is not a servant is, therefore, an independent contractor when he contracts to act on account of the principal. Thus, a broker who contracts to sell goods for his principal is an independent contractor as distinguished from a servant. Although, under some circumstances, the principal is bound by the broker's unauthorized contracts and representations, the principal is not liable to third persons for tangible harm resulting from his unauthorized physical conduct within the scope of the employment, as the principal would be for similar conduct by a servant; nor does the principal have the duties or immunities of a master towards the broker. Although an agent who contracts to act and who is not a servant is therefore an independent contractor, not all independent contractors are agents. Thus, one who contracts for a stipulated price to build a house for another and who reserves no direction over the conduct of the work is an independent contractor; but he is not an agent, since he is not a fiduciary, has no power to make the one employing him a party to a transaction, and is subject to no control over his conduct....

c. Servants not necessarily menials. As stated more fully in Section 220, the term servant does not denote menial or manual service. Many servants perform exacting work requiring intelligence rather than muscle. Thus the officers of a corporation or a ship, the interne in a hospital, all of whom give their time to their employers, are servants equally with the janitor and others performing manual labor....

§ 3. General Agent; Special Agent

(1) A general agent is an agent authorized to conduct a series of transactions involving a continuity of service.

(2) A special agent is an agent authorized to conduct a single transaction or a series of transactions not involving continuity of service.

§ 4. Disclosed Principal; Partially Disclosed Principal; Undisclosed Principal

(1) If, at the time of a transaction conducted by an agent, the other party thereto has notice that the agent is acting for a principal and of the principal's identity, the principal is a disclosed principal.

(2) If the other party has notice that the agent is or may be acting for a principal but has no notice of the principal's identity, the principal for whom the agent is acting is a partially disclosed principal.

(3) If the other party has no notice that the agent is acting for a principal, the one for whom he acts is an undisclosed principal.

§ 7. Authority

Authority is the power of the agent to affect the legal relations of the principal by acts done in accordance with the principal's manifestations of consent to him.

§ 8. Apparent Authority

Apparent authority is the power to affect the legal relations of another person by transactions with third persons, professedly as agent for the other, arising from and in accordance with the other's manifestations to such third persons.

§ 8A. Inherent Agency Power

Inherent agency power is a term used in the restatement of this subject to indicate the power of an agent which is derived not from authority, apparent authority or estoppel, but solely from the agency relation and exists for the protection of persons harmed by or dealing with a servant or other agent.

§ 8B. Estoppel; Change of Position

(1) A person who is not otherwise liable as a party to a transaction purported to be done on his account, is nevertheless subject to liability to persons who have changed their positions because of their belief that the transaction was entered into by or for him, if

(a) he intentionally or carelessly caused such belief, or

(b) knowing of such belief and that others might change their positions because of it, he did not take reasonable steps to notify them of the facts.

(2) An owner of property who represents to third persons that another is the owner of the property or who permits the other so to represent, or who realizes that third persons believe that another is the owner of the property, and that he could easily inform the third persons of the facts, is subject to the loss of the property if the other disposes of it to third persons who, in ignorance of the facts, purchase the property or otherwise change their position with reference to it.

(3) Change of position, as the phrase is used in the restatement of this subject, indicates payment of money, expenditure of labor, suffering a loss or subjection to legal liability.

TOPIC 3.   ESSENTIAL CHARACTERISTICS OF RELATION

§ 13.   Agent as a Fiduciary

An agent is a fiduciary with respect to matters within the scope of his agency.

§ 14.   Control by Principal

A principal has the right to control the conduct of the agent with respect to matters entrusted to him.

TOPIC 4.   AGENCY DISTINGUISHED FROM OTHER RELATIONS

§ 14H.   Agents or Holders of a Power Given for Their Benefit

One who holds a power created in the form of an agency authority, but given for the benefit of the power holder or of a third person, is not an agent of the one creating the power.

§ 14O.   Security Holder Becoming a Principal

A creditor who assumes control of his debtor's business for the mutual benefit of himself and his debtor, may become a principal, with liability for the acts and transactions of the debtor in connection with the business.

Chapter 2

CREATION OF RELATION

TOPIC 1.   MUTUAL CONSENT AND CONSIDERATION

§ 15.   Manifestations of Consent

An agency relation exists only if there has been a manifestation by the principal to the agent that the agent may act on his account, and consent by the agent so to act.

TOPIC 3.   CAPACITY OF PARTIES TO RELATION

§ 23.   Agent Having Interests Adverse to Principal

One whose interests are adverse to those of another can be authorized to act on behalf of the other; it is a breach of duty for him so to act without revealing the existence and extent of such adverse interests.

Chapter 3

CREATION AND INTERPRETATION OF AUTHORITY AND APPARENT AUTHORITY

TOPIC 1.   METHODS OF MANIFESTING CONSENT

§ 26.   Creation of Authority;   General Rule

Except for the execution of instruments under seal or for the performance of transactions required by statute to be authorized in a particular way, authority to do an act can be created by written or spoken words or other conduct of the principal which, reasonably interpreted, causes the agent to believe that the principal desires him so to act on the principal's account.

§ 27.   Creation of Apparent Authority: General Rule

Except for the execution of instruments under seal or for the conduct of transactions required by statute to be authorized in a particular way, apparent authority to do an act is created as to a third person by written or spoken words or any other conduct of the principal which, reasonably interpreted, causes the third person to believe that the principal consents to have the act done on his behalf by the person purporting to act for him.

TOPIC 2.   INTERPRETATION OF AUTHORITY
AND APPARENT AUTHORITY

TITLE A.   AUTHORITY

§ 32.   Applicability of Rules for Interpretation of Agreements

Except to the extent that the fiduciary relation between principal and agent requires special rules, the rules for the interpretation of contracts apply to the interpretation of authority.

§ 33. General Principle of Interpretation

An agent is authorized to do, and to do only, what it is reasonable for him to infer that the principal desires him to do in the light of the principal's manifestations and the facts as he knows or should know them at the time he acts.

Comment:

a. Authority an ambulatory power. The agency relation is normally the result of a contract and is always the result of an agreement between the parties. For the purpose of interpreting the words used, the effect of customs and all similar matters, the normal rules for the interpretation of contracts are applicable, as stated in Section 32. Nevertheless, an agreement creating an agency relation has elements different from those of other contracts. The implicit, basic understanding of the parties to the agency relation is that the agent is to act only in accordance with the principal's desires as manifested to him. . . . Whatever the original agreement or authority may have been, he is authorized at any given moment to do, and to do only, what he reasonably believes the principal desires him to do, in the light of what he knows or should know of the principal's purpose and the existing circumstances. . . .

Illustrations:

1. P, a mill owner, directs A, his purchasing agent, to purchase a large quantity of raw material, to be used in executing an order for goods. The following day the order for goods is rescinded, as A learns. Without inquiry as to whether or not P still wishes the material, A has no authority to purchase the raw material.

2. P, the owner of a factory running on half time for lack of orders, before leaving for his vacation, directs his purchasing agent to "put in our usual monthly coal supply of 1000 tons." The following day a large order comes in which will immediately put the factory on full running time. It may be found that A is authorized to purchase sufficient coal to keep the factory running, this depending upon whether or not P can easily be reached, the amount of discretion usually given to A, the condition of P's bank balance, and other factors.

3. Same facts as in Illustration 2, except that P is present when the large order is received. A has no authority to order more than 1000 tons.

b. Authority distinct from contract of agency. An agent is a fiduciary under a duty to obey the will of the principal as he knows it or should know it. This will may change, either with or without a change in events. Whatever it is at any given time, if the agent has reason to know it, his duty is not to act contrary to it. The fact that in changing his mind the principal is violating his contract with the agent does not diminish the agent's duty of obedience to it. Hence the rule applicable to the interpretation of authority must be as flexible as the will of the principal may be. Thus, whether or not the agent is authorized to do a particular act at a particular time depends, not only on what the principal told the agent, but upon a great variety of other factors, including changes in the situation after the instructions were given. The interpretation of authority, therefore, differs in this respect from the interpretation of a contract, even the contract of agency.

The agent's authority may therefore be increased, diminished, become dormant or be destroyed, not only by further manifestations by the principal but also by the happening of events, dependent, in many situations, upon what the agent knows or should know as to the principal's purposes. This does not mean that the agent can do anything merely because he believes it to be of advantage to the principal. Nor does it mean that the agent is authorized to act if he believes the principal would authorize him to act if he knew the facts. The agent's scope of authority is limited to the authorized subject matter and the kind of transaction contemplated. An agent of a dealer in property, whose function is limited to selling, is not authorized to buy property even if he reasonably believes the principal would authorize its purchase if he knew of the opportunity. The ordinary store manager, in the absence of an emergency, is not authorized to borrow, even though he knows the principal would welcome the opportunity.

It is in accordance with this continuous comparison between the communication to the agent and the circumstances under which he acts, that his authority may broaden . . . or may be diminished, suspended or terminated . . . , however irrevocable the terms in which the authority is expressed. Whether or not the principal is liable for a breach of contract for revoking the authority, nevertheless he can do so. . . . Further, because the agent is under a duty to protect the principal's interests within the authorized field, if the circumstances are or become ambiguous, either intrinsically or because of extrinsic facts, and he cannot communicate with the principal, the agent is autho-

rized to act reasonably in accordance with the facts as he knows
or should know them. . . .

§ 35. When Incidental Authority Is Inferred

Unless otherwise agreed, authority to conduct a transaction
includes authority to do acts which are incidental to it, usually
accompany it, or are reasonably necessary to accomplish it.

§ 39. Inference That Agent Is to Act Only for Principal's Benefit

Unless otherwise agreed, authority to act as agent includes only
authority to act for the benefit of the principal.

§ 43. Acquiescence by Principal in Agent's Conduct

(1) Acquiescence by the principal in conduct of an agent whose
previously conferred authorization reasonably might include it, indicates that the conduct was authorized; if clearly not included in the
authorization, acquiescence in it indicates affirmance.

(2) Acquiescence by the principal in a series of acts by the
agent indicates authorization to perform similar acts in the future.

TITLE B.   APPARENT AUTHORITY

§ 49. Interpretation of Apparent Authority Compared with Interpretation of Authority

The rules applicable to the interpretation of authority are
applicable to the interpretation of apparent authority except that:

(a) manifestations of the principal to the other party to the
transaction are interpreted in light of what the other party
knows or should know instead of what the agent knows or
should know . . . .

.   .   .

Chapter 4

RATIFICATION

TOPIC 1.   DEFINITIONS

§ 82. Ratification

Ratification is the affirmance by a person of a prior act which
did not bind him but which was done or professedly done on his

account, whereby the act, as to some or all persons, is given effect as if originally authorized by him.

§ 83. Affirmance

Affirmance is either

(a) a manifestation of an election by one on whose account an unauthorized act has been done to treat the act as authorized, or

(b) conduct by him justifiable only if there were such an election.

TOPIC 2. WHEN AFFIRMANCE RESULTS IN RATIFICATION

§ 84. What Acts Can Be Ratified

(1) An act which, when done, could have been authorized by a purported principal, or if an act of service by an intended principal, can be ratified if, at the time of affirmance, he could authorize such an act.

(2) An act which, when done, the purported or intended principal could not have authorized, he cannot ratify, except an act affirmed by a legal representative whose appointment relates back to or before the time of such act.

§ 85. Purporting to Act as Agent as a Requisite for Ratification

(1) Ratification does not result from the affirmance of a transaction with a third person unless the one acting purported to be acting for the ratifier.

(2) An act of service not involving a transaction with a third person is subject to ratification if, but only if, the one doing the act intends or purports to perform it as the servant of another.

§ 87. Who Can Affirm

To become effective as ratification, the affirmance must be by the person identified as the principal at the time of the original act or, if no person was then identified, by the one for whom the agent intended to act.

§ 88. Affirmance after Withdrawal of Other Party or Other Termination of Original Transaction

To constitute ratification, the affirmance of a transaction must occur before the other party has manifested his withdrawal from it either to the purported principal or to the agent, and before the offer or agreement has otherwise terminated or been discharged.

§ 89. Affirmance after Change of Circumstances

If the affirmance of a transaction occurs at a time when the situation has so materially changed that it would be inequitable to subject the other party to liability thereon, the other party has an election to avoid liability.

§ 90. Affirmance after Rights Have Crystallized

If an act to be effective in creating a right against another or to deprive him of a right must be performed before a specific time, an affirmance is not effective against the other unless made before such time.

TOPIC 3.   WHAT CONSTITUTES AFFIRMANCE

§ 93. Methods and Formalities of Affirmance

(1) Except as stated in Subsection (2), affirmance can be established by any conduct of the purported principal manifesting that he consents to be a party to the transaction, or by conduct justifiable only if there is ratification.

(2) Where formalities are requisite for the authorization of an act, its affirmance must be by the same formalities in order to constitute a ratification.

(3) The affirmance can be made by an agent authorized so to do.

§ 94. Failure to Act as Affirmance

An affirmance of an unauthorized transaction can be inferred from a failure to repudiate it.

§ 97. Bringing Suit or Basing Defense as Affirmance

There is affirmance if the purported principal, with knowledge of the facts, in an action in which the third person or the purported agent is an adverse party:

> (a) brings suit to enforce promises which were part of the unauthorized transaction or to secure interests which were the fruit of such transaction and to which he would be entitled only if the act had been authorized; or

> (b) bases a defense upon the unauthorized transaction as though it were authorized; or

(c) continues to maintain such suit or base such defense.

§ 98. Receipt of Benefits as Affirmance

The receipt by a purported principal, with knowledge of the facts, of something to which he would not be entitled unless an act purported to be done for him were affirmed, and to which he makes no claim except through such act, constitutes an affirmance unless at the time of such receipt he repudiates the act. If he repudiates the act, his receipt of benefits constitutes an affirmance at the election of the other party to the transaction.

§ 99. Retention of Benefits as Affirmance

The retention by a purported principal, with knowledge of the facts and before he has changed his position, of something which he is not entitled to retain unless an act purported to be done on his account is affirmed, and to which he makes no claim except through such act, constitutes an affirmance unless at the time of such retention he repudiates the act. Even if he repudiates the act, his retention constitutes an affirmance at the election of the other party to the transaction.

TOPIC 4. LIABILITIES

§ 100. Effect of Ratification; in General

[T]he liabilities resulting from ratification are the same as those resulting from authorization if, between the time when the original act was performed and when it was affirmed, there has been no change in the capacity of the principal or third person or in the legality of authorizing or performing the original act.

§ 100A. Relation Back in Time and Place

The liabilities of the parties to a ratified act or contract are determined in accordance with the law governing the act or contract at the time and place it was done or made. Whether the conduct of the purported principal is an affirmance depends upon the law at the time and place when and where the principal consents or acts.

Chapter 5

TERMINATION OF AGENCY POWERS

TOPIC 1. TERMINATION OF AUTHORITY

TITLE B. TERMINATION BY MUTUAL CONSENT, REVOCATION, OR RENUNCIATION

§ 118. Revocation or Renunciation

Authority terminates if the principal or the agent manifests to the other dissent to its continuance.

Comment:

a. Such termination by act of the principal is revocation; by act of the agent, it is renunciation.

b. Power to revoke or renounce. The principal has power to revoke and the agent has power to renounce, although doing so is in violation of a contract between the parties and although the authority is expressed to be irrevocable. A statement in a contract that the authority cannot be terminated by either party is effective only to create liability for its wrongful termination.

Illustrations:

1. In consideration of A's agreement to advertise and give his best energies to the sale of Blackacre, its owner, P, grants to A "a power of attorney, irrevocable for one year" to sell it. A advertises and spends time trying to sell Blackacre. At the end of three months P informs A that he revokes. A's authority is terminated.

2. In consideration of $1000 and A's promise to endeavor to sell, P grants to A for a period of one year a power of attorney to sell property, with compensation at 25 per cent. of the selling price, the power of attorney ending with this phrase: "Hereby intending and agreeing that this power shall be irrevocable during one year, and that during this period A shall have a power coupled with an interest which shall not be affected by my death or other circumstances." At the end of three months P informs A that he revokes. A's authority is terminated.

Comment:

c. Liabilities. If there is a contract between principal and agent that the authority shall not be revoked or renounced, a party who revokes or renounces, unless privileged by the conduct of the other or by supervening circumstances, is subject to liability to the other. ...

d. Non-agency powers. A power in the form of an agency authority given for the protection of a person described as an agent, but who is not one, is not an agency authority and cannot be revoked by the power giver; if such a power is held for the benefit of a third person, it can be terminated neither by revocation nor renunciation. See § 139. ...

. . .

TOPIC 5. TERMINATION OF POWERS GIVEN AS SECURITY

§ 138. Definition

A power given as security is a power to affect the legal relations of another, created in the form of an agency authority, but held for the benefit of the power holder or a third person and given to secure the performance of a duty or to protect a title, either legal or equitable, such power being given when the duty or title is created or given for consideration.

Comment:

a. A power given as security arises when a person manifests consent that the one to whom it is given can properly act to create liability against him, or to dispose of some of his interests, or to perfect or otherwise protect a title already in the power holder or in the person for whom he is to act. If the power is given as security for the performance of a duty, it must be supported by consideration, but consideration is not necessary if the power is in aid of and accompanies a transfer of a title to the power holder.

b. Distinguished from authority. A power given as security is one held for the benefit of a person other than the power giver. ...

. . .

§ 139. Termination of Powers Given as Security

(1) Unless otherwise agreed, a power given as security is not terminated by:

(a) revocation by the creator of the power;

(b) surrender by the holder of the power, if he holds for the benefit of another;

(c) the loss of capacity during the lifetime of either the creator of the power or the holder of the power; or

(d) the death of the holder of the power, or, if the power is given as security for a duty which does not terminate at the death of the creator of the power, by his death.

(2) A power given as security is terminated by its surrender by the beneficiary, if of full capacity; or by the happening of events which, by its terms, discharges the obligations secured by it, or which makes its execution illegal or impossible.

Chapter 6

LIABILITY OF PRINCIPAL TO THIRD PERSONS; CONTRACTS AND CONVEYANCES

TOPIC 1. GENERAL PRINCIPLES

§ 140. Liability Based Upon Agency Principles

The liability of the principal to a third person upon a transaction conducted by an agent, or the transfer of his interests by an agent, may be based upon the fact that:

(a) the agent was authorized;

(b) the agent was apparently authorized; or

(c) the agent had a power arising from the agency relation and not dependent upon authority or apparent authority.

§ 143. Effect of Ratification

Upon ratification with knowledge of the material facts, the principal becomes responsible for contracts and conveyances made for him by one purporting to act on his account as if the transaction had been authorized, if there has been no supervening loss of capacity by the principal or change in the law which would render illegal the authorization or performance of such a transaction.

TOPIC 2. DISCLOSED OR PARTIALLY DISCLOSED PRINCIPAL

TITLE A. CREATION OF LIABILITY BY AUTHORIZED ACTS

§ 144. General Rule

A disclosed or partially disclosed principal is subject to liability upon contracts made by an agent acting within his authority if made in proper form and with the understanding that the principal is a party.

TITLE C.   CREATION OF LIABILITY BY UNAUTHORIZED ACTS

§ 159. Apparent Authority

A disclosed or partially disclosed principal is subject to liability upon contracts made by an agent acting within his apparent authority if made in proper form and with the understanding that the apparent principal is a party.   The rules as to the liability of a principal for authorized acts, are applicable to unauthorized acts which are apparently authorized.

§ 160. Violation of Secret Instructions

A disclosed or partially disclosed principal authorizing an agent to make a contract, but imposing upon him limitations as to incidental terms intended not to be revealed, is subject to liability upon a contract made in violation of such limitations with a third person who has no notice of them.

§ 161. Unauthorized Acts of General Agent

A general agent for a disclosed or partially disclosed principal subjects his principal to liability for acts done on his account which usually accompany or are incidental to transactions which the agent is authorized to conduct if, although they are forbidden by the principal, the other party reasonably believes that the agent is authorized to do them and has no notice that he is not so authorized.

§ 161A. Unauthorized Acts of Special Agents

A special agent for a disclosed or partly disclosed principal has no power to bind his principal by contracts or conveyances which he is not authorized or apparently authorized to make, unless the principal is estopped, or unless:

(a) the agent's only departure from his authority or apparent authority is

i.   in naming or disclosing the principal, or

ii.   in having an improper motive, or

iii.   in being negligent in determining the facts upon which his authority is based, or

iv.   in making misrepresentations; or

(b) the agent is given possession of goods or commercial documents with authority to deal with them.

TITLE D. DEFENSES AND LIABILITY AFFECTED BY SUBSEQUENT EVENTS

§ 179. Rights Between Third Person and Agent

Unless otherwise agreed, the liability of a disclosed or partially disclosed principal is not affected by any rights or liabilities existing between the other party and the agent at the time the contract is made.

§ 180. Defenses of Principal—In General

A disclosed or partially disclosed principal is entitled to all defenses arising out of a transaction between his agent and a third person. He is not entitled to defenses which are personal to the agent.

TOPIC 3. UNDISCLOSED PRINCIPAL

TITLE A. CREATION OF LIABILITY BY AUTHORIZED ACTS

§ 186. General Rule

An undisclosed principal is bound by contracts and conveyances made on his account by an agent acting within his authority, except that the principal is not bound by a contract which is under seal or which is negotiable, or upon a contract which excludes him.

TITLE B. CREATION OF LIABILITY BY UNAUTHORIZED ACTS

§ 194. Acts of General Agents

A general agent for an undisclosed principal authorized to conduct transactions subjects his principal to liability for acts done on his account, if usual or necessary in such transactions, although forbidden by the principal to do them.

§ 195. Acts of Manager Appearing to Be Owner

An undisclosed principal who entrusts an agent with the management of his business is subject to liability to third persons with whom the agent enters into transactions usual in such businesses and on the principal's account, although contrary to the directions of the principal.

§ 195A. Unauthorized Acts of Special Agents

A special agent for an undisclosed principal has no power to bind his principal by contracts or conveyances which he is not authorized to make unless:

(a) the agent's only departure from his authority is

(i) in not disclosing his principal, or

(ii) in having an improper motive, or

(iii) in being negligent in determining the facts upon which his authority is based, or

(iv) in making misrepresentations; or

(b) the agent is given possession of goods or commercial documents with authority to deal with them.

TITLE C. DEFENSES AND LIABILITY AFFECTED BY SUBSEQUENT EVENTS

§ 203. Defenses of Undisclosed Principal—In General

An undisclosed principal is entitled to all defenses arising out of a transaction with an agent, but not defenses which are personal to the agent.

§ 205. Power of Agent to Modify Contract Before Disclosure of Principal

Until the existence of the principal is disclosed, an agent who has made a contract for an undisclosed principal has power to cancel the contract and to modify it with binding effect upon the principal if the contract or conveyance, as modified, is authorized or is within the inherent power of the agent to make.

Chapter 7

LIABILITY OF PRINCIPAL TO THIRD PERSON; TORTS

TOPIC 2. LIABILITY FOR AUTHORIZED CONDUCT OR CONDUCT INCIDENTAL THERETO

TITLE B. TORTS OF SERVANTS

§ 219. When Master is Liable for Torts of His Servants

(1) A master is subject to liability for the torts of his servants committed while acting in the scope of their employment.

(2) A master is not subject to liability for the torts of his servants acting outside the scope of their employment, unless:

(a) the master intended the conduct or the consequences, or

(b) the master was negligent or reckless, or

(c) the conduct violated a non-delegable duty of the master, or

(d) the servant purported to act or to speak on behalf of the principal and there was reliance upon apparent authority, or he was aided in accomplishing the tort by the existence of the agency relation.

WHO IS A SERVANT

§ 220. Definition of Servant

(1) A servant is a person employed to perform services in the affairs of another and who with respect to the physical conduct in the performance of the services is subject to the other's control or right to control.

(2) In determining whether one acting for another is a servant or an independent contractor, the following matters of fact, among others, are considered:

(a) the extent of control which, by the agreement, the master may exercise over the details of the work;

(b) whether or not the one employed is engaged in a distinct occupation or business;

(c) the kind of occupation, with reference to whether, in the locality, the work is usually done under the direction of the employer or by a specialist without supervision;

(d) the skill required in the particular occupation;

(e) whether the employer or the workman supplies the instrumentalities, tools, and the place of work for the person doing the work;

(f) the length of time for which the person is employed;

(g) the method of payment, whether by the time or by the job;

(h) whether or not the work is a part of the regular business of the employer;

(i) whether or not the parties believe they are creating the relation of master and servant; and

(j) whether the principal is or is not in business.

SCOPE OF EMPLOYMENT

§ 228. General Statement

(1) Conduct of a servant is within the scope of employment if, but only if:

(a) it is of the kind he is employed to perform;

(b) it occurs substantially within the authorized time and space limits;

(c) it is actuated, at least in part, by a purpose to serve the master, and

(d) if force is intentionally used by the servant against another, the use of force is not unexpectable by the master.

(2) Conduct of a servant is not within the scope of employment if it is different in kind from that authorized, far beyond the authorized time or space limits, or too little actuated by a purpose to serve the master.

§ 229. Kind of Conduct Within Scope of Employment

(1) To be within the scope of the employment, conduct must be of the same general nature as that authorized, or incidental to the conduct authorized.

(2) In determining whether or not the conduct, although not authorized, is nevertheless so similar to or incidental to the conduct authorized as to be within the scope of employment, the following matters of fact are to be considered:

(a) whether or not the act is one commonly done by such servants;

(b) the time, place and purpose of the act;

(c) the previous relations between the master and the servant;

(d) the extent to which the business of the master is apportioned between different servants;

(e) whether or not the act is outside the enterprise of the master or, if within the enterprise, has not been entrusted to any servant;

(f) whether or not the master has reason to expect that such an act will be done;

(g) the similarity in quality of the act done to the act authorized;

(h) whether or not the instrumentality by which the harm is done has been furnished by the master to the servant;

(i) the extent of departure from the normal method of accomplishing an authorized result; and

(j) whether or not the act is seriously criminal.

§ 230. Forbidden Acts

An act, although forbidden, or done in a forbidden manner, may be within the scope of employment.

§ 231. Criminal or Tortious Acts

An act may be within the scope of employment although consciously criminal or tortious.

TITLE C.   AGENTS' TORTS—LIABILITY NOT DEPENDENT UPON RELATION OF MASTER AND SERVANT

IN GENERAL

§ 250. Non-liability for Physical Harm by Non-servant Agents

A principal is not liable for physical harm caused by the negligent physical conduct of a non-servant agent during the performance of the principal's business, if he neither intended nor authorized the result nor the manner of performance, unless he was under a duty to have the act performed with due care.

Chapter 10

LIABILITY OF THIRD PERSON TO PRINCIPAL

TOPIC 1.   CONTRACTS; DISCLOSED AGENCY

§ 292. General Rule

The other party to a contract made by an agent for a disclosed or partially disclosed principal, acting within his authority, apparent authority or other agency power, is liable to the principal as if he had contracted directly with the principal, unless the principal is excluded as a party by the form or terms of the contract.

§ 298. Defenses of Other Party

The other party to a contract made by an agent on behalf of a disclosed or partially disclosed principal has all the defenses which he would have had against the principal if the principal had made the contract under the same circumstances.

§ 299. Rights Between Other Party and Agent

Unless otherwise agreed, the liability of the other party to a disclosed or partially disclosed principal upon a contract made by an agent is not affected by any rights or liabilities then existing between the other party and the agent.

TOPIC 2. CONTRACTS; UNDISCLOSED AGENCY

§ 302. General Rule

A person who makes a contract with an agent of an undisclosed principal, intended by the agent to be on account of his principal and within the power of such agent to bind his principal, is liable to the principal as if the principal himself had made the contract with him, unless he is excluded by the form or terms of the contract, unless his existence is fraudulently concealed or unless there is set-off or a similar defense against the agent.

§ 303. Principal Excluded From Transaction

A person with whom an agent makes a contract on account of an undisclosed principal is not liable in an action at law brought upon the contract by such principal:

(a) if the contract is in the form of a sealed or negotiable instrument; or

(b) if the terms of the contract exclude liability to any undisclosed principal or to the particular principal.

§ 306. Rights Between Other Party and Agent

(1) If the agent has been authorized to conceal the existence of the principal, the liability to an undisclosed principal of a person dealing with the agent within his power to bind the principal is diminished by any claim which such person may have against the agent at the time of making the contract and until the existence of the principal becomes known to him, if he could set off such claim in an action against the agent.

(2) If the agent is authorized only to contract in the principal's name, the other party does not have set-off for a claim due him from the agent unless the agent has been entrusted with the possession of chattels which he disposes of as directed or unless the principal has otherwise misled the third person into extending credit to the agent.

§ 308. Defenses of Other Party

In an action by an undisclosed principal against the other party to a contract, the other party has all the defenses, except those of a purely procedural nature:

(a) which he would have had against the principal if the principal had made the contract under the same circumstances,

(b) which he had against the agent until the discovery of the principal, unless the agent was authorized to contract only in the principal's name.

TOPIC 5. EFFECT OF RATIFICATION

§ 319. General Rule

Where a purported servant or other agent has entered into a transaction with a third person, its ratification by the purported master or other principal has the same effect upon the liabilities of the third person to the principal as an original authorization.

Chapter 11

LIABILITY OF AGENT TO THIRD PERSONS

TOPIC 1. CONTRACTS AND CONVEYANCES

TITLE A. AGENT A PARTY TO A TRANSACTION CONDUCTED BY HIMSELF

§ 320. Principal Disclosed

Unless otherwise agreed, a person making or purporting to make a contract with another as agent for a disclosed principal does not become a party to the contract.

§ 321. Principal Partially Disclosed

Unless otherwise agreed, a person purporting to make a contract with another for a partially disclosed principal is a party to the contract.

§ 322. Principal Undisclosed

An agent purporting to act upon his own account, but in fact making a contract on account of an undisclosed principal, is a party to the contract.

§ 326. Principal Known to Be Nonexistent or Incompetent

Unless otherwise agreed, a person who, in dealing with another, purports to act as agent for a principal whom both know to be nonexistent or wholly incompetent, becomes a party to such a contract.

Comment:

. . .

b. Promoters. The classic illustration of the rule stated in this Section is the promoter. When a promoter makes an agreement with another on behalf of a corporation to be formed, the following alternatives may represent the intent of the parties:

(1) They may understand that the other party is making a revocable offer to the nonexistent corporation which will result in a contract if the corporation is formed and accepts the offer prior to withdrawal. This is the normal understanding.

(2) They may understand that the other party is making an irrevocable offer for a limited time. Consideration to support the promise to keep the offer open can be found in an express or limited promise by the promoter to organize the corporation and use his best efforts to cause it to accept the offer.

(3) They may agree to a present contract by which the promoter is bound, but with an agreement that his liability terminates if the corporation is formed and manifests its willingness to become a party. There can be no ratification by the newly formed corporation, since it was not in existence when the agreement was made . . . .

(4) They may agree to a present contract on which, even though the corporation becomes a party, the promoter remains liable either primarily or as surety for the performance of the corporation's obligation.

Which one of these possible alternatives, or variants thereof, is intended is a matter of interpretation on the facts of the individual case.

TITLE B.   AGENT NOT PARTY TO TRANSACTION CONDUCTED BY HIMSELF

§ 328.   Liability of Authorized Agent for Performance of Contract

An agent, by making a contract only on behalf of a competent disclosed or partially disclosed principal whom he has power so to bind, does not thereby become liable for its nonperformance.

§ 329.   Agent Who Warrants Authority

A person who purports to make a contract, conveyance or representation on behalf of another who has full capacity but whom he has no power to bind, thereby becomes subject to liability to the other party thereto upon an implied warranty of authority, unless he has manifested that he does not make such warranty or the other party knows that the agent is not so authorized.

§ 330.   Liability for Misrepresentation of Authority

A person who tortiously misrepresents to another that he has authority to make a contract, conveyance, or representation on behalf of a principal whom he has no power to bind, is subject to liability to the other in an action of tort for loss caused by reliance upon such misrepresentation.

TITLE C.   DEFENSES AND EFFECTS OF SUBSEQUENT EVENTS

§ 333.   Rights Between Other Party and Principal

Unless otherwise agreed, the liability of an agent upon a contract between a third person and the principal to which the agent is a party is not affected by any rights or liabilities existing between the third person and the principal not arising from the transaction, except that, with the consent of the principal, the agent can set off a claim which the principal would have in an action brought against him.

§ 334.   Defenses of Agent—In General

In an action against an agent upon a contract between a third person and the principal to which the agent is a party, the agent has all the defenses which arise out of the transaction itself and also those which he has personally against the third person; defenses which are personal to the principal are not available to the agent.

§ 335. Agent Surety for Principal

In an action brought against an agent upon a contract to which the agent is a party but under which the primary duty of performance rests upon the principal, the agent has the defenses available to a surety.

§ 336. Election by Other Party to Hold Principal; Agency Disclosed

Unless otherwise agreed, the agent of a disclosed or partially disclosed principal who is a party to a contract made by another with such principal is not relieved from liability upon the contract by the determination of the other party to look to the principal alone, nor, unless the agent and the principal are joint contractors, by the fact that the other gets a judgment against the principal. He is relieved from liability to the extent that he is prejudiced thereby if he changes his position in justifiable reliance upon a manifestation of the other that he will look solely to the principal for performance.

§ 337. Election by Other Party to Hold Principal; Agency Undisclosed

An agent who has made a contract on behalf of an undisclosed principal is not relieved from liability by the determination of the other party thereto to look to the principal alone for the performance of the contract. He is discharged from liability if the other obtains a judgment against the principal, or, to the extent that he is prejudiced thereby, if he changes his position in justifiable reliance upon the other's manifestation that he will look solely to the principal for payment.

Chapter 13

DUTIES AND LIABILITIES OF AGENT TO PRINCIPAL

TOPIC 1. DUTIES

TITLE B. DUTIES OF SERVICE AND OBEDIENCE

§ 377. Contractual Duties

A person who makes a contract with another to perform services as an agent for him is subject to a duty to act in accordance with his promise.

§ 379. Duty of Care and Skill

(1) Unless otherwise agreed, a paid agent is subject to a duty to the principal to act with standard care and with the skill which is standard in the locality for the kind of work which he is employed to perform and, in addition, to exercise any special skill that he has.

(2) Unless otherwise agreed, a gratuitous agent is under a duty to the principal to act with the care and skill which is required of persons not agents performing similar gratuitous undertakings for others.

TITLE C. DUTIES OF LOYALTY

§ 387. General Principle

Unless otherwise agreed, an agent is subject to a duty to his principal to act solely for the benefit of the principal in all matters connected with his agency.

§ 388. Duty to Account for Profits Arising Out of Employment

Unless otherwise agreed, an agent who makes a profit in connection with transactions conducted by him on behalf of the principal is under a duty to give such profit to the principal.

Comment:

a. Ordinarily, the agent's primary function is to make profits for the principal, and his duty to account includes accounting for any unexpected and incidental accretions whether or not received in violation of duty. Thus, an agent who, without the knowledge of the principal, receives something in connection with, or because of, a transaction conducted for the principal, has a duty to pay this to the principal even though otherwise he has acted with perfect fairness to the principal and violates no duty of loyalty in receiving the amount. . . .

Illustrations:

1. A, a real estate broker acting for P, the seller, in order to assure himself of his commission, makes a contract with T, a purchaser, by which, if T cancels the contract with P, as he is given the right to do, T is to pay A the amount of A's commission. T repudiates the contract with P but pays A. A holds his commission as a constructive trustee for P.

2. P authorizes A to sell land held in A's name for a fixed sum. A makes a contract to sell the land to T, who makes a deposit which is to be forfeited if the transaction is

not carried out. T forfeits the amount. A sells the land to another person at the price fixed by P. A is under a duty to account to P for the amount received from T....

Comment:

b. Gratuities to agent. An agent can properly retain gratuities received on account of the principal's business if, because of custom or otherwise, an agreement to this effect is found. Except in such a case, the receipt and retention of a gratuity by an agent from a party with interests adverse to those of the principal is evidence that the agent is committing a breach of duty to the principal by not acting in his interests.

Illustrations:

4. A, the purchasing agent for the P railroad, purchases honestly and for a fair price fifty trucks from T, who is going out of business. In gratitude for A's favorable action and without ulterior motive or agreement, T makes A a gift of a car. A holds the automobile as a constructive trustee for P, although A is not otherwise liable to P....

Comment:

c. Use of confidential information. An agent who acquires confidential information in the course of his employment or in violation of his duties has a duty not to use it to the disadvantage of the principal.... He also has a duty to account for any profits made by the use of such information, although this does not harm the principal. Thus, where a corporation has decided to operate an enterprise at a place where land values will be increased because of such operation, a corporate officer who takes advantage of his special knowledge to buy land in the vicinity is accountable for the profits he makes, even though such purchases have no adverse effect upon the enterprise. So, if he has "inside" information that the corporation is about to purchase or sell securities, or to declare or to pass a dividend, profits made by him in stock transactions undertaken because of his knowledge are held in constructive trust for the principal. He is also liable for profits made by selling confidential information to third persons, even though the principal is not adversely affected.

§ 389. Acting as Adverse Party Without Principal's Consent

Unless otherwise agreed, an agent is subject to a duty not to deal with his principal as an adverse party in a transaction connected with his agency without the principal's knowledge.

Comment:

a. The rule stated in this Section applies to transactions which the agent conducts for his principal, dealing therein with himself, and also to transactions in which the agent deals with his principal, who acts in person or through another agent; it is applicable to transactions in which the agent is acting entirely for himself and to those in which he has such a substantial interest that it reasonably might affect his judgment. Thus, an agent who is appointed to sell or to give advice concerning sales violates his duty if, without the principal's knowledge, he sells to himself or purchases from the principal through the medium of a "straw," or induces his principal to sell to a corporation in which he has a large concealed interest....

. . .

c. Where no harm to principal. The rule stated in this Section is not based upon the existence of harm to the principal in the particular case. It exists to prevent a conflict of opposing interests in the minds of agents whose duty it is to act solely for the benefit of their principals. The rule applies, therefore, even though the transaction between the principal and the agent is beneficial to the principal. Thus, in the absence of a known custom or an agreement, an agent employed to sell at the market price cannot, without disclosure to the principal, properly buy the goods on his own account, even though he pays a higher price for them than the principal could obtain elsewhere. The rule applies also although the transaction is a public sale and the price received is above that stated by the principal to be adequate. Likewise, ordinarily, an agent appointed to buy or to sell at a fixed price violates his duty to the principal if, without the principal's acquiescence, he buys from or sells the specified article to himself at the specified price, even though it is impossible to obtain more or as much. However, if a broker is employed to sell property with an agreement that he is to retain all above a specified price, it may be inferred that the transaction gives him an option to purchase at that price without notice to the principal that he is acting for himself....

. . .

§ 390. Acting as Adverse Party With Principal's Consent

An agent who, to the knowledge of the principal, acts on his own account in a transaction in which he is employed has a duty to deal fairly with the principal and to disclose to him all facts which the agent knows or should know would reasonably affect the principal's judgment, unless the principal has manifested that he knows such facts or that he does not care to know them.

Comment:

a. Facts to be disclosed. One employed as agent violates no duty to the principal by acting for his own benefit if he makes a full disclosure of the facts to an acquiescent principal and takes no unfair advantage of him. Before dealing with the principal on his own account, however, an agent has a duty, not only to make no misstatements of fact, but also to disclose to the principal all relevant facts fully and completely. A fact is relevant if it is one which the agent should realize would be likely to affect the judgment of the principal in giving his consent to the agent to enter into the particular transaction on the specified terms. Hence, the disclosure must include not only the fact that the agent is acting on his own account (see § 389), but also all other facts which he should realize have or are likely to have a bearing upon the desirability of the transaction from the viewpoint of the principal. This includes, in the case of sales to him by the principal, not only the price which can be obtained, but also all facts affecting the desirability of sale, such as the likelihood of a higher price being obtained later, the possibilities of dealing with the property in another way, and all other matters which a disinterested and skillful agent advising the principal would think reasonably relevant.

If the principal has limited business experience, an agent cannot properly fail to give such information merely because the principal says he does not care for it; the agent's duty of fair dealing is satisfied only if he reasonably believes that the principal understands the implications of the transaction.

Illustrations:

1. P employs A to sell Blackacre for $1,000. A, having sought a customer, is unable to find one and reports such fact to P. He then states that he is willing to pay $1,000, telling P truthfully that he believes that a better sale might be made later in view of the chance that the locality will develop. A pays P $1,000. A month later, A sells the land for $1,500. In the absence of other facts, A has violated no duty to P.

2. P employs A to purchase a suitable manufacturing site for him. A owns one which is suitable and sells it to P at the fair price of $25,000, telling P all relevant facts

except that, a short time previously, he purchased the land for $15,000. The transaction can be rescinded by P. . . .

Comment:

c. Fairness. The agent must not take advantage of his position to persuade the principal into making a hard or improvident bargain. If the agent is one upon whom the principal naturally would rely for advice, the fact that the agent discloses that he is acting as an adverse party does not relieve him from the duty of giving the principal impartial advice based upon a carefully formed judgment as to the principal's interests. If he cannot or does not wish to do so, he has a duty to see that the principal secures the advice of a competent and disinterested third person. An agent who is in a close confidential relation to the principal, such as a family attorney, has the burden of proving that a substantial gift to him was not the result of undue influence. Even though an agent employed to sell is not in such a position, payment of less than the reasonable market value for property he buys from the principal is evidence that the bargain was unfair. If the principal is not in a dependent position, however, and the agent fully performs his duties of disclosure, a transaction of purchase and sale between them is not voidable merely because the principal receives an inadequate price or pays too great a price.

Illustrations:

4. P, a young physician with some inherited wealth and no business experience, places his property in charge of A to manage. Desiring a particular piece of land which represents a large share of P's assets, A waits until there is a slump in the price of land and, believing correctly that the slump is only temporary, suggests to P that it be sold, offering as an incentive that P's income from his profession will increase and that, although the price to be obtained is low, P can well afford to get more enjoyment from the proceeds now than from a larger amount later. P thereupon agrees to sell to A at a price which is as much as could be obtained at that time for the property. It may be found that A violated his duty of dealing fairly with P.

5. Same facts as in Illustration 4, except that A provides P with an independent experienced adviser, who gives disinterested advice, setting out the possibilities of

accretion in values. It may be found that A has satisfied his
duty of loyalty....

. . .

e. Agreements for compensation. A person is not ordinarily subject to a fiduciary duty in making terms as to compensation with a prospective principal....

. . .

§ 391. Acting for Adverse Party Without Principal's Consent

Unless otherwise agreed, an agent is subject to a duty to his
principal not to act on behalf of an adverse party in a transaction
connected with his agency without the principal's knowledge.

§ 392. Acting for Adverse Party With Principal's Consent

An agent who, to the knowledge of two principals, acts for both
of them in a transaction between them, has a duty to act with
fairness to each and to disclose to each all facts which he knows or
should know would reasonably affect the judgment of each in
permitting such dual agency, except as to a principal who has
manifested that he knows such facts or does not care to know them.

§ 393. Competition as to Subject Matter of Agency

Unless otherwise agreed, an agent is subject to a duty not to
compete with the principal concerning the subject matter of his
agency.

§ 394. Acting for One With Conflicting Interests

Unless otherwise agreed, an agent is subject to a duty not to act
or to agree to act during the period of his agency for persons whose
interests conflict with those of the principal in matters in which the
agent is employed.

§ 395. Using or Disclosing Confidential Information

Unless otherwise agreed, an agent is subject to a duty to the
principal not to use or to communicate information confidentially
given him by the principal or acquired by him during the course of
or on account of his agency or in violation of his duties as agent, in
competition with or to the injury of the principal, on his own
account or on behalf of another, although such information does
not relate to the transaction in which he is then employed, unless
the information is a matter of general knowledge.

§ 396. Using Confidential Information After Termination of Agency

Unless otherwise agreed, after the termination of the agency, the agent:

(a) has no duty not to compete with the principal;

(b) has a duty to the principal not to use or to disclose to third persons, on his own account or on account of others, in competition with the principal or to his injury, trade secrets, written lists of names, or other similar confidential matters given to him only for the principal's use or acquired by the agent in violation of duty. The agent is entitled to use general information concerning the method of business of the principal and the names of the customers retained in his memory, if not acquired in violation of his duty as agent;

(c) has a duty to account for profits made by the sale or use of trade secrets and other confidential information, whether or not in competition with the principal;

(d) has a duty to the principal not to take advantage of a still subsisting confidential relation created during the prior agency relation.

TOPIC 2.   LIABILITIES

§ 401. Liability for Loss Caused

An agent is subject to liability for loss caused to the principal by any breach of duty.

§ 403. Liability for Things Received in Violation of Duty of Loyalty

If an agent receives anything as a result of his violation of a duty of loyalty to the principal, he is subject to a liability to deliver it, its value, or its proceeds, to the principal.

§ 404. Liability for Use of Principal's Assets

An agent who, in violation of duty to his principal, uses for his own purposes or those of a third person assets of the principal's business is subject to liability to the principal for the value of the use. If the use predominates in producing a profit he is subject to liability, at the principal's election, for such profit; he is not, however, liable for profits made by him merely by the use of time which he has contracted to devote to the principal unless he violates his duty not to act adversely or in competition with the principal.

Comment:

a. The rule stated in this Section applies whether or not the agent uses the principal's facilities or other assets in competition with him. It applies irrespective of any harm done to the things used and irrespective of the use which the principal would have made of them.

Illustration:

1. P employs A to take care of the horses which P uses for driving purposes. P does not use them for a month and, during this period, without P's consent, A rents the horses to various persons who benefit the horses by the exercise thereby given them. A is subject to liability to P for the amount which he has received as rental.

Comment:

b. What are assets of the principal. The agent is subject to liability not only for the use of tangible things but also for the use of trade secrets, good-will, credit, and other intangible assets of the principal. Thus, an agent is subject to liability if, in selling his own goods, he uses the principal's trade-mark in territory in which the trade-mark is known but in which the principal does not sell and does not intend to sell similar goods.

Although the right to the services of an agent is a business asset of the principal, the agent's liability for profits made by his use of the principal's assets does not include a liability for profits made by him during hours which he should have devoted to the principal's service, unless he has thereby violated a fiduciary duty owed by him to the principal.

Illustration:

2. P employs A to give his full time to P as a bookkeeper. A uses portions of the time which he should have devoted to P's service in keeping the books for another employer, deriving thereby a greater salary than he receives from P. P cannot recover from A the amount of salary which A receives from the other employer.

c. Whether use of principal's assets predominates. Whether or not the use of assets of the principal predominates in producing a profit is a question of fact. Where an agent conducts a business upon the principal's premises, the location and facilities of the principal or the services of the agent may predominate in the creation of profits. If a ship captain uses the ship to carry heavy packages of his own, by selling which he makes a substantial profit, the owner is entitled to it; if the captain carries a box of trinkets for personal sale at ports of call, the ivory he thereby obtains does not necessarily go to the shipowner.

Illustration:

> 3. A soldier uses his official uniform and position to smuggle forbidden goods into a friendly country and thereby makes large profits. The country by which he is employed is entitled to the profits.

Comment:

d. Other remedies of principal. In addition to the rights which the principal has under the rule stated in this Section, the principal may have a cause of action for breach of contract or for a tort by the agent, or he may be entitled to a decree declaring a constructive trust in the specific proceeds of the use of an asset. These rights may be in the alternative or they may be cumulative, in accordance with the rules stated in Section 407. Thus, if the agent improperly uses the principal's chattels, the principal is entitled to recover their value, plus any damages caused to the business by their use, if the use amounts to a conversion; or he can recover the chattels in specie together with any profit which the agent has made from them, plus any damage to them or to the business caused by their use.

§ 407. Principal's Choice of Remedies

(1) If an agent has received a benefit as a result of violating his duty of loyalty, the principal is entitled to recover from him what he has so received, its value, or its proceeds, and also the amount of damage thereby caused; except that, if the violation consists of the wrongful disposal of the principal's property, the principal cannot recover its value and also what the agent received in exchange therefor.

(2) A principal who has recovered damages from a third person because of an agent's violation of his duty of loyalty is entitled nevertheless to obtain from the agent any profit which the agent improperly received as a result of the transaction.

Chapter 14

DUTIES AND LIABILITIES OF PRINCIPAL TO AGENT

TOPIC 1. CONTRACTUAL AND RESTITUTIONAL DUTIES AND LIABILITIES

TITLE A. INTERPRETATION OF CONTRACTS AND LIABILITIES THEREUNDER

§ 438. Duty of Indemnity; the Principle

(1) A principal is under a duty to indemnify the agent in accordance with the terms of the agreement with him.

(2) In the absence of terms to the contrary in the agreement of employment, the principal has a duty to indemnify the agent where the agent

(a) makes a payment authorized or made necessary in executing the principal's affairs or, unless he is officious, one beneficial to the principal, or

(b) suffers a loss which, because of their relation, it is fair that the principal should bear.

§ 439. When Duty of Indemnity Exists

Unless otherwise agreed, a principal is subject to a duty to exonerate an agent who is not barred by the illegality of his conduct to indemnify him for:

(a) authorized payments made by the agent on behalf of the principal;

(b) payments upon contracts upon which the agent is authorized to make himself liable, and upon obligations arising from the possession or ownership of things which he is authorized to hold on account of the principal;

(c) payments of damages to third persons which he is required to make on account of the authorized performance of an act which constitutes a tort or a breach of contract;

(d) expenses of defending actions by third persons brought because of the agent's authorized conduct, such actions being unfounded but not brought in bad faith; and

(e) payments resulting in benefit to the principal, made by the agent under such circumstances that it would be inequitable for indemnity not to be made.

§ 440. When No Duty of Indemnity

Unless otherwise agreed, the principal is not subject to a duty to indemnify an agent:

(a) for pecuniary loss or other harm, not of benefit to the principal, arising from the performance of unauthorized acts or resulting solely from the agent's negligence or other fault; or

(b) if the principal has otherwise performed his duties to the agent, for physical harm caused by the performance of authorized acts, for harm suffered as a result of torts, other than the tortious institution of suits, committed upon the agent by third persons because of his employment, or for harm suffered by the refusal of third persons to deal with him; or

(c) if the agent's loss resulted from an enterprise which he knew to be illegal.

§ 442. Period of Employment

Unless otherwise agreed, mutual promises by principal and agent to employ and to serve create obligations to employ and to serve which are terminable upon notice by either party; if neither party terminates the employment, it may terminate by lapse of time or by supervening events.

UNIFORM PARTNERSHIP ACT

PART I. PRELIMINARY PROVISIONS

PART II. NATURE OF PARTNERSHIP

PART III. RELATIONS OF PARTNERS TO PERSONS DEALING WITH THE PARTNERSHIP

PART IV. RELATIONS OF PARTNERS TO ONE ANOTHER

PART V. PROPERTY RIGHTS OF A PARTNER

PART VI. DISSOLUTION AND WINDING UP

PART VII. MISCELLANEOUS PROVISIONS

PART I

PRELIMINARY PROVISIONS

§ 1. Name of Act

This act may be cited as Uniform Partnership Act.

§ 2. Definition of Terms

In this act, "Court" includes every court and judge having jurisdiction in the case.

"Business" includes every trade, occupation, or profession.

"Person" includes individuals, partnerships, corporations, and other associations.

"Bankrupt" includes bankrupt under the Federal Bankruptcy Act or insolvent under any state insolvent act.

"Conveyance" includes every assignment, lease, mortgage, or encumbrance.

"Real property" includes land and any interest or estate in land.

* Omitted.

166

§ 3. Interpretation of Knowledge and Notice

(1) A person has "knowledge" of a fact within the meaning of this act not only when he has actual knowledge thereof, but also when he has knowledge of such other facts as in the circumstances shows bad faith.

(2) A person has "notice" of a fact within the meaning of this act when the person who claims the benefit of the notice:

(a) States the fact to such person, or

(b) Delivers through the mail, or by other means of communication, a written statement of the fact to such person or to a proper person at his place of business or residence.

§ 4. Rules of Construction

(1) The rule that statutes in derogation of the common law are to be strictly construed shall have no application to this act.

(2) The law of estoppel shall apply under this act.

(3) The law of agency shall apply under this act.

(4) This act shall be so interpreted and construed as to effect its general purpose to make uniform the law of those states which enact it.

(5) This act shall not be construed so as to impair the obligations of any contract existing when the act goes into effect, nor to affect any action or proceedings begun or right accrued before this act takes effect.

§ 5. Rules for Cases Not Provided for in This Act

In any case not provided for in this act the rules of law and equity, including the law merchant, shall govern.

PART II

NATURE OF PARTNERSHIP

§ 6. Partnership Defined

(1) A partnership is an association of two or more persons to carry on as co-owners a business for profit.

(2) But any association formed under any other statute of this state, or any statute adopted by authority, other than the authority of this state, is not a partnership under this act, unless such association would have been a partnership in this state prior to the

adoption of this act; but this act shall apply to limited partnerships except in so far as the statutes relating to such partnerships are inconsistent herewith.

§ 7. Rules for Determining the Existence of a Partnership

In determining whether a partnership exists, these rules shall apply:

(1) Except as provided by section 16 persons who are not partners as to each other are not partners as to third persons.

(2) Joint tenancy, tenancy in common, tenancy by the entireties, joint property, common property, or part ownership does not of itself establish a partnership, whether such co-owners do or do not share any profits made by the use of the property.

(3) The sharing of gross returns does not of itself establish a partnership, whether or not the persons sharing them have a joint or common right or interest in any property from which the returns are derived.

(4) The receipt by a person of a share of the profits of a business is prima facie evidence that he is a partner in the business, but no such inference shall be drawn if such profits were received in payment:

(a) As a debt by installments or otherwise,

(b) As wages of an employee or rent to a landlord,

(c) As an annuity to a widow or representative of a deceased partner,

(d) As interest on a loan, though the amount of payment vary with the profits of the business,

(e) As the consideration for the sale of a good-will of a business or other property by installments or otherwise.

§ 8. Partnership Property

(1) All property originally brought into the partnership stock or subsequently acquired by purchase or otherwise, on account of the partnership, is partnership property.

(2) Unless the contrary intention appears, property acquired with partnership funds is partnership property.

(3) Any estate in real property may be acquired in the partnership name. Title so acquired can be conveyed only in the partnership name.

(4) A conveyance to a partnership in the partnership name, though without words of inheritance, passes the entire estate of the grantor unless a contrary intent appears.

PART III

RELATIONS OF PARTNERS TO PERSONS DEALING WITH THE PARTNERSHIP

§ 9. Partner Agent of Partnership as to Partnership Business

(1) Every partner is an agent of the partnership for the purpose of its business, and the act of every partner, including the execution in the partnership name of any instrument, for apparently carrying on in the usual way the business of the partnership of which he is a member binds the partnership, unless the partner so acting has in fact no authority to act for the partnership in the particular matter, and the person with whom he is dealing has knowledge of the fact that he has no such authority.

(2) An act of a partner which is not apparently for the carrying on of the business of the partnership in the usual way does not bind the partnership unless authorized by the other partners.

(3) Unless authorized by the other partners or unless they have abandoned the business, one or more but less than all the partners have no authority to:

(a) Assign the partnership property in trust for creditors or on the assignee's promise to pay the debts of the partnership,

(b) Dispose of the good-will of the business,

(c) Do any other act which would make it impossible to carry on the ordinary business of a partnership,

(d) Confess a judgment,

(e) Submit a partnership claim or liability to arbitration or reference.

(4) No act of a partner in contravention of a restriction on authority shall bind the partnership to persons having knowledge of the restriction.

§ 10. Conveyance of Real Property of the Partnership

(1) Where title to real property is in the partnership name, any partner may convey title to such property by a conveyance executed in the partnership name; but the partnership may recover such property unless the partner's act binds the partnership under the

provisions of paragraph (1) of section 9, or unless such property has been conveyed by the grantee or a person claiming through such grantee to a holder for value without knowledge that the partner, in making the conveyance, has exceeded his authority.

(2) Where title to real property is in the name of the partnership, a conveyance executed by a partner, in his own name, passes the equitable interest of the partnership, provided the act is one within the authority of the partner under the provisions of paragraph (1) of section 9.

(3) Where title to real property is in the name of one or more but not all the partners, and the record does not disclose the right of the partnership, the partners in whose name the title stands may convey title to such property, but the partnership may recover such property if the partners' act does not bind the partnership under the provisions of paragraph (1) of section 9, unless the purchaser or his assignee, is a holder for value, without knowledge.

(4) Where the title to real property is in the name of one or more or all the partners, or in a third person in trust for the partnership, a conveyance executed by a partner in the partnership name, or in his own name, passes the equitable interest of the partnership, provided the act is one within the authority of the partner under the provisions of paragraph (1) of section 9.

(5) Where the title to real property is in the names of all the partners a conveyance executed by all the partners passes all their rights in such property.

§ 11. Partnership Bound by Admission of Partner

An admission or representation made by any partner concerning partnership affairs within the scope of his authority as conferred by this act is evidence against the partnership.

§ 12. Partnership Charged With Knowledge of or Notice to Partner

Notice to any partner of any matter relating to partnership affairs, and the knowledge of the partner acting in the particular matter, acquired while a partner or then present to his mind, and the knowledge of any other partner who reasonably could and should have communicated it to the acting partner, operate as notice to or knowledge of the partnership, except in the case of a fraud on the partnership committed by or with the consent of that partner.

§ 13. Partnership Bound by Partner's Wrongful Act

Where, by any wrongful act or omission of any partner acting in the ordinary course of the business of the partnership or with the authority of his co-partners, loss or injury is caused to any person, not being a partner in the partnership, or any penalty is incurred, the partnership is liable therefor to the same extent as the partner so acting or omitting to act.

§ 14. Partnership Bound by Partner's Breach of Trust

The partnership is bound to make good the loss:

(a) Where one partner acting within the scope of his apparent authority receives money or property of a third person and misapplies it; and

(b) Where the partnership in the course of its business receives money or property of a third person and the money or property so received is misapplied by any partner while it is in the custody of the partnership.

§ 15. Nature of Partner's Liability

All partners are liable

(a) Jointly and severally for everything chargeable to the partnership under sections 13 and 14.

(b) Jointly for all other debts and obligations of the partnership; but any partner may enter into a separate obligation to perform a partnership contract.

§ 16. Partner by Estoppel

(1) When a person, by words spoken or written or by conduct, represents himself, or consents to another representing him to any one, as a partner in an existing partnership or with one or more persons not actual partners, he is liable to any such person to whom such representation has been made, who has, on the faith of such representation, given credit to the actual or apparent partnership, and if he has made such representation or consented to its being made in a public manner he is liable to such person, whether the representation has or has not been made or communicated to such person so giving credit by or with the knowledge of the apparent partner making the representation or consenting to its being made.

(a) When a partnership liability results, he is liable as though he were an actual member of the partnership.

(b) When no partnership liability results, he is liable jointly with the other persons, if any, so consenting to the contract or representation as to incur liability, otherwise separately.

(2) When a person has been thus represented to be a partner in an existing partnership, or with one or more persons not actual partners, he is an agent of the persons consenting to such representation to bind them to the same extent and in the same manner as though he were a partner in fact, with respect to persons who rely upon the representation. Where all the members of the existing partnership consent to the representation, a partnership act or obligation results; but in all other cases it is the joint act or obligation of the person acting and the persons consenting to the representation.

§ 17. Liability of Incoming Partner

A person admitted as a partner into an existing partnership is liable for all the obligations of the partnership arising before his admission as though he had been a partner when such obligations were incurred, except that this liability shall be satisfied only out of partnership property.

PART IV

RELATIONS OF PARTNERS TO ONE ANOTHER

§ 18. Rules Determining Rights and Duties of Partners

The rights and duties of the partners in relation to the partnership shall be determined, subject to any agreement between them, by the following rules:

(a) Each partner shall be repaid his contributions, whether by way of capital or advances to the partnership property and share equally in the profits and surplus remaining after all liabilities, including those to partners, are satisfied; and must contribute towards the losses, whether of capital or otherwise, sustained by the partnership according to his share in the profits.

(b) The partnership must indemnify every partner in respect of payments made and personal liabilities reasonably incurred by him in the ordinary and proper conduct of its business, or for the preservation of its business or property.

(c) A partner, who in aid of the partnership makes any payment or advance beyond the amount of capital which he agreed to contribute, shall be paid interest from the date of the payment or advance.

(d) A partner shall receive interest on the capital contributed by him only from the date when repayment should be made.

(e) All partners have equal rights in the management and conduct of the partnership business.

(f) No partner is entitled to remuneration for acting in the partnership business, except that a surviving partner is entitled to reasonable compensation for his services in winding up the partnership affairs.

(g) No person can become a member of a partnership without the consent of all the partners.

(h) Any difference arising as to ordinary matters connected with the partnership business may be decided by a majority of the partners; but no act in contravention of any agreement between the partners may be done rightfully without the consent of all the partners.

§ 19. Partnership Books

The partnership books shall be kept, subject to any agreement between the partners, at the principal place of business of the partnership, and every partner shall at all times have access to and may inspect and copy any of them.

§ 20. Duty of Partners to Render Information

Partners shall render on demand true and full information of all things affecting the partnership to any partner or the legal representative of any deceased partner or partner under legal disability.

§ 21. Partner Accountable as a Fiduciary

(1) Every partner must account to the partnership for any benefit, and hold as trustee for it any profits derived by him without the consent of the other partners from any transaction connected with the formation, conduct, or liquidation of the partnership or from any use by him of its property.

(2) This section applies also to the representatives of a deceased partner engaged in the liquidation of the affairs of the partnership as the personal representatives of the last surviving partner.

§ 22. Right to an Account

Any partner shall have the right to a formal account as to partnership affairs:

(a) If he is wrongfully excluded from the partnership business or possession of its property by his co-partners,

(b) If the right exists under the terms of any agreement,

(c) As provided by section 21,

(d) Whenever other circumstances render it just and reasonable.

§ 23. Continuation of Partnership Beyond Fixed Term

(1) When a partnership for a fixed term or particular undertaking is continued after the termination of such term or particular undertaking without any express agreement, the rights and duties of the partners remain the same as they were at such termination, so far as is consistent with a partnership at will.

(2) A continuation of the business by the partners or such of them as habitually acted therein during the term, without any settlement or liquidation of the partnership affairs, is prima facie evidence of a continuation of the partnership.

PART V

PROPERTY RIGHTS OF A PARTNER

§ 24. Extent of Property Rights of a Partner

The property rights of a partner are (1) his rights in specific partnership property, (2) his interest in the partnership, and (3) his right to participate in the management.

§ 25. Nature of a Partner's Right in Specific Partnership Property

(1) A partner is co-owner with his partners of specific partnership property holding as a tenant in partnership.

(2) The incidents of this tenancy are such that:

(a) A partner, subject to the provisions of this act and to any agreement between the partners, has an equal right with his partners to possess specific partnership property for partnership purposes; but he has no right to possess such property for any other purpose without the consent of his partners.

(b) A partner's right in specific partnership property is not assignable except in connection with the assignment of rights of all the partners in the same property.

(c) A partner's right in specific partnership property is not subject to attachment or execution, except on a claim against the partnership. When partnership property is attached for a partnership debt the partners, or any of them, or the representatives of a deceased partner, cannot claim any right under the homestead or exemption laws.

(d) On the death of a partner his right in specific partnership property vests in the surviving partner or partners, except where the deceased was the last surviving partner, when his right in such property vests in his legal representative. Such surviving partner or partners, or the legal representative of the last surviving partner, has no right to possess the partnership property for any but a partnership purpose.

(e) A partner's right in specific partnership property is not subject to dower, curtesy, or allowances to widows, heirs, or next of kin.

§ 26. Nature of Partner's Interest in the Partnership

A partner's interest in the partnership is his share of the profits and surplus, and the same is personal property.

§ 27. Assignment of Partner's Interest

(1) A conveyance by a partner of his interest in the partnership does not of itself dissolve the partnership, nor, as against the other partners in the absence of agreement, entitle the assignee, during the continuance of the partnership, to interfere in the management or administration of the partnership business or affairs, or to require any information or account of partnership transactions, or to inspect the partnership books; but it merely entitles the assignee to receive in accordance with his contract the profits to which the assigning partner would otherwise be entitled.

(2) In case of a dissolution of the partnership, the assignee is entitled to receive his assignor's interest and may require an account from the date only of the last account agreed to by all the partners.

§ 28. Partner's Interest Subject to Charging Order

(1) On due application to a competent court by any judgment creditor of a partner, the court which entered the judgment, order,

or decree, or any other court, may charge the interest of the debtor partner with payment of the unsatisfied amount of such judgment debt with interest thereon; and may then or later appoint a receiver of his share of the profits, and of any other money due or to fall due to him in respect of the partnership, and make all other orders, directions, accounts and inquiries which the debtor partner might have made, or which the circumstances of the case may require.

(2) The interest charged may be redeemed at any time before foreclosure, or in case of a sale being directed by the court may be purchased without thereby causing a dissolution:

(a) With separate property, by any one or more of the partners, or

(b) With partnership property, by any one or more of the partners with the consent of all the partners whose interests are not so charged or sold.

(3) Nothing in this act shall be held to deprive a partner of his right, if any, under the exemption laws, as regards his interest in the partnership.

PART VI

DISSOLUTION AND WINDING UP

§ 29. Dissolution Defined

The dissolution of a partnership is the change in the relation of the partners caused by any partner ceasing to be associated in the carrying on as distinguished from the winding up of the business.

Official Comment

... In this act dissolution designates the point in time when the partners cease to carry on the business together; termination is the point in time when all the partnership affairs are wound up; winding up, the process of settling partnership affairs after dissolution.

§ 30. Partnership Not Terminated by Dissolution

On dissolution the partnership is not terminated, but continues until the winding up of partnership affairs is completed.

§ 31. Causes of Dissolution

Dissolution is caused:

(1) Without violation of the agreement between the partners,

(a) By the termination of the definite term or particular undertaking specified in the agreement,

(b) By the express will of any partner when no definite term or particular undertaking is specified,

(c) By the express will of all the partners who have not assigned their interests or suffered them to be charged for their separate debts, either before or after the termination of any specified term or particular undertaking,

(d) By the expulsion of any partner from the business bona fide in accordance with such a power conferred by the agreement between the partners;

(2) In contravention of the agreement between the partners, where the circumstances do not permit a dissolution under any other provision of this section, by the express will of any partner at any time;

(3) By any event which makes it unlawful for the business of the partnership to be carried on or for the members to carry it on in partnership;

(4) By the death of any partner;

(5) By the bankruptcy of any partner or the partnership;

(6) By decree of court under section 32.

Official Comment

Paragraph (2) will settle a matter on which at present considerable confusion and uncertainty exists. The paragraph as drawn allows a partner to dissolve a partnership in contravention of the agreement between the partners....

The relation of partners is one of agency. The agency is such a personal one that equity cannot enforce it even where the agreement provides that the partnership shall continue for a definite time. The power of any partner to terminate the relation, even though in doing so he breaks a contract, should, it is submitted, be recognized.

The rights of the parties upon a dissolution in contravention of the agreement are safeguarded by section 38(2), infra.

§ 32. Dissolution by Decree of Court

(1) On application by or for a partner the court shall decree a dissolution whenever:

(a) A partner has been declared a lunatic in any judicial proceeding or is shown to be of unsound mind,

(b) A partner becomes in any other way incapable of performing his part of the partnership contract,

(c) A partner has been guilty of such conduct as tends to affect prejudicially the carrying on of the business,

(d) A partner wilfully or persistently commits a breach of the partnership agreement, or otherwise so conducts himself in matters relating to the partnership business that it is not reasonably practicable to carry on the business in partnership with him,

(e) The business of the partnership can only be carried on at a loss,

(f) Other circumstances render a dissolution equitable.

(2) On the application of the purchaser of a partner's interest under sections 28 or 29: [1]

(a) After the termination of the specified term or particular undertaking,

(b) At any time if the partnership was a partnership at will when the interest was assigned or when the charging order was issued.

§ 33. General Effect of Dissolution on Authority of Partner

Except so far as may be necessary to wind up partnership affairs or to complete transactions begun but not then finished, dissolution terminates all authority of any partner to act for the partnership,

(1) With respect to the partners,

(a) When the dissolution is not by the act, bankruptcy or death of a partner; or

(b) When the dissolution is by such act, bankruptcy or death of a partner, in cases where section 34 so requires.

(2) With respect to persons not partners, as declared in section 35.

§ 34. Right of Partner to Contribution From Co-partners After Dissolution

Where the dissolution is caused by the act, death or bankruptcy of a partner, each partner is liable to his co-partners for his share of any liability created by any partner acting for the partnership as if the partnership had not been dissolved unless

(a) The dissolution being by act of any partner, the partner acting for the partnership had knowledge of the dissolution, or

----

1. So in original. Probably should read "sections 27 or 28."

(b) The dissolution being by the death or bankruptcy of a partner, the partner acting for the partnership had knowledge or notice of the death or bankruptcy.

§ 35. Power of Partner to Bind Partnership to Third Persons After Dissolution

(1) After dissolution a partner can bind the partnership except as provided in Paragraph (3)

(a) By any act appropriate for winding up partnership affairs or completing transactions unfinished at dissolution;

(b) By any transaction which would bind the partnership if dissolution had not taken place, provided the other party to the transaction

(I) Had extended credit to the partnership prior to dissolution and had no knowledge or notice of the dissolution; or

(II) Though he had not so extended credit, had nevertheless known of the partnership prior to dissolution, and, having no knowledge or notice of dissolution, the fact of dissolution had not been advertised in a newspaper of general circulation in the place (or in each place if more than one) at which the partnership business was regularly carried on.

(2) The liability of a partner under Paragraph (1b) shall be satisfied out of partnership assets alone when such partner had been prior to dissolution

(a) Unknown as a partner to the person with whom the contract is made; and

(b) So far unknown and inactive in partnership affairs that the business reputation of the partnership could not be said to have been in any degree due to his connection with it.

(3) The partnership is in no case bound by any act of a partner after dissolution

(a) Where the partnership is dissolved because it is unlawful to carry on the business, unless the act is appropriate for winding up partnership affairs; or

(b) Where the partner has become bankrupt; or

(c) Where the partner has no authority to wind up partnership affairs; except by a transaction with one who

(I) Had extended credit to the partnership prior to dissolution and had no knowledge or notice of his want of authority; or

(II) Had not extended credit to the partnership prior to dissolution, and, having no knowledge or notice of his want of authority, the fact of his want of authority has not been advertised in the manner provided for advertising the fact of dissolution in Paragraph (1bII).

(4) Nothing in this section shall affect the liability under Section 16 of any person who after dissolution represents himself or consents to another representing him as a partner in a partnership engaged in carrying on business.

§ 36. Effect of Dissolution on Partner's Existing Liability

(1) The dissolution of the partnership does not of itself discharge the existing liability of any partner.

(2) A partner is discharged from any existing liability upon dissolution of the partnership by an agreement to that effect between himself, the partnership creditor and the person or partnership continuing the business; and such agreement may be inferred from the course of dealing between the creditor having knowledge of the dissolution and the person or partnership continuing the business.

(3) Where a person agrees to assume the existing obligations of a dissolved partnership, the partners whose obligations have been assumed shall be discharged from any liability to any creditor of the partnership who, knowing of the agreement, consents to a material alteration in the nature or time of payment of such obligations.

(4) The individual property of a deceased partner shall be liable for all obligations of the partnership incurred while he was a partner but subject to the prior payment of his separate debts.

§ 37. Right to Wind Up

Unless otherwise agreed the partners who have not wrongfully dissolved the partnership or the legal representative of the last surviving partner, not bankrupt, has the right to wind up the partnership affairs; provided, however, that any partner, his legal representative or his assignee, upon cause shown, may obtain winding up by the court.

§ 38. Rights of Partners to Application of Partnership Property

(1) When dissolution is caused in any way, except in contravention of the partnership agreement, each partner, as against his co-partners and all persons claiming through them in respect of their interests in the partnership, unless otherwise agreed, may have the

partnership property applied to discharge its liabilities, and the surplus applied to pay in cash the net amount owing to the respective partners. But if dissolution is caused by expulsion of a partner, bona fide under the partnership agreement and if the expelled partner is discharged from all partnership liabilities, either by payment or agreement under section 36(2), he shall receive in cash only the net amount due him from the partnership.

(2) When dissolution is caused in contravention of the partnership agreement the rights of the partners shall be as follows:

(a) Each partner who has not caused dissolution wrongfully shall have,

I. All the rights specified in paragraph (1) of this section, and

II. The right, as against each partner who has caused the dissolution wrongfully, to damages for breach of the agreement.

(b) The partners who have not caused the dissolution wrongfully, if they all desire to continue the business in the same name, either by themselves or jointly with others, may do so, during the agreed term for the partnership and for that purpose may possess the partnership property, provided they secure the payment by bond approved by the court, or pay to any partner who has caused the dissolution wrongfully, the value of his interest in the partnership at the dissolution, less any damages recoverable under clause (2aII) of this section, and in like manner indemnify him against all present or future partnership liabilities.

(c) A partner who has caused the dissolution wrongfully shall have:

I. If the business is not continued under the provisions of paragraph (2b) all the rights of a partner under paragraph (1), subject to clause (2aII), of this section,

II. If the business is continued under paragraph (2b) of this section the right as against his co-partners and all claiming through them in respect of their interests in the partnership, to have the value of his interest in the partnership, less any damages caused to his co-partners by the dissolution, ascertained and paid to him in cash, or the payment secured by bond approved by the court, and to be released from all existing liabilities of the partnership; but in ascertaining the value of the partner's interest the value of the goodwill of the business shall not be considered.

Official Comment

The right given to each partner, where no agreement to the contrary has been made, to have his share of the surplus paid to him in cash makes certain an existing uncertainty. At present it is not certain whether a partner may or may not insist on a physical partition of the property remaining after third persons have been paid.

§ 39. Rights Where Partnership Is Dissolved for Fraud or Misrepresentation

Where a partnership contract is rescinded on the ground of the fraud or misrepresentation of one of the parties thereto, the party entitled to rescind is, without prejudice to any other right, entitled,

(a) To a lien on, or a right of retention of, the surplus of the partnership property after satisfying the partnership liabilities to third persons for any sum of money paid by him for the purchase of an interest in the partnership and for any capital or advances contributed by him; and

(b) To stand, after all liabilities to third persons have been satisfied, in the place of the creditors of the partnership for any payments made by him in respect of the partnership liabilities; and

(c) To be indemnified by the person guilty of the fraud or making the representation against all debts and liabilities of the partnership.

§ 40. Rules for Distribution

In settling accounts between the partners after dissolution, the following rules shall be observed, subject to any agreement to the contrary:

(a) The assets of the partnership are:

I.   The partnership property,

II.   The contributions of the partners necessary for the payment of all the liabilities specified in clause (b) of this paragraph.

(b) The liabilities of the partnership shall rank in order of payment, as follows:

I.   Those owing to creditors other than partners,

II.   Those owing to partners other than for capital and profits,

III.   Those owing to partners in respect of capital,

IV.   Those owing to partners in respect of profits.

(c) The assets shall be applied in order of their declaration in clause (a) of this paragraph to the satisfaction of the liabilities.

(d) The partners shall contribute, as provided by section 18(a) the amount necessary to satisfy the liabilities; but if any, but not all, of the partners are insolvent, or, not being subject to process, refuse to contribute, the other partners shall contribute their share of the liabilities, and, in the relative proportions in which they share the profits, the additional amount necessary to pay the liabilities.

(e) An assignee for the benefit of creditors or any person appointed by the court shall have the right to enforce the contributions specified in clause (d) of this paragraph.

(f) Any partner or his legal representative shall have the right to enforce the contributions specified in clause (d) of this paragraph, to the extent of the amount which he has paid in excess of his share of the liability.

(g) The individual property of a deceased partner shall be liable for the contributions specified in clause (d) of this paragraph.

(h) When partnership property and the individual properties of the partners are in possession of a court for distribution, partnership creditors shall have priority on partnership property and separate creditors on individual property, saving the rights of lien or secured creditors as heretofore.

(i) Where a partner has become bankrupt or his estate is insolvent the claims against his separate property shall rank in the following order:

   I.   Those owing to separate creditors,

   II.   Those owing to partnership creditors,

   III.   Those owing to partners by way of contribution.

§ 41. Liability of Persons Continuing the Business in Certain Cases

(1) When any new partner is admitted into an existing partnership, or when any partner retires and assigns (or the representative of the deceased partner assigns) his rights in partnership property to two or more of the partners, or to one or more of the partners and one or more third persons, if the business is continued without liquidation of the partnership affairs, creditors of the first or dissolved partnership are also creditors of the partnership so continuing the business.

(2) When all but one partner retire and assign (or the representative of a deceased partner assigns) their rights in partnership property to the remaining partner, who continues the business without liquidation of partnership affairs, either alone or with others, creditors of the dissolved partnership are also creditors of the person or partnership so continuing the business.

(3) When any partner retires or dies and the business of the dissolved partnership is continued as set forth in paragraphs (1) and (2) of this section, with the consent of the retired partners or the representative of the deceased partner, but without any assignment of his right in partnership property, rights of creditors of the dissolved partnership and of the creditors of the person or partnership continuing the business shall be as if such assignment had been made.

(4) When all the partners or their representatives assign their rights in partnership property to one or more third persons who promise to pay the debts and who continue the business of the dissolved partnership, creditors of the dissolved partnership are also creditors of the person or partnership continuing the business.

(5) When any partner wrongfully causes a dissolution and the remaining partners continue the business under the provisions of section 38(2b), either alone or with others, and without liquidation of the partnership affairs, creditors of the dissolved partnership are also creditors of the person or partnership continuing the business.

(6) When a partner is expelled and the remaining partners continue the business either alone or with others, without liquidation of the partnership affairs, creditors of the dissolved partnership are also creditors of the person or partnership continuing the business.

(7) The liability of a third person becoming a partner in the partnership continuing the business, under this section, to the creditors of the dissolved partnership shall be satisfied out of partnership property only.

(8) When the business of a partnership after dissolution is continued under any conditions set forth in this section the creditors of the dissolved partnership, as against the separate creditors of the retiring or deceased partner or the representative of the deceased partner, have a prior right to any claim of the retired partner or the representative of the deceased partner against the person or partnership continuing the business, on account of the retired or deceased partner's interest in the dissolved partnership or on account of any consideration promised for such interest or for his right in partnership property.

(9) Nothing in this section shall be held to modify any right of creditors to set aside any assignment on the ground of fraud.

(10) The use by the person or partnership continuing the business of the partnership name, or the name of a deceased partner as part thereof, shall not of itself make the individual

property of the deceased partner liable for any debts contracted by such person or partnership.

§ 42. Rights of Retiring or Estate of Deceased Partner When the Business Is Continued

When any partner retires or dies, and the business is continued under any of the conditions set forth in section 41(1, 2, 3, 5, 6), or section 38(2b) without any settlement of accounts as between him or his estate and the person or partnership continuing the business, unless otherwise agreed, he or his legal representative as against such persons or partnership may have the value of his interest at the date of dissolution ascertained, and shall receive as an ordinary creditor an amount equal to the value of his interest in the dissolved partnership with interest, or, at his option or at the option of his legal representative, in lieu of interest, the profits attributable to the use of his right in the property of the dissolved partnership; provided that the creditors of the dissolved partnership as against the separate creditors, or the representative of the retired or deceased partner, shall have priority on any claim arising under this section, as provided by section 41(8) of this act.

§ 43. Accrual of Actions

The right to an account of his interest shall accrue to any partner, or his legal representative, as against the winding up partners or the surviving partners or the person or partnership continuing the business, at the date of dissolution, in the absence of any agreement to the contrary.

REVISED UNIFORM PARTNERSHIP ACT (1994)

ARTICLE 1. GENERAL PROVISIONS

ARTICLE 2. NATURE OF PARTNERSHIP

ARTICLE 3. RELATIONS OF PARTNERS TO PERSONS DEALING WITH PARTNERSHIP

ARTICLE 4. RELATIONS OF PARTNERS TO EACH OTHER AND TO PARTNERSHIP

ARTICLE 1

GENERAL PROVISIONS

Section 101. Definitions.
Section 102. Knowledge and Notice.
Section 103. Effect of Partnership Agreement; Nonwaivable Provisions.
Section 104. Supplemental Principles of Law.
Section 105. Execution, Filing, and Recording of Statements.
Section 106. Law Governing Internal Relations.
Section 107. Partnership Subject to Amendment or Repeal of [Act].

SECTION 101. DEFINITIONS.

In this [Act]:

(1) "Business" includes every trade, occupation, and profession.

(2) "Debtor in bankruptcy" means a person who is the subject of:

(i) an order for relief under Title 11 of the United States Code or a comparable order under a successor statute of general application; or

(ii) a comparable order under federal, state, or foreign law governing insolvency.

(3) "Distribution" means a transfer of money or other property from a partnership to a partner in the partner's capacity as a partner or to the partner's transferee.

(4) "Partnership" means an association of two or more persons to carry on as co-owners a business for profit formed under Section 202, predecessor law, or comparable law of another jurisdiction.

(5) "Partnership agreement" means the agreement, whether written, oral, or implied, among the partners concerning the partnership, including amendments to the partnership agreement.

(6) "Partnership at will" means a partnership in which the partners have not agreed to remain partners until the expiration of a definite term or the completion of a particular undertaking.

(7) "Partnership interest" or "partner's interest in the partnership" means all of a partner's interests in the partnership, including the partner's transferable interest and all management and other rights.

(8) "Person" means an individual, corporation, business trust, estate, trust, partnership, association, joint venture, government, governmental subdivision, agency, or instrumentality, or any other legal or commercial entity.

(9) "Property" means all property, real, personal, or mixed, tangible or intangible, or any interest therein.

(10) "State" means a State of the United States, the District of Columbia, the Commonwealth of Puerto Rico, or any territory or insular possession subject to the jurisdiction of the United States.

(11) "Statement" means a statement of partnership authority under Section 303, a statement of denial under Section 304, a statement of dissociation under Section 704, a statement of dissolution under Section 805, a statement of merger under Section 907, or an amendment or cancellation of any of the foregoing.

(12) "Transfer" includes an assignment, conveyance, lease, mortgage, deed, and encumbrance.

SECTION 102. KNOWLEDGE AND NOTICE.

(a) A person knows a fact if the person has actual knowledge of it.

(b) A person has notice of a fact if the person:

(1) knows of it;

(2) has received a notification of it; or

(3) has reason to know it exists from all of the facts known to the person at the time in question.

(c) A person notifies or gives a notification to another by taking steps reasonably required to inform the other person in ordinary course, whether or not the other person learns of it.

(d) A person receives a notification when the notification:

(1) comes to the person's attention; or

(2) is duly delivered at the person's place of business or at any other place held out by the person as a place for receiving communications.

(e) Except as otherwise provided in subsection (f), a person other than an individual knows, has notice, or receives a notification of a fact for purposes of a particular transaction when the individual

189

conducting the transaction knows, has notice, or receives a notification of the fact, or in any event when the fact would have been brought to the individual's attention if the person had exercised reasonable diligence.   The person exercises reasonable diligence if it maintains reasonable routines for communicating significant information to the individual conducting the transaction and there is reasonable compliance with the routines.   Reasonable diligence does not require an individual acting for the person to communicate information unless the communication is part of the individual's regular duties or the individual has reason to know of the transaction and that the transaction would be materially affected by the information.

(f) A partner's knowledge, notice, or receipt of a notification of a fact relating to the partnership is effective immediately as knowledge by, notice to, or receipt of a notification by the partnership, except in the case of a fraud on the partnership committed by or with the consent of that partner.

SECTION 103. EFFECT OF PARTNERSHIP AGREEMENT; NONWAIVABLE PROVISIONS.

(a) Except as otherwise provided in subsection (b), relations among the partners and between the partners and the partnership are governed by the partnership agreement.   To the extent the partnership agreement does not otherwise provide, this [Act] governs relations among the partners and between the partners and the partnership.

(b) The partnership agreement may not:

(1) vary the rights and duties under Section 105 except to eliminate the duty to provide copies of statements to all of the partners;

(2) unreasonably restrict the right of access to books and records under Section 403(b);

(3) eliminate the duty of loyalty under Section 404(b) or 603(b)(3), but:

(i) the partnership agreement may identify specific types or categories of activities that do not violate the duty of loyalty, if not manifestly unreasonable; or

(ii) all of the partners or a number or percentage specified in the partnership agreement may authorize or ratify, after full disclosure of all material facts, a specific act or transaction that otherwise would violate the duty of loyalty;

(4) unreasonably reduce the duty of care under Section 404(c) or 603(b)(3);

(5) eliminate the obligation of good faith and fair dealing under Section 404(d), but the partnership agreement may prescribe the standards by which the performance of the obligation is to be measured, if the standards are not manifestly unreasonable;

(6) vary the power to dissociate as a partner under Section 602(a), except to require the notice under Section 601(1) to be in writing;

(7) vary the right of a court to expel a partner in the events specified in Section 601(5);

(8) vary the requirement to wind up the partnership business in cases specified in Section 801(4), (5), or (6); or

(9) restrict rights of third parties under this [Act].

SECTION 104. SUPPLEMENTAL PRINCIPLES OF LAW.

(a) Unless displaced by particular provisions of this [Act], the principles of law and equity supplement this [Act].

(b) If an obligation to pay interest arises under this [Act] and the rate is not specified, the rate is that specified in [applicable statute].

SECTION 105. EXECUTION, FILING, AND RECORDING OF STATEMENTS.

(a) A statement may be filed in the office of [the Secretary of State]. A certified copy of a statement that is filed in an office in another State may be filed in the office of [the Secretary of State]. Either filing has the effect provided in this [Act] with respect to partnership property located in or transactions that occur in this State.

(b) A certified copy of a statement that has been filed in the office of the [Secretary of State] and recorded in the office for recording transfers of real property has the effect provided for recorded statements in this [Act]. A recorded statement that is not a certified copy of a statement filed in the office of the [Secretary of State] does not have the effect provided for recorded statements in this [Act].

(c) A statement filed by a partnership must be executed by at least two partners. Other statements must be executed by a partner or other person authorized by this [Act]. An individual who executes a statement as, or on behalf of, a partner or other person named as a partner in a statement shall personally declare under penalty of perjury that the contents of the statement are accurate.

(d) A person authorized by this [Act] to file a statement may amend or cancel the statement by filing an amendment or cancellation that names the partnership, identifies the statement, and states the substance of the amendment or cancellation.

(e) A person who files a statement pursuant to this section shall promptly send a copy of the statement to every nonfiling partner and to any other person named as a partner in the statement. Failure to send a copy of a statement to a partner or other person does not limit the effectiveness of the statement as to a person not a partner.

(f) The [Secretary of State] may collect a fee for filing or providing a certified copy of a statement. The [officer responsible for] recording transfers of real property may collect a fee for recording a statement.

Comment:

1. . . .

No filings are mandatory under RUPA. In all cases, the filing of a statement is optional and voluntary. A system of mandatory filing and disclosure for partnerships, similar to that required for corporations and limited partnerships, was rejected for several reasons. First, RUPA is designed to accommodate the needs of small partnerships, which often have unwritten or sketchy agreements and limited resources. Furthermore, inadvertent partnerships are also governed by the Act, as the default form of business organization, in which case filing would be unlikely.

SECTION 106. LAW GOVERNING INTERNAL RELATIONS.

The law of the jurisdiction in which a partnership has its chief executive office governs relations among the partners and between the partners and the partnership.

SECTION 107. PARTNERSHIP SUBJECT TO AMENDMENT OR REPEAL OF [ACT].

A partnership governed by this [Act] is subject to any amendment to or repeal of this [Act].

ARTICLE 2

NATURE OF PARTNERSHIP

SECTION 201. PARTNERSHIP AS ENTITY.

A partnership is an entity distinct from its partners.

SECTION 202. FORMATION OF PARTNERSHIP.

(a) Except as otherwise provided in subsection (b), the association of two or more persons to carry on as co-owners a business for profit forms a partnership, whether or not the persons intend to form a partnership.

(b) An association formed under a statute other than this [Act], a predecessor statute, or a comparable statute of another jurisdiction is not a partnership under this [Act].

(c) In determining whether a partnership is formed, the following rules apply:

(1) Joint tenancy, tenancy in common, tenancy by the entireties, joint property, common property, or part ownership does not by itself establish a partnership, even if the co-owners share profits made by the use of the property.

(2) The sharing of gross returns does not by itself establish a partnership, even if the persons sharing them have a joint or common right or interest in property from which the returns are derived.

(3) A person who receives a share of the profits of a business is presumed to be a partner in the business, unless the profits were received in payment:

(i) of a debt by installments or otherwise;

(ii) for services as an independent contractor or of wages or other compensation to an employee;

(iii) of rent;

(iv) of an annuity or other retirement or health benefit to a beneficiary, representative, or designee of a deceased or retired partner;

(v) of interest or other charge on a loan, even if the amount of payment varies with the profits of the business, including a direct or indirect present or future ownership of the collateral, or rights to income, proceeds, or increase in value derived from the collateral; or

(vi) for the sale of the goodwill of a business or other property by installments or otherwise.

SECTION 203. PARTNERSHIP PROPERTY.

Property acquired by a partnership is property of the partnership and not of the partners individually.

SECTION 204. WHEN PROPERTY IS PARTNERSHIP PROPERTY.

(a) Property is partnership property if acquired in the name of:

(1) the partnership; or

(2) one or more partners with an indication in the instrument transferring title to the property of the person's capacity as a partner or of the existence of a partnership but without an indication of the name of the partnership.

(b) Property is acquired in the name of the partnership by a transfer to:

(1) the partnership in its name; or

(2) one or more partners in their capacity as partners in the partnership, if the name of the partnership is indicated in the instrument transferring title to the property.

(c) Property is presumed to be partnership property if purchased with partnership assets, even if not acquired in the name of the partnership or of one or more partners with an indication in the instrument transferring title to the property of the person's capacity as a partner or of the existence of a partnership.

(d) Property acquired in the name of one or more of the partners, without an indication in the instrument transferring title to the property of the person's capacity as a partner or of the existence of a partnership and without use of partnership assets, is presumed to be separate property, even if used for partnership purposes.

ARTICLE 3

RELATIONS OF PARTNERS TO PERSONS DEALING WITH PARTNERSHIP

SECTION 301. PARTNER AGENT OF PARTNERSHIP.

Subject to the effect of a statement of partnership authority under Section 303:

(1) Each partner is an agent of the partnership for the purpose of its business. An act of a partner, including the execution of an instrument in the partnership name, for apparently carrying on in the ordinary course the partnership business or business of the kind carried on by the partnership binds the partnership, unless the partner had no authority to act for the partnership in the particular matter and the person with whom the partner was dealing knew or had received a notification that the partner lacked authority.

(2) An act of a partner which is not apparently for carrying on in the ordinary course the partnership business or business of the kind carried on by the partnership binds the partnership only if the act was authorized by the other partners.

Comment: ...

2. Section 301(1) retains the basic principles reflected in UPA Section 9(1). It declares that each partner is an agent of the partnership and that, by virtue of partnership status, each partner has apparent authority to bind the partnership in ordinary course transactions. The effect of Section 301(1) is to characterize a partner as a general managerial agent having both actual and apparent authority co-extensive in scope with the firm's ordinary business, at least in the absence of a contrary partnership agreement.

Section 301(1) effects two changes from UPA Section 9(1). First, it clarifies that a partner's apparent authority includes acts for carrying on in the ordinary course "business of the kind

195

carried on by the partnership," not just the business of the particular partnership in question. The UPA is ambiguous on this point, but there is some authority for an expanded construction in accordance with the so-called English rule. See, e.g., Burns v. Gonzalez, 439 S.W.2d 128, 131 (Tex.Civ.App. 1969) (dictum); Commercial Hotel Co. v. Weeks, 254 S.W. 521 (Tex.Civ.App.1923). No substantive change is intended by use of the more customary phrase "carrying on in the ordinary course" in lieu of the UPA phrase "in the usual way." The UPA and the case law use both terms without apparent distinction....

SECTION 302. TRANSFER OF PARTNERSHIP PROPERTY.

(a) Partnership property may be transferred as follows:

(1) Subject to the effect of a statement of partnership authority under Section 303, partnership property held in the name of the partnership may be transferred by an instrument of transfer executed by a partner in the partnership name.

(2) Partnership property held in the name of one or more partners with an indication in the instrument transferring the property to them of their capacity as partners or of the existence of a partnership, but without an indication of the name of the partnership, may be transferred by an instrument of transfer executed by the persons in whose name the property is held.

(3) Partnership property held in the name of one or more persons other than the partnership, without an indication in the instrument transferring the property to them of their capacity as partners or of the existence of a partnership, may be transferred by an instrument of transfer executed by the persons in whose name the property is held.

(b) A partnership may recover partnership property from a transferee only if it proves that execution of the instrument of initial transfer did not bind the partnership under Section 301 and:

(1) as to a subsequent transferee who gave value for property transferred under subsection (a)(1) and (2), proves that the subsequent transferee knew or had received a notification that the person who executed the instrument of initial transfer lacked authority to bind the partnership; or

(2) as to a transferee who gave value for property transferred under subsection (a)(3), proves that the transferee knew or had received a notification that the property was partnership property and that the person who executed the instrument of initial transfer lacked authority to bind the partnership.

(c) A partnership may not recover partnership property from a subsequent transferee if the partnership would not have been entitled to recover the property, under subsection (b), from any earlier transferee of the property.

(d) If a person holds all of the partners' interests in the partnership, all of the partnership property vests in that person. The person may execute a document in the name of the partnership to evidence vesting of the property in that person and may file or record the document.

SECTION 303. STATEMENT OF PARTNERSHIP AUTHORITY.

(a) A partnership may file a statement of partnership authority, which:

(1) must include:

(i) the name of the partnership;

(ii) the street address of its chief executive office and of one office in this State, if there is one;

(iii) the names and mailing addresses of all of the partners or of an agent appointed and maintained by the partnership for the purpose of subsection (b); and

(iv) the names of the partners authorized to execute an instrument transferring real property held in the name of the partnership; and

(2) may state the authority, or limitations on the authority, of some or all of the partners to enter into other transactions on behalf of the partnership and any other matter.

(b) If a statement of partnership authority names an agent, the agent shall maintain a list of the names and mailing addresses of all of the partners and make it available to any person on request for good cause shown.

(c) If a filed statement of partnership authority is executed pursuant to Section 105(c) and states the name of the partnership but does not contain all of the other information required by subsection (a), the statement nevertheless operates with respect to a person not a partner as provided in subsections (d) and (e).

(d) Except as otherwise provided in subsection (g), a filed statement of partnership authority supplements the authority of a partner to enter into transactions on behalf of the partnership as follows:

(1) Except for transfers of real property, a grant of authority contained in a filed statement of partnership authority is

197

conclusive in favor of a person who gives value without knowledge to the contrary, so long as and to the extent that a limitation on that authority is not then contained in another filed statement. A filed cancellation of a limitation on authority revives the previous grant of authority.

(2) A grant of authority to transfer real property held in the name of the partnership contained in a certified copy of a filed statement of partnership authority recorded in the office for recording transfers of that real property is conclusive in favor of a person who gives value without knowledge to the contrary, so long as and to the extent that a certified copy of a filed statement containing a limitation on that authority is not then of record in the office for recording transfers of that real property. The recording in the office for recording transfers of that real property of a certified copy of a filed cancellation of a limitation on authority revives the previous grant of authority.

(e) A person not a partner is deemed to know of a limitation on the authority of a partner to transfer real property held in the name of the partnership if a certified copy of the filed statement containing the limitation on authority is of record in the office for recording transfers of that real property.

(f) Except as otherwise provided in subsections (d) and (e) and Sections 704 and 805, a person not a partner is not deemed to know of a limitation on the authority of a partner merely because the limitation is contained in a filed statement.

(g) Unless earlier canceled, a filed statement of partnership authority is canceled by operation of law five years after the date on which the statement, or the most recent amendment, was filed with the [Secretary of State].

SECTION 304. STATEMENT OF DENIAL.

A partner or other person named as a partner in a filed statement of partnership authority or in a list maintained by an agent pursuant to Section 303(b) may file a statement of denial stating the name of the partnership and the fact that it is being denied, which may include denial of a person's authority or status as a partner. A statement of denial is a limitation on authority as provided in Section 303(d) and (e).

SECTION 305. PARTNERSHIP LIABLE FOR PARTNER'S ACTIONABLE CONDUCT.

(a) A partnership is liable for loss or injury caused to a person, or for a penalty incurred, as a result of a wrongful act or omission, or other actionable conduct, of a partner acting in the ordinary course of business of the partnership or with authority of the partnership.

(b) If, in the course of the partnership's business or while acting with authority of the partnership, a partner receives or causes the partnership to receive money or property of a person not a partner, and the money or property is misapplied by a partner, the partnership is liable for the loss.

SECTION 306. PARTNER'S LIABILITY.

(a) Except as otherwise provided in subsection (b), all partners are liable jointly and severally for all obligations of the partnership unless otherwise agreed by the claimant or provided by law.

(b) A person admitted as a partner into an existing partnership is not personally liable for any partnership obligation incurred before the person's admission as a partner.

Comment:

1. Section 306(a) changes the UPA rule by imposing joint and several liability on the partners for all partnership obligations. Under UPA Section 15, partners' liability for torts is joint and several, while their liability for contracts is joint but not several. About ten States that have adopted the UPA already provide for joint and several liability. The UPA reference to "debts and obligations" is redundant, and no change is intended by RUPA's reference solely to "obligations."

Joint and several liability under RUPA differs, however, from the classic model, which permits a judgment creditor to proceed immediately against any of the joint and several judgment debtors. Generally, Section 307(d) requires the judgment creditor to exhaust the partnership's assets before enforcing a judgment against the separate assets of a partner. . . .

SECTION 307. ACTIONS BY AND AGAINST PARTNERSHIP AND PARTNERS.

(a) A partnership may sue and be sued in the name of the partnership.

(b) An action may be brought against the partnership and any or all of the partners in the same action or in separate actions.

(c) A judgment against a partnership is not by itself a judgment against a partner. A judgment against a partnership may not be satisfied from a partner's assets unless there is also a judgment against the partner.

(d) A judgment creditor of a partner may not levy execution against the assets of the partner to satisfy a judgment based on a claim against the partnership unless:

(1) a judgment based on the same claim has been obtained against the partnership and a writ of execution on the judgment has been returned unsatisfied in whole or in part;

(2) the partnership is a debtor in bankruptcy;

(3) the partner has agreed that the creditor need not exhaust partnership assets;

(4) a court grants permission to the judgment creditor to levy execution against the assets of a partner based on a finding that partnership assets subject to execution are clearly insufficient to satisfy the judgment, that exhaustion of partnership assets is excessively burdensome, or that the grant of permission is an appropriate exercise of the court's equitable powers; or

(5) liability is imposed on the partner by law or contract independent of the existence of the partnership.

(e) This section applies to any partnership liability or obligation resulting from a representation by a partner or purported partner under Section 308.

SECTION 308. LIABILITY OF PURPORTED PARTNER.

(a) If a person, by words or conduct, purports to be a partner, or consents to being represented by another as a partner, in a partnership or with one or more persons not partners, the purported partner is liable to a person to whom the representation is made, if that person, relying on the representation, enters into a transaction with the actual or purported partnership. If the representation, either by the purported partner or by a person with the purported partner's consent, is made in a public manner, the purported partner is liable to a person who relies upon the purported partnership even if the purported partner is not aware of being held out as a partner to the claimant. If partnership liability results, the purported partner is liable with respect to that liability as if the purported partner were a partner. If no partnership liability results, the purported partner is liable with respect to that liability jointly and severally with any other person consenting to the representation.

(b) If a person is thus represented to be a partner in an existing partnership, or with one or more persons not partners, the purported partner is an agent of persons consenting to the representation to bind them to the same extent and in the same manner as if the purported partner were a partner, with respect to persons who enter into transactions in reliance upon the representation. If all of the partners of the existing partnership consent to the representation, a partnership act or obligation results. If fewer than all of the partners of the existing partnership consent to the representation, the person acting and the partners consenting to the representation are jointly and severally liable.

(c) A person is not liable as a partner merely because the person is named by another in a statement of partnership authority.

(d) A person does not continue to be liable as a partner merely because of a failure to file a statement of dissociation or to amend a statement of partnership authority to indicate the partner's dissociation from the partnership.

(e) Except as otherwise provided in subsections (a) and (b), persons who are not partners as to each other are not liable as partners to other persons.

ARTICLE 4

RELATIONS OF PARTNERS TO EACH OTHER AND TO PARTNERSHIP

SECTION 401. PARTNER'S RIGHTS AND DUTIES.

(a) Each partner is deemed to have an account that is:

(1) credited with an amount equal to the money plus the value of any other property, net of the amount of any liabilities, the partner contributes to the partnership and the partner's share of the partnership profits; and

(2) charged with an amount equal to the money plus the value of any other property, net of the amount of any liabilities, distributed by the partnership to the partner and the partner's share of the partnership losses.

(b) Each partner is entitled to an equal share of the partnership profits and is chargeable with a share of the partnership losses in proportion to the partner's share of the profits.

(c) A partnership shall reimburse a partner for payments made and indemnify a partner for liabilities incurred by the partner in the ordinary course of the business of the partnership or for the preservation of its business or property.

(d) A partnership shall reimburse a partner for an advance to the partnership beyond the amount of capital the partner agreed to contribute.

(e) A payment or advance made by a partner which gives rise to a partnership obligation under subsection (c) or (d) constitutes a loan to the partnership which accrues interest from the date of the payment or advance.

(f) Each partner has equal rights in the management and conduct of the partnership business.

(g) A partner may use or possess partnership property only on behalf of the partnership.

(h) A partner is not entitled to remuneration for services performed for the partnership, except for reasonable compensation for services rendered in winding up the business of the partnership.

(i) A person may become a partner only with the consent of all of the partners.

(j) A difference arising as to a matter in the ordinary course of business of a partnership may be decided by a majority of the partners. An act outside the ordinary course of business of a partnership and an amendment to the partnership agreement may be undertaken only with the consent of all of the partners.

(k) This section does not affect the obligations of a partnership to other persons under Section 301.

Comment: ...

3. Subsection (b) establishes the default rules for the sharing of partnership profits and losses. The UPA Section 18(a) rules that profits are shared equally and that losses, whether capital or operating, are shared in proportion to each partner's share of the profits are continued. Thus, under the default rule, partners share profits per capita and not in proportion to capital contribution as do corporate shareholders or partners in limited partnerships. Compare RULPA Section 504. With respect to losses, the qualifying phrase, "whether capital or operating," has been deleted as inconsistent with contempo-

rary partnership accounting practice and terminology; no substantive change is intended.

If partners agree to share profits other than equally, losses will be shared similarly to profits, absent agreement to do otherwise. That rule, carried over from the UPA, is predicated on the assumption that partners would likely agree to share losses on the same basis as profits, but may fail to say so. Of course, by agreement, they may share losses on a different basis from profits.

The default rules apply, as does UPA Section 18(a), where one or more of the partners contribute no capital, although there is case law to the contrary. See, e.g., Kovacik v. Reed, 49 Cal.2d 166, 315 P.2d 314 (1957); Becker v. Killarney, 177 Ill.App.3d 793, 127 Ill.Dec. 102, 532 N.E.2d 931 (1988). It may seem unfair that the contributor of services, who contributes little or no capital, should be obligated to contribute toward the capital loss of the large contributor who contributed no services. In entering a partnership with such a capital structure, the partners should foresee that application of the default rule may bring about unusual results and take advantage of their power to vary by agreement the allocation of capital losses. . . .

SECTION 402. DISTRIBUTIONS IN KIND.

A partner has no right to receive, and may not be required to accept, a distribution in kind.

Comment: . . .

This section is complemented by Section 807(a) which provides that, in winding up the partnership business on dissolution, any surplus after the payment of partnership obligations must be applied to pay in cash the net amount distributable to each partner.

SECTION 403. PARTNER'S RIGHTS AND DUTIES WITH RESPECT TO INFORMATION.

(a) A partnership shall keep its books and records, if any, at its chief executive office.

(b) A partnership shall provide partners and their agents and attorneys access to its books and records. It shall provide former partners and their agents and attorneys access to books and records pertaining to the period during which they were partners. The right of access provides the opportunity to inspect and copy books and records during ordinary business hours. A partnership may impose a reasonable charge, covering the costs of labor and material, for copies of documents furnished.

(c) Each partner and the partnership shall furnish to a partner, and to the legal representative of a deceased partner or partner under legal disability:

(1) without demand, any information concerning the partnership's business and affairs reasonably required for the proper exercise of the partner's rights and duties under the partnership agreement or this [Act]; and

(2) on demand, any other information concerning the partnership's business and affairs, except to the extent the demand or the information demanded is unreasonable or otherwise improper under the circumstances.

SECTION 404. GENERAL STANDARDS OF PARTNER'S CONDUCT.

(a) The only fiduciary duties a partner owes to the partnership and the other partners are the duty of loyalty and the duty of care set forth in subsections (b) and (c).

(b) A partner's duty of loyalty to the partnership and the other partners is limited to the following:

(1) to account to the partnership and hold as trustee for it any property, profit, or benefit derived by the partner in the conduct and winding up of the partnership business or derived from a use by the partner of partnership property, including the appropriation of a partnership opportunity;

(2) to refrain from dealing with the partnership in the conduct or winding up of the partnership business as or on behalf of a party having an interest adverse to the partnership; and

(3) to refrain from competing with the partnership in the conduct of the partnership business before the dissolution of the partnership.

(c) A partner's duty of care to the partnership and the other partners in the conduct and winding up of the partnership business is limited to refraining from engaging in grossly negligent or reckless conduct, intentional misconduct, or a knowing violation of law.

(d) A partner shall discharge the duties to the partnership and the other partners under this [Act] or under the partnership agreement and exercise any rights consistently with the obligation of good faith and fair dealing.

(e) A partner does not violate a duty or obligation under this [Act] or under the partnership agreement merely because the partner's conduct furthers the partner's own interest.

(f) A partner may lend money to and transact other business with the partnership, and as to each loan or transaction the rights and obligations of the partner are the same as those of a person who is not a partner, subject to other applicable law.

(g) This section applies to a person winding up the partnership business as the personal or legal representative of the last surviving partner as if the person were a partner.

Comment:

1. Section 404 is new. The title, "General Standards of Partner's Conduct," is drawn from RMBCA Section 8.30. Section 404 is both comprehensive and exclusive. In that regard, it is structurally different from the UPA which touches only sparingly on a partner's duty of loyalty and leaves any further development of the fiduciary duties of partners to the common law of agency. Compare UPA Sections 4(3) and 21.

Section 404 begins by stating that the **only** fiduciary duties a partner owes to the partnership and the other partners are the duties of loyalty and care set forth in subsections (b) and (c) of the Act. Those duties may not be waived or eliminated in the partnership agreement, but the agreement may identify activities and determine standards for measuring performance of the duties, if not manifestly unreasonable. See Sections 103(b)(3)–(5)....

[2.] Under Section 103(b)(3), the partnership agreement may not "eliminate" the duty of loyalty. Section 103(b)(3)(i) expressly empowers the partners, however, to identify specific types or categories of activities that do not violate the duty of loyalty, if not manifestly unreasonable. As under UPA Section 21, the other partners may also consent to a specific act or transaction that otherwise violates one of the rules. For the consent to be effective under Section 103(b)(3)(ii), there must be full disclosure of all material facts regarding the act or transaction and the partner's conflict of interest. See Comment 5 to Section 103.

3. Subsection (c) is new and establishes the duty of care that partners owe to the partnership and to the other partners. There is no statutory duty of care under the UPA, although a

common law duty of care is recognized by some courts. See, e.g., Rosenthal v. Rosenthal, 543 A.2d 348, 352 (Me.1988) (duty of care limited to acting in a manner that does not constitute gross negligence or wilful misconduct).

The standard of care imposed by RUPA is that of gross negligence, which is the standard generally recognized by the courts. See, e.g., Rosenthal v. Rosenthal, supra. Section 103(b)(4) provides that the duty of care may not be eliminated entirely by agreement, but the standard may be reasonably reduced. See Comment 6 to Section 103.

4.   Subsection (d) is also new. It provides that partners have an obligation of good faith and fair dealing in the discharge of all their duties, including those arising under the Act, such as their fiduciary duties of loyalty and care, and those arising under the partnership agreement. The exercise of any rights by a partner is also subject to the obligation of good faith and fair dealing. The obligation runs to the partnership and to the other partners in all matters related to the conduct and winding up of the partnership business.

The obligation of good faith and fair dealing is a contract concept, imposed on the partners because of the consensual nature of a partnership. See Restatement (Second) of Contracts § 205 (1981). It is not characterized, in RUPA, as a fiduciary duty arising out of the partners' special relationship. Nor is it a separate and independent obligation. It is an ancillary obligation that applies whenever a partner discharges a duty or exercises a right under the partnership agreement or the Act.

The meaning of "good faith and fair dealing" is not firmly fixed under present law. "Good faith" clearly suggests a subjective element, while "fair dealing" implies an objective component. It was decided to leave the terms undefined in the Act and allow the courts to develop their meaning based on the experience of real cases....

In some situations the obligation of good faith includes a disclosure component. Depending on the circumstances, a partner may have an affirmative disclosure obligation that supplements the Section 403 duty to render information.

Under Section 103(b)(5), the obligation of good faith and fair dealing may not be eliminated by agreement, but the partners by agreement may determine the standards by which the performance of the obligation is to be measured, if the standards are not manifestly unreasonable. See Comment 7 to Section 103....

SECTION 405. ACTIONS BY PARTNERSHIP AND PARTNERS.

(a) A partnership may maintain an action against a partner for a breach of the partnership agreement, or for the violation of a duty to the partnership, causing harm to the partnership.

(b) A partner may maintain an action against the partnership or another partner for legal or equitable relief, with or without an accounting as to partnership business, to:

(1) enforce the partner's rights under the partnership agreement;

(2) enforce the partner's rights under this [Act], including:

(i) the partner's rights under Sections 401, 403, or 404;

(ii) the partner's right on dissociation to have the partner's interest in the partnership purchased pursuant to Section 701 or enforce any other right under [Article] 6 or 7; or

(iii) the partner's right to compel a dissolution and winding up of the partnership business under Section 801 or enforce any other right under [Article] 8; or

(3) enforce the rights and otherwise protect the interests of the partner, including rights and interests arising independently of the partnership relationship.

(c) The accrual of, and any time limitation on, a right of action for a remedy under this section is governed by other law. A right to an accounting upon a dissolution and winding up does not revive a claim barred by law.

SECTION 406. CONTINUATION OF PARTNERSHIP BEYOND DEFINITE TERM OR PARTICULAR UNDERTAKING.

(a) If a partnership for a definite term or particular undertaking is continued, without an express agreement, after the expiration of the term or completion of the undertaking, the rights and duties of the partners remain the same as they were at the expiration or completion, so far as is consistent with a partnership at will.

(b) If the partners, or those of them who habitually acted in the business during the term or undertaking, continue the business without any settlement or liquidation of the partnership, they are presumed to have agreed that the partnership will continue.

ARTICLE 5

TRANSFEREES AND CREDITORS OF PARTNER

Section 501.   Partner Not Co–Owner of Partnership Property.
Section 502.   Partner's Transferable Interest in Partnership.
Section 503.   Transfer of Partner's Transferable Interest.
Section 504.   Partner's Transferable Interest Subject to Charging Order.

SECTION 501. PARTNER NOT CO–OWNER OF PARTNERSHIP PROPERTY.

A partner is not a co-owner of partnership property and has no interest in partnership property which can be transferred, either voluntarily or involuntarily.

SECTION 502. PARTNER'S TRANSFERABLE INTEREST IN PARTNERSHIP.

The only transferable interest of a partner in the partnership is the partner's share of the profits and losses of the partnership and the partner's right to receive distributions. The interest is personal property.

SECTION 503. TRANSFER OF PARTNER'S TRANSFERABLE INTEREST.

(a) A transfer, in whole or in part, of a partner's transferable interest in the partnership:

(1) is permissible;

(2) does not by itself cause the partner's dissociation or a dissolution and winding up of the partnership business; and

(3) does not, as against the other partners or the partnership, entitle the transferee, during the continuance of the partnership, to participate in the management or conduct of the partnership business, to require access to information concerning partnership transactions, or to inspect or copy the partnership books or records.

(b) A transferee of a partner's transferable interest in the partnership has a right:

(1) to receive, in accordance with the transfer, distributions to which the transferor would otherwise be entitled;

(2) to receive upon the dissolution and winding up of the partnership business, in accordance with the transfer, the net amount otherwise distributable to the transferor; and

(3) to seek under Section 801(6) a judicial determination that it is equitable to wind up the partnership business.

(c) In a dissolution and winding up, a transferee is entitled to an account of partnership transactions only from the date of the latest account agreed to by all of the partners.

(d) Upon transfer, the transferor retains the rights and duties of a partner other than the interest in distributions transferred.

(e) A partnership need not give effect to a transferee's rights under this section until it has notice of the transfer.

(f) A transfer of a partner's transferable interest in the partnership in violation of a restriction on transfer contained in the partnership agreement is ineffective as to a person having notice of the restriction at the time of transfer.

SECTION 504. PARTNER'S TRANSFERABLE INTEREST SUBJECT TO CHARGING ORDER.

(a) On application by a judgment creditor of a partner or of a partner's transferee, a court having jurisdiction may charge the transferable interest of the judgment debtor to satisfy the judgment. The court may appoint a receiver of the share of the distributions due or to become due to the judgment debtor in respect of the partnership and make all other orders, directions, accounts, and inquiries the judgment debtor might have made or which the circumstances of the case may require.

(b) A charging order constitutes a lien on the judgment debtor's transferable interest in the partnership. The court may order a foreclosure of the interest subject to the charging order at any time. The purchaser at the foreclosure sale has the rights of a transferee.

(c) At any time before foreclosure, an interest charged may be redeemed:

(1) by the judgment debtor;

(2) with property other than partnership property, by one or more of the other partners; or

(3) with partnership property, by one or more of the other partners with the consent of all of the partners whose interests are not so charged.

(d) This [Act] does not deprive a partner of a right under exemption laws with respect to the partner's interest in the partnership.

(e) This section provides the exclusive remedy by which a judgment creditor of a partner or partner's transferee may satisfy a judgment out of the judgment debtor's transferable interest in the partnership.

ARTICLE 6

PARTNER'S DISSOCIATION

SECTION 601. EVENTS CAUSING PARTNER'S DISSOCIATION.

A partner is dissociated from a partnership upon the occurrence of any of the following events:

(1) the partnership's having notice of the partner's express will to withdraw as a partner [as of the time of notice] or on a later date specified by the partner;

(2) an event agreed to in the partnership agreement as causing the partner's dissociation;

(3) the partner's expulsion pursuant to the partnership agreement;

(4) the partner's expulsion by the unanimous vote of the other partners if:

(i) it is unlawful to carry on the partnership business with that partner;

(ii) there has been a transfer of all or substantially all of that partner's transferable interest in the partnership, other than a transfer for security purposes, or a court order charging the partner's interest, which has not been foreclosed;

(iii) within 90 days after the partnership notifies a corporate partner that it will be expelled because it has filed a certificate of dissolution or the equivalent, its charter has been revoked, or its right to conduct business has been suspended by the jurisdiction of its incorporation, [and] there is no revocation of the certificate of dissolution or no reinstatement of its charter or its right to conduct business; or

(iv) a partnership that is a partner has been dissolved and its business is being wound up;

(5) on application by the partnership or another partner, the partner's expulsion by judicial determination because:

(i) the partner engaged in wrongful conduct that adversely and materially affected the partnership business;

(ii) the partner willfully or persistently committed a material breach of the partnership agreement or of a duty owed to the partnership or the other partners under Section 404; or

(iii) the partner engaged in conduct relating to the partnership business which makes it not reasonably practicable to carry on the business in partnership with the partner;

(6) the partner's:

(i) becoming a debtor in bankruptcy;

(ii) executing an assignment for the benefit of creditors;

(iii) seeking, consenting to, or acquiescing in the appointment of a trustee, receiver, or liquidator of that partner or of all or substantially all of that partner's property; or

(iv) failing, within 90 days after the appointment, to have vacated or stayed the appointment of a trustee, receiver, or liquidator of the partner or of all or substantially all of the partner's property obtained without the partner's consent or acquiescence, or failing within 90 days after the expiration of a stay to have the appointment vacated;

(7) in the case of a partner who is an individual:

(i) the partner's death;

(ii) the appointment of a guardian or general conservator for the partner; or

(iii) a judicial determination that the partner has otherwise become incapable of performing the partner's duties under the partnership agreement;

(8) in the case of a partner that is a trust or is acting as a partner by virtue of being a trustee of a trust, distribution of the trust's entire transferable interest in the partnership, but not merely by reason of the substitution of a successor trustee;

(9) in the case of a partner that is an estate or is acting as a partner by virtue of being a personal representative of an estate, distribution of the estate's entire transferable interest in the partnership, but not merely by reason of the substitution of a successor personal representative; or

(10) termination of a partner who is not an individual, partnership, corporation, trust, or estate.

Comment:

1. RUPA dramatically changes the law governing partnership breakups and dissolution. An entirely new concept, "dissociation," is used in lieu of the UPA term "dissolution" to denote the change in the relationship caused by a partner's ceasing to be associated in the carrying on of the business. "Dissolution" is retained but with a different meaning. See Section 802. The entity theory of partnership provides a conceptual basis for continuing the firm itself despite a partner's withdrawal from the firm.

Under RUPA, unlike the UPA, the dissociation of a partner does not necessarily cause a dissolution and winding up of the business of the partnership. Section 801 identifies the situations in which the dissociation of a partner causes a winding up of the business. Section 701 provides that in all other situations there is a buyout of the partner's interest in the partnership, rather than a windup of the partnership business. In those other situations, the partnership entity continues, unaffected by the partner's dissociation. . . .

Section 601 enumerates all of the events that cause a partner's dissociation. . . .

2. Section 601(1) provides that a partner is dissociated when the partnership has notice of the partner's express will to withdraw as a partner, unless a later date is specified by the partner. If a future date is specified by the partner, other partners may dissociate before that date; specifying a future date does not bind the others to remain as partners until that date. See also Section 801(2)(i).

Section 602(a) provides that a partner has the power to withdraw at any time. The power to withdraw is immutable under Section 103(b)(6), with the exception that the partners may agree the notice must be in writing. This continues the present rule that a partner has the power to withdraw at will, even if not the right. See UPA Section 31(2). Since no writing is required to create a partner relationship, it was felt unnecessarily formalistic, and a trap for the unwary, to require a writing to end one. If a written notification is given, Section 102(d) clarifies when it is deemed received.

RUPA continues the UPA "express will" concept, thus preserving existing case law. Section 601(1) clarifies existing law by providing that the partnership must have notice of the partner's expression of will before the dissociation is effective. See Section 102(b) for the meaning of "notice." ...

4. Section 601(3) provides that a partner may be expelled by the other partners pursuant to a power of expulsion contained in the partnership agreement. That continues the basic rule of UPA Section 31(1)(d). The expulsion can be with or without cause. As under existing law, the obligation of good faith under Section 404(d) does not require prior notice, specification of cause, or an opportunity to be heard. See Holman v. Coie, 11 Wash.App. 195, 522 P.2d 515, cert. denied, 420 U.S. 984, 95 S.Ct. 1415, 43 L.Ed.2d 666 (1975)....

6. ... Subsection (5)(iii) provides for judicial expulsion of a partner who engaged in conduct relating to the partnership business that makes it not reasonably practicable to carry on the business in partnership with that partner. Expulsion for such misconduct makes the partner's dissociation wrongful under Section 602(a)(ii) and may also support a judicial decree of dissolution under Section 801(5)(ii)....

SECTION 602. PARTNER'S POWER TO DISSOCIATE; WRONGFUL DISSOCIATION.

(a) A partner has the power to dissociate at any time, rightfully or wrongfully, by express will pursuant to Section 601(1).

(b) A partner's dissociation is wrongful only if:

(1) it is in breach of an express provision of the partnership agreement; or

(2) in the case of a partnership for a definite term or particular undertaking, before the expiration of the term or the completion of the undertaking;

(i) the partner withdraws by express will, unless the withdrawal follows within 90 days after another partner's dissociation by death or otherwise under Section 601(6) through (10) or wrongful dissociation under this subsection;

(ii) the partner is expelled by judicial determination under Section 601(5);

(iii) the partner is dissociated by becoming a debtor in bankruptcy; or

(iv) in the case of a partner who is not an individual, trust other than a business trust, or estate, the partner is expelled or otherwise dissociated because it willfully dissolved or terminated.

(c) A partner who wrongfully dissociates is liable to the partnership and to the other partners for damages caused by the dissociation. The liability is in addition to any other obligation of the partner to the partnership or to the other partners.

Comment:

1. Subsection (a) states explicitly what is implicit in UPA Section 31(2) and RUPA Section 601(1)—that a partner has the power to dissociate at any time by expressing a will to withdraw, even in contravention of the partnership agreement. The phrase "rightfully or wrongfully" reflects the distinction between a partner's *power* to withdraw in contravention of the partnership agreement and a partner's *right* to do so. In this context, although a partner can not be enjoined from exercising the power to dissociate, the dissociation may be wrongful under subsection (b).

2. Subsection (b) provides that a partner's dissociation is wrongful only if it results from one of the enumerated events. The significance of a wrongful dissociation is that it may give rise to damages under subsection (c) and, if it results in the dissolution of the partnership, the wrongfully dissociating partner is not entitled to participate in winding up the business under Section 804.

Under subsection (b), a partner's dissociation is wrongful if (1) it breaches an express provision of the partnership agreement or (2), in a term partnership, before the expiration of the term or the completion of the undertaking (i) the partner voluntarily withdraws by express will, except a withdrawal following *another* partner's wrongful dissociation or dissociation by death or otherwise under Section 601(6) through (10); (ii) the partner is expelled for misconduct under Section 601(5); (iii) the partner becomes a debtor in bankruptcy (see Section 101(2)); or (iv) a partner that is an entity (other than a trust or estate) is expelled or otherwise dissociated because its dissolution or termination was willful. Since subsection (b) is merely a default rule, the partnership agreement may eliminate or expand the dissociations that are wrongful or modify the effects of wrongful dissociation.

The exception in subsection (b)(2)(i) is intended to protect a partner's reactive withdrawal from a term partnership after the premature departure of another partner, such as the partnership's rainmaker or main supplier of capital, under the same circumstances that may result in the dissolution of the partnership under Section 801(2)(i). Under that section, a term partnership is dissolved 90 days after the bankruptcy, incapacity, death (or similar dissociation of a partner that is an entity), or wrongful dissociation of any partner, unless a majority in interest (see Comment 5(i) to Section 801 for a discussion of the term "majority in interest") of the remaining partners agree to continue the partnership. Under Section 602(b)(2)(i), a partner's exercise of the right of withdrawal by express will under those circumstances is rendered "rightful," even if the partnership is continued by others, and does not expose the withdrawing partner to damages for wrongful dissociation under Section 602(c).

A partner wishing to withdraw prematurely from a term partnership for any other reason, such as another partner's misconduct, can avoid being treated as a wrongfully dissociating partner by applying to a court under Section 601(5)(iii) to have the offending partner expelled. Then, the partnership could be dissolved under Section 801(2)(i) or the remaining partners could, by unanimous vote, dissolve the partnership under Section 801(2)(ii).

3. Subsection (c) provides that a wrongfully dissociating partner is liable to the partnership and to the other partners for any damages caused by the wrongful nature of the dissociation. That liability is in addition to any other obligation of the partner to the partnership or to the other partners. For example, the partner would be liable for any damage caused by breach of the partnership agreement or other misconduct. The partnership might also incur substantial expenses resulting from a partner's premature withdrawal from a term partnership, such as replacing the partner's expertise or obtaining new financing. The wrongfully dissociating partner would be liable to the partnership for those and all other expenses and damages that are causally related to the wrongful dissociation.

Section 701(c) provides that any damages for wrongful dissociation may be offset against the amount of the buyout price due to the partner under Section 701(a), and Section 701(h) provides that a partner who wrongfully dissociates from a term partnership is not entitled to payment of the buyout price until the term expires.

Under UPA Section 38(2)(c)(II), in addition to an offset for damages, the goodwill value of the partnership is excluded in determining the value of a wrongfully dissociating partner's partnership interest. Under RUPA, however, unless the partnership's goodwill is damaged by the wrongful dissociation, the value of the wrongfully dissociating partner's interest will include any goodwill value of the partnership. If the firm's goodwill is damaged, the amount of the damages suffered by the partnership and the remaining partners will be offset against the buyout price. See Section 701 and Comments.

SECTION 603. EFFECT OF PARTNER'S DISSOCIATION.

(a) If a partner's dissociation results in a dissolution and winding up of the partnership business, [Article] 8 applies; otherwise, [Article] 7 applies.

(b) Upon a partner's dissociation:

(1) the partner's right to participate in the management and conduct of the partnership business terminates, except as otherwise provided in Section 803;

(2) the partner's duty of loyalty under Section 404(b)(3) terminates; and

(3) the partner's duty of loyalty under Section 404(b)(1) and (2) and duty of care under Section 404(c) continue only with regard to matters arising and events occurring before the partner's dissociation, unless the partner participates in winding up the partnership's business pursuant to Section 803.

Comment:

1. Section 603(a) is a "switching" provision. It provides that, after a partner's dissociation, the partner's interest in the partnership must be purchased pursuant to the buyout rules in Article 7 *unless* there is a dissolution and winding up of the partnership business under Article 8. Thus, a partner's dissociation will always result in either a buyout of the dissociated partner's interest or a dissolution and winding up of the business.

By contrast, under the UPA, every partner dissociation results in the dissolution of the partnership, most of which trigger a right to have the business wound up unless the partnership agreement provides otherwise. See UPA § 38. The only exception in which the remaining partners have a statutory right to continue the business is when a partner wrongfully dissolves the partnership in breach of the partnership agreement. See UPA § 38(2)(b).

2. Section 603(b) is new and deals with some of the internal effects of a partner's dissociation. Subsection (b)(1) makes it clear that one of the consequences of a partner's dissociation is the immediate loss of the right to participate in the management of the business, unless it results in a dissolution and winding up of the business. In that case, Section 804(a) provides that all of the partners who have not wrongfully dissociated may participate in winding up the business....

ARTICLE 7

PARTNER'S DISSOCIATION WHEN BUSINESS NOT WOUND UP

SECTION 701. PURCHASE OF DISSOCIATED PARTNER'S INTEREST.

(a) If a partner is dissociated from a partnership without resulting in a dissolution and winding up of the partnership business under Section 801, the partnership shall cause the dissociated partner's interest in the partnership to be purchased for a buyout price determined pursuant to subsection (b).

(b) The buyout price of a dissociated partner's interest is the amount that would have been distributable to the dissociating partner under Section 807(b) if, on the date of dissociation, the assets of the partnership were sold at a price equal to the greater of the liquidation value or the value based on a sale of the entire business as a going concern without the dissociated partner and the partnership were wound up as of that date. Interest must be paid from the date of dissociation to the date of payment.

(c) Damages for wrongful dissociation under Section 602(b), and all other amounts owing, whether or not presently due, from the dissociated partner to the partnership, must be offset against the buyout price. Interest must be paid from the date the amount owed becomes due to the date of payment.

(d) A partnership shall indemnify a dissociated partner whose interest is being purchased against all partnership liabilities, whether incurred before or after the dissociation, except liabilities incurred by an act of the dissociated partner under Section 702.

(e) If no agreement for the purchase of a dissociated partner's interest is reached within 120 days after a written demand for payment, the partnership shall pay, or cause to be paid, in cash to the dissociated partner the amount the partnership estimates to be the buyout price and accrued interest, reduced by any offsets and accrued interest under subsection (c).

(f) If a deferred payment is authorized under subsection (h), the partnership may tender a written offer to pay the amount it estimates to be the buyout price and accrued interest, reduced by any offsets under subsection (c), stating the time of payment, the amount and type of security for payment, and the other terms and conditions of the obligation.

(g) The payment or tender required by subsection (e) or (f) must be accompanied by the following:

    (1) a statement of partnership assets and liabilities as of the date of dissociation;

    (2) the latest available partnership balance sheet and income statement, if any;

    (3) an explanation of how the estimated amount of the payment was calculated; and

    (4) written notice that the payment is in full satisfaction of the obligation to purchase unless, within 120 days after the written notice, the dissociated partner commences an action to determine the buyout price, any offsets under subsection (c), or other terms of the obligation to purchase.

(h) A partner who wrongfully dissociates before the expiration of a definite term or the completion of a particular undertaking is not entitled to payment of any portion of the buyout price until the expiration of the term or completion of the undertaking, unless the partner establishes to the satisfaction of the court that earlier payment will not cause undue hardship to the business of the partnership. A deferred payment must be adequately secured and bear interest.

(i) A dissociated partner may maintain an action against the partnership, pursuant to Section 405(b)(2)(ii), to determine the buyout price of that partner's interest, any offsets under subsection (c), or other terms of the obligation to purchase. The action must be commenced within 120 days after the partnership has tendered payment or an offer to pay or within one year after written demand for payment if no payment or offer to pay is tendered. The court shall determine the buyout price of the dissociated partner's interest, any offset due under subsection (c), and accrued interest, and enter judgment for any additional payment or refund. If deferred payment is authorized under subsection (h), the court shall also determine the security for payment and other terms of the obligation to purchase. The court may assess reasonable attorney's fees and the fees and expenses of appraisers or other experts for a party to the action, in amounts the court finds equitable, against a party that the court finds acted arbitrarily, vexatiously, or not in good faith. The finding may be based on the partnership's failure to tender payment or an offer to pay or to comply with subsection (g).

Comment:

1. Article 7 is new and provides for the buyout of a dissociated partner's interest in the partnership when the partner's dissociation does not result in a dissolution and winding up of its business under Article 8. See Section 603(a). If there is no dissolution, the remaining partners have a right to continue the business and the dissociated partner has a right to be paid the value of his partnership interest. These rights can, of course, be varied in the partnership agreement. See Section 103. A dissociated partner has a continuing relationship with the partnership and third parties as provided in Sections 603(b), 702, and 703. See also Section 403(b) (former partner's access to partnership books and records).

2. Subsection (a) provides that, if a partner's dissociation does not result in a windup of the business, the partnership shall cause the interest of the dissociating partner to be purchased for a buyout price determined pursuant to subsection (b). The buyout is mandatory. The "cause to be purchased" language is intended to accommodate a purchase by the partnership, one or more of the remaining partners, or a third party. . . .

3. Subsection (b) provides how the "buyout price" is to be determined. The terms "fair market value" or "fair value" were not used because they are often considered terms of art having a special meaning depending on the context, such as in tax or corporate law. "Buyout price" is a new term. It is intended that the term be developed as an independent concept appropriate to the partnership buyout situation, while drawing on valuation principles developed elsewhere.

Under subsection (b), the buyout price is the amount that would have been distributable to the dissociating partner under Section 807(b) if, on the date of dissociation, the assets of the partnership were sold at a price equal to the greater of liquidation value or going concern value without the departing partner. Liquidation value is not intended to mean distress sale value. Under general principles of valuation, the hypothetical selling price in either case should be the price that a willing and informed buyer would pay a willing and informed seller, with neither being under any compulsion to deal. The notion of a minority discount in determining the buyout price is negated by valuing the business as a going concern. Other discounts, such as for a lack of marketability or the loss of a key partner, may be appropriate, however.

Since the buyout price is based on the value of the business at the time of dissociation, the partnership must pay interest on the amount due from the date of dissociation until payment to compensate the dissociating partner for the use of his interest in the firm. Section 104(b) provides that interest shall be at the legal rate unless otherwise provided in the partnership agreement. . . .

UPA Section 38(2)(c)(II) provides that the good will of the business not be considered in valuing a wrongfully dissociating partner's interest. The forfeiture of good will rule is implicitly rejected by RUPA. See Section 602(c) and Comment 3.

The Section 701 rules are merely default rules. The partners may, in the partnership agreement, fix the method or formula for determining the buyout price and all of the other terms and conditions of the buyout right. Indeed, the very right to a buyout itself may be modified, although a provision providing for a complete forfeiture would probably not be enforceable. See Section 104(a).

4. Subsection (c) provides that the partnership may offset against the buyout price all amounts owing by the dissociated partner to the partnership, whether or not presently due, including any damages for wrongful dissociation under Section 602(c). This has the effect of accelerating payment of amounts not yet due from the departing partner to the partnership, including a long-term loan by the partnership to the dissociated partner. Where appropriate, the amounts not yet due should be discounted to present value. A dissociating partner, on the other hand, is not entitled to an add-on for amounts owing to him by the partnership. Thus, a departing partner who has made a long-term loan to the partnership must wait for repayment, unless the terms of the loan agreement provide for acceleration upon dissociation. . . .

6. Subsection (e) provides that, if no agreement for the purchase of the dissociated partner's interest is reached within 120 days after the dissociated partner's written demand for payment, the partnership must pay, or cause to be paid, in cash the amount it estimates to be the buyout price, adjusted for any offsets allowed and accrued interest. Thus, the dissociating partner will receive in cash within 120 days of dissociation the undisputed minimum value of the partner's partnership interest. If the dissociated partner claims that the buyout price should be higher, suit may thereafter be brought as provided in subsection (i) to have the amount of the buyout price determined by the court. This is similar to the procedure for determining the value of dissenting shareholders' shares under RMBCA Sections 13.20–13.28. . . .

9. Subsection (h) replaces UPA Section 38(2)(c) and provides a somewhat different rule for payment to a partner whose dissociation before the expiration of a definite term or the completion of a particular undertaking is wrongful under Section 602(b). Under subsection (h), a wrongfully dissociating partner is not entitled to receive any portion of the buyout price before the expiration of the term or completion of the undertaking, unless the dissociated partner establishes to the satisfaction of the court that earlier payment will not cause undue hardship to the business of the partnership. In all other cases, there must be an immediate payment in cash. . . .

If the parties fail to reach agreement, the court must determine the buyout price of the partner's interest, any offsets, including damages for wrongful dissociation, and the amount of interest accrued. If payment to a wrongfully dissociated partner is deferred, the court may also require security for payment and determine the other terms of the obligation. . . .

SECTION 702. DISSOCIATED PARTNER'S POWER TO BIND AND LIABILITY TO PARTNERSHIP.

(a) For two years after a partner dissociates without resulting in a dissolution and winding up of the partnership business, the partnership, including a surviving partnership under [Article] 9, is bound by an act of the dissociated partner which would have bound the partnership under Section 301 before dissociation only if at the time of entering into the transaction the other party:

(1) reasonably believed that the dissociated partner was then a partner;

(2) did not have notice of the partner's dissociation; and

(3) is not deemed to have had knowledge under Section 303(e) or notice under Section 704(c).

(b) A dissociated partner is liable to the partnership for any damage caused to the partnership arising from an obligation incurred by the dissociated partner after dissociation for which the partnership is liable under subsection (a).

SECTION 703. DISSOCIATED PARTNER'S LIABILITY TO OTHER PERSONS.

(a) A partner's dissociation does not of itself discharge the partner's liability for a partnership obligation incurred before dissociation. A dissociated partner is not liable for a partnership obligation incurred after dissociation, except as otherwise provided in subsection (b).

(b) A partner who dissociates without resulting in a dissolution and winding up of the partnership business is liable as a partner to the other party in a transaction entered into by the partnership, or a surviving partnership under [Article] 9, within two years after the partner's dissociation, only if at the time of entering into the transaction the other party:

(1) reasonably believed that the dissociated partner was then a partner;

(2) did not have notice of the partner's dissociation; and

(3) is not deemed to have had knowledge under Section 303(e) or notice under Section 704(c).

(c) By agreement with the partnership creditor and the partners continuing the business, a dissociated partner may be released from liability for a partnership obligation.

(d) A dissociated partner is released from liability for a partnership obligation if a partnership creditor, with notice of the partner's dissociation but without the partner's consent, agrees to a material alteration in the nature or time of payment of a partnership obligation.

SECTION 704. STATEMENT OF DISSOCIATION.

(a) A dissociated partner or the partnership may file a statement of dissociation stating the name of the partnership and that the partner is dissociated from the partnership.

(b) A statement of dissociation is a limitation on the authority of a dissociated partner for the purposes of Section 303(d) and (e).

(c) For the purposes of Sections 702(a)(3) and 703(b)(3), a person not a partner is deemed to have notice of the dissociation 90 days after the statement of dissociation is filed.

SECTION 705. CONTINUED USE OF PARTNERSHIP NAME.

Continued use of a partnership name, or a dissociated partner's name as part thereof, by partners continuing the business does not of itself make the dissociated partner liable for an obligation of the partners or the partnership continuing the business.

ARTICLE 8

WINDING UP PARTNERSHIP BUSINESS

SECTION 801. EVENTS CAUSING DISSOLUTION AND WINDING UP OF PARTNERSHIP BUSINESS.

A partnership is dissolved, and its business must be wound up, only upon the occurrence of any of the following events:

(1) in a partnership at will, the partnership's having notice from a partner, other than a partner who is dissociated under Section 601(2) through (10), of that partner's express will to withdraw as a partner [as of the time of the notice] or on a later date specified by the partner;

(2) in a partnership for a definite term or particular undertaking:

(i) the expiration of 90 days after a partner's dissociation by death or otherwise under Section 601(6) through (10) or wrongful dissociation under Section 602(b), unless before that time a majority in interest of the remaining partners, including partners who have rightfully dissociated pursuant to Section 602(b)(2)(i), agree to continue the partnership;

(ii) the express will of all of the partners to wind up the partnership business; or

(iii) the expiration of the term or the completion of the undertaking;

(3) an event agreed to in the partnership agreement resulting in the winding up of the partnership business;

(4) an event that makes it unlawful for all or substantially all of the business of the partnership to be continued, but a cure of illegality within 90 days after notice to the partnership of the event is effective retroactively to the date of the event for purposes of this section;

(5) on application by a partner, a judicial determination that:

(i) the economic purpose of the partnership is likely to be unreasonably frustrated;

(ii) another partner has engaged in conduct relating to the partnership business which makes it not reasonably practicable to carry on the business in partnership with that partner; or

(iii) it is not otherwise reasonably practicable to carry on the partnership business in conformity with the partnership agreement; or

(6) on application by a transferee of a partner's transferable interest, a judicial determination that it is equitable to wind up the partnership business:

(i) after the expiration of the term or completion of the undertaking, if the partnership was for a definite term or particular undertaking at the time of the transfer or entry of the charging order that gave rise to the transfer; or

(ii) at any time, if the partnership was a partnership at will at the time of the transfer or entry of the charging order that gave rise to the transfer.

Comment:

1.   Under UPA Section 29, a partnership is dissolved every time a partner leaves. That reflects the aggregate nature of the partnership under the UPA. Even if the business of the partnership is continued by some of the partners, it is technically a new partnership. The dissolution of the old partnership and creation of a new partnership causes many unnecessary problems. . . .

RUPA's move to the entity theory is driven in part by the need to prevent a technical dissolution or its consequences. Under RUPA, not every partner dissociation causes a dissolution of the partnership. Only certain departures trigger a dissolution. The basic rule is that a partnership is dissolved, and its business must be wound up, only upon the occurrence of one of the events listed in Section 801. All other dissociations result in a buyout of the partner's interest under Article 7 and a continuation of the partnership entity and business by the remaining partners. See Section 603(a).

With only three exceptions, the provisions of Section 801 are merely default rules and may by agreement be varied or eliminated as grounds for dissolution. The first exception is dissolution under Section 801(4) resulting from carrying on an illegal business. The other two exceptions cover the power of a court to dissolve a partnership under Section 801(5) on application of a partner and under Section 801(6) on application of a transferee. . . .

2. Under RUPA, "dissolution" is merely the commencement of the winding up process. The partnership continues for the limited purpose of winding up the business. In effect, that means the scope of the partnership business contracts to completing work in process and taking such other actions as may be necessary to wind up the business. Winding up the partnership business entails selling its assets, paying its debts, and distributing the net balance, if any, to the partners in cash according to their interests. The partnership entity continues, and the partners are associated in the winding up of the business until winding up is completed. When the winding up is completed, the partnership entity terminates.

3. Section 801 continues two basic rules from the UPA. First, it continues the rule that any member of an *at-will* partnership has the right to force a liquidation. Second, by negative implication, it continues the rule that the partners who wish to continue the business of a *term* partnership can not be forced to liquidate the business by a partner who withdraws prematurely in violation of the partnership agreement. . . .

4. Section 801(1) provides that a partnership at will is dissolved and its business must be wound up upon the partnership's having notice of a partner's express will to withdraw as a partner, unless a later effective date is specified by the partner. . . .

If, after dissolution, none of the partners wants the partnership wound up, Section 802(b) provides that, with the consent of all the partners, including the withdrawing partner, the remaining partners may continue the business. In that event, although there is a technical dissolution of the partnership and, at least in theory, a temporary contraction of the scope of the business, the partnership entity continues and the scope of its business is restored.   See Section 802(b) and Comment 2.

5. Section 801(2) provides three ways in which a term partnership may be dissolved before the expiration of the term:

(i) Subsection (2)(i) provides for dissolution upon the expiration of 90 days after any partner's dissociation by death or otherwise under Section 601(6) to (10) or wrongful dissociation under Section 602(b), unless within that 90–day period a majority in interest of the remaining partners agree to continue the partnership.   This reactive dissolution of a term partnership protects the remaining partners where the dissociating partner is crucial to the successful continuation of the business.   The corresponding UPA Section 38(2)(b) rule requires unanimous consent of the remaining partners to continue the business, thus giving each partner an absolute right to a reactive liquidation.   Under RUPA, if the partnership is continued by the majority, any dissenting partner who wants to withdraw may do so rightfully under the exception to Section 602(b)(2)(i), in which case his interest in the partnership will be bought out under Article 7.   By itself, however, a partner's vote not to continue the business is not necessarily an expression of the partner's will to withdraw, and a dissenting partner may still elect to remain a partner and continue in the business.

The Section 601 dissociations giving rise to a reactive dissolution are: (6) a partner's bankruptcy or similar financial impairment; (7) a partner's death or incapacity; (8) the distribution by a trust-partner of its entire partnership interest; (9) the distribution by an estate-partner of its entire partnership interest; and (10) the termination of an entity-partner.   Any dissociation during the term of the partnership that is wrongful under Section 602(b), including a partner's voluntary withdrawal, expulsion or bankruptcy, also gives rise to a reactive dissolution.   Those statutory grounds may be varied by agreement or the reactive dissolution may be abolished entirely.

Under subsection (2)(i), a term partnership is dissolved 90 days after the first partner's dissociation unless within that time a majority in interest of the remaining partners have agreed to continue the partnership.   Continuation under subsection (2)(i) requires the agreement of at least a majority in interest of the remaining partners.   The interest and vote of a partner who dissociates rightfully under Section 602(b)(2)(i) is counted in determining whether a majority in interest agrees to continue. . . .

SECTION 802. PARTNERSHIP CONTINUES AFTER DISSOLUTION.

(a) Subject to subsection (b), a partnership continues after dissolution only for the purpose of winding up its business. The partnership is terminated when the winding up of its business is completed.

(b) At any time after the dissolution of a partnership and before the winding up of its business is completed, all of the partners, including any dissociating partner other than a wrongfully dissociating partner, may waive the right to have the partnership's business wound up and the partnership terminated. In that event:

> (1) the partnership resumes carrying on its business as if dissolution had never occurred, and any liability incurred by the partnership or a partner after the dissolution and before the waiver is determined as if dissolution had never occurred; and

> (2) the rights of a third party accruing under Section 804(1) or arising out of conduct in reliance on the dissolution before the third party knew or received a notification of the waiver may not be adversely affected.

SECTION 803. RIGHT TO WIND UP PARTNERSHIP BUSINESS.

(a) After dissolution, a partner who has not wrongfully dissociated may participate in winding up the partnership's business, but on application of any partner, partner's legal representative, or transferee, the [designate the appropriate court], for good cause shown, may order judicial supervision of the winding up.

(b) The legal representative of the last surviving partner may wind up a partnership's business.

(c) A person winding up a partnership's business may preserve the partnership business or property as a going concern for a reasonable time, prosecute and defend actions and proceedings, whether civil, criminal, or administrative, settle and close the partnership's business, dispose of and transfer the partnership's property, discharge the partnership's liabilities, distribute the assets of the partnership pursuant to Section 807, settle disputes by mediation or arbitration, and perform other necessary acts.

SECTION 804. PARTNER'S POWER TO BIND PARTNERSHIP AFTER DISSOLUTION.

Subject to Section 805, a partnership is bound by a partner's act after dissolution that:

(1) is appropriate for winding up the partnership business; or

(2) would have bound the partnership under Section 301 before dissolution, if the other party to the transaction did not have notice of the dissolution.

SECTION 805. STATEMENT OF DISSOLUTION.

(a) After dissolution, a partner who has not wrongfully dissociated may file a statement of dissolution stating the name of the partnership and that the partnership has dissolved and is winding up its business.

(b) A statement of dissolution cancels a filed statement of partnership authority for the purposes of Section 303(d) and is a limitation on authority for the purposes of Section 303(e).

(c) For the purposes of Sections 301 and 804, a person not a partner is deemed to have notice of the dissolution and the limitation on the partners' authority as a result of the statement of dissolution 90 days after it is filed.

(d) After filing and, if appropriate, recording a statement of dissolution, a dissolved partnership may file and, if appropriate, record a statement of partnership authority which will operate with respect to a person not a partner as provided in Section 303(d) and (e) in any transaction, whether or not the transaction is appropriate for winding up the partnership business.

SECTION 806. PARTNER'S LIABILITY TO OTHER PARTNERS AFTER DISSOLUTION.

(a) Except as otherwise provided in subsection (b), after dissolution a partner is liable to the other partners for the partner's share of any partnership liability incurred under Section 804.

(b) A partner who, with knowledge of the dissolution, incurs a partnership liability under Section 804(2) by an act that is not appropriate for winding up the partnership business is liable to the partnership for any damage caused to the partnership arising from the liability.

SECTION 807. SETTLEMENT OF ACCOUNTS AND CONTRIBUTIONS AMONG PARTNERS.

(a) In winding up a partnership's business, the assets of the partnership, including the contributions of the partners required by this section, must be applied to discharge its obligations to creditors, including, to the extent permitted by law, partners who are creditors. Any surplus must be applied to pay in cash the net amount distributable to partners in accordance with their right to distributions under subsection (b).

(b) Each partner is entitled to a settlement of all partnership accounts upon winding up the partnership business. In settling accounts among the partners, the profits and losses that result from the liquidation of the partnership assets must be credited and charged to the partners' accounts. The partnership shall make a distribution to a partner in an amount equal to any excess of the credits over the charges in the partner's account. A partner shall contribute to the partnership an amount equal to any excess of the charges over the credits in the partner's account.

(c) If a partner fails to contribute, all of the other partners shall contribute, in the proportions in which those partners share partnership losses, the additional amount necessary to satisfy the partnership obligations. A partner or partner's legal representative may recover from the other partners any contributions the partner makes to the extent the amount contributed exceeds that partner's share of the partnership obligations.

(d) After the settlement of accounts, each partner shall contribute, in the proportion in which the partner shares partnership losses, the amount necessary to satisfy partnership obligations that were not known at the time of the settlement.

(e) The estate of a deceased partner is liable for the partner's obligation to contribute to the partnership.

(f) An assignee for the benefit of creditors of a partnership or a partner, or a person appointed by a court to represent creditors of a partnership or a partner, may enforce a partner's obligation to contribute to the partnership.

Comment:

1. Section 807 provides the default rules for the settlement of accounts and contributions among the partners in winding up the business. It is derived in part from UPA Sections 38(1) and 40.

2. Subsection (a) continues the rule in UPA Section 38(1) that, in winding up the business, the partnership assets must first be applied to discharge partnership liabilities to creditors. For this purpose, any required contribution by the partners is treated as an asset of the partnership. After the payment of all partnership liabilities, any surplus must be applied to pay in

cash the net amount due the partners under subsection (b) by way of a liquidating distribution.

RUPA continues the "in-cash" rule of UPA Section 38(1) and is consistent with Section 402, which provides that a partner has no right to receive, and may not be required to accept, a distribution in kind, unless otherwise agreed. The in-cash rule avoids the valuation problems that afflict unwanted in-kind distributions.

The partnership must apply its assets to discharge the obligations of partners who are creditors on a parity with other creditors. See Section 404(f).... In effect, that abolishes the priority rules in UPA Section 40(b) and (c) which subordinate the payment of inside debt to outside debt. Both RULPA and the RMBCA do likewise. See RULPA § 804; RMBCA §§ 6.40(f), 14.05(a). Ultimately, however, a partner whose "debt" has been repaid by the partnership is personally liable, as a partner, for any outside debt remaining unsatisfied, unlike a limited partner or corporate shareholder. Accordingly, the obligation to contribute sufficient funds to satisfy the claims of outside creditors may result in the equitable subordination of inside debt when partnership assets are insufficient to satisfy all obligations to non-partners.

RUPA in effect abolishes the "dual priority" or "jingle" rule of UPA Section 40(h) and (i). Those sections gave partnership creditors priority as to partnership property and separate creditors priority as to separate property. The jingle rule has already been preempted by the Bankruptcy Code, at least as to Chapter 7 partnership liquidation proceedings. Under Section 723(c) of the Bankruptcy Code, and under RUPA, partnership creditors share pro rata with the partners' individual creditors in the assets of the partners' estates....

ARTICLE 9

CONVERSIONS AND MERGERS

SECTION 901. DEFINITIONS.

In this [article]:

(1) "General partner" means a partner in a partnership and a general partner in a limited partnership.

(2) "Limited partner" means a limited partner in a limited partnership.

(3) "Limited partnership" means a limited partnership created under the [State Limited Partnership Act], predecessor law, or comparable law of another jurisdiction.

(4) "Partner" includes both a general partner and a limited partner.

Comment: ...

2. As Section 908 makes clear, the requirements of Article 9 are not mandatory, and a partnership may convert or merge in any other manner provided by law. Article 9 is merely a "safe harbor." If the requirements of the article are followed, the conversion or merger is legally valid. Since most States have no other established procedure for the conversion or merger of partnerships, it is likely that the Article 9 procedures will be used in virtually all cases....

SECTION 902. CONVERSION OF PARTNERSHIP TO LIMITED PARTNERSHIP.

(a) A partnership may be converted to a limited partnership pursuant to this section.

(b) The terms and conditions of a conversion of a partnership to a limited partnership must be approved by all of the partners or by a number or percentage specified for conversion in the partnership agreement.

(c) After the conversion is approved by the partners, the partnership shall file a certificate of limited partnership in the jurisdiction in which the limited partnership is to be formed. The certificate must include:

(1) a statement that the partnership was converted to a limited partnership from a partnership;

(2) its former name; and

(3) a statement of the number of votes cast by the partners for and against the conversion and, if the vote is less than

unanimous, the number or percentage required to approve the conversion under the partnership agreement.

(d) The conversion takes effect when the certificate of limited partnership is filed or at any later date specified in the certificate.

(e) A general partner who becomes a limited partner as a result of the conversion remains liable as a general partner for an obligation incurred by the partnership before the conversion takes effect. If the other party to a transaction with the limited partnership reasonably believes when entering the transaction that the limited partner is a general partner, the limited partner is liable for an obligation incurred by the limited partnership within 90 days after the conversion takes effect. The limited partner's liability for all other obligations of the limited partnership incurred after the conversion takes effect is that of a limited partner as provided in the [State Limited Partnership Act].

SECTION 903. CONVERSION OF LIMITED PARTNERSHIP TO PARTNERSHIP.

(a) A limited partnership may be converted to a partnership pursuant to this section.

(b) Notwithstanding a provision to the contrary in a limited partnership agreement, the terms and conditions of a conversion of a limited partnership to a partnership must be approved by all of the partners.

(c) After the conversion is approved by the partners, the limited partnership shall cancel its certificate of limited partnership.

(d) The conversion takes effect when the certificate of limited partnership is canceled.

(e) A limited partner who becomes a general partner as a result of the conversion remains liable only as a limited partner for an obligation incurred by the limited partnership before the conversion takes effect. The partner is liable as a general partner for an obligation of the partnership incurred after the conversion takes effect.

SECTION 904. EFFECT OF CONVERSION; ENTITY UN-CHANGED.

(a) A partnership or limited partnership that has been converted pursuant to this [article] is for all purposes the same entity that existed before the conversion.

(b) When a conversion takes effect:

(1) all property owned by the converting partnership or limited partnership remains vested in the converted entity;

(2) all obligations of the converting partnership or limited partnership continue as obligations of the converted entity; and

(3) an action or proceeding pending against the converting partnership or limited partnership may be continued as if the conversion had not occurred.

SECTION 905. MERGER OF PARTNERSHIPS.

(a) Pursuant to a plan of merger approved as provided in subsection (c), a partnership may be merged with one or more partnerships or limited partnerships.

(b) The plan of merger must set forth:

(1) the name of each partnership or limited partnership that is a party to the merger;

(2) the name of the surviving entity into which the other partnerships or limited partnerships will merge;

(3) whether the surviving entity is a partnership or a limited partnership and the status of each partner;

(4) the terms and conditions of the merger;

(5) the manner and basis of converting the interests of each party to the merger into interests or obligations of the surviving entity, or into money or other property in whole or part; and

(6) the street address of the surviving entity's chief executive office.

(c) The plan of merger must be approved:

(1) in the case of a partnership that is a party to the merger, by all of the partners, or a number or percentage specified for merger in the partnership agreement; and

(2) in the case of a limited partnership that is a party to the merger, by the vote required for approval of a merger by the law of the State or foreign jurisdiction in which the limited partnership is organized and, in the absence of such a specifically applicable law, by all of the partners, notwithstanding a provision to the contrary in the partnership agreement.

(d) After a plan of merger is approved and before the merger takes effect, the plan may be amended or abandoned as provided in the plan.

(e) The merger takes effect on the later of:

(1) the approval of the plan of merger by all parties to the merger, as provided in subsection (c);

(2) the filing of all documents required by law to be filed as a condition to the effectiveness of the merger; or

(3) any effective date specified in the plan of merger.

SECTION 906. EFFECT OF MERGER.

(a) When a merger takes effect:

(1) the separate existence of every partnership or limited partnership that is a party to the merger, other than the surviving entity, ceases;

(2) all property owned by each of the merged partnerships or limited partnerships vests in the surviving entity;

(3) all obligations of every partnership or limited partnership that is a party to the merger become the obligations of the surviving entity; and

(4) an action or proceeding pending against a partnership or limited partnership that is a party to the merger may be continued as if the merger had not occurred, or the surviving entity may be substituted as a party to the action or proceeding.

(b) The [Secretary of State] of this State is the agent for service of process in an action or proceeding against a surviving foreign partnership or limited partnership to enforce an obligation of a domestic partnership or limited partnership that is a party to a merger. The surviving entity shall promptly notify the [Secretary of State] of the mailing address of its chief executive office and of any change of address. Upon receipt of process, the [Secretary of State] shall mail a copy of the process to the surviving foreign partnership or limited partnership.

(c) A partner of the surviving partnership or limited partnership is liable for:

(1) all obligations of a party to the merger for which the partner was personally liable before the merger;

(2) all other obligations of the surviving entity incurred before the merger by a party to the merger, but those obligations may be satisfied only out of property of the entity; and

(3) all obligations of the surviving entity incurred after the merger takes effect, but those obligations may be satisfied only out of property of the entity if the partner is a limited partner.

234

(d) If the obligations incurred before the merger by a party to the merger are not satisfied out of the property of the surviving partnership or limited partnership, the general partners of that party immediately before the effective date of the merger shall contribute the amount necessary to satisfy that party's obligations to the surviving entity, in the manner provided in Section 807 or in the [Limited Partnership Act] of the jurisdiction in which the party was formed, as the case may be, as if the merged party were dissolved.

(e) A partner of a party to a merger who does not become a partner of the surviving partnership or limited partnership is dissociated from the entity, of which that partner was a partner, as of the date the merger takes effect. The surviving entity shall cause the partner's interest in the entity to be purchased under Section 701 or another statute specifically applicable to that partner's interest with respect to a merger. The surviving entity is bound under Section 702 by an act of a general partner dissociated under this subsection, and the partner is liable under Section 703 for transactions entered into by the surviving entity after the merger takes effect.

SECTION 907. STATEMENT OF MERGER.

(a) After a merger, the surviving partnership or limited partnership may file a statement that one or more partnerships or limited partnerships have merged into the surviving entity.

(b) A statement of merger must contain:

(1) the name of each partnership or limited partnership that is a party to the merger;

(2) the name of the surviving entity into which the other partnerships or limited partnership were merged;

(3) the street address of the surviving entity's chief executive office and of an office in this State, if any; and

(4) whether the surviving entity is a partnership or a limited partnership.

(c) Except as otherwise provided in subsection (d), for the purposes of Section 302, property of the surviving partnership or limited partnership which before the merger was held in the name of another party to the merger is property held in the name of the surviving entity upon filing a statement of merger.

(d) For the purposes of Section 302, real property of the surviving partnership or limited partnership which before the merger was held in the name of another party to the merger is property held in the name of the surviving entity upon recording a certified

235

copy of the statement of merger in the office for recording transfers of that real property.

(e) A filed and, if appropriate, recorded statement of merger, executed and declared to be accurate pursuant to Section 105(c), stating the name of a partnership or limited partnership that is a party to the merger in whose name property was held before the merger and the name of the surviving entity, but not containing all of the other information required by subsection (b), operates with respect to the partnerships or limited partnerships named to the extent provided in subsections (c) and (d).

SECTION 908. NONEXCLUSIVE.

This [article] is not exclusive. Partnerships or limited partnerships may be converted or merged in any other manner provided by law.

ARTICLE 10

MISCELLANEOUS PROVISIONS

SECTION 1001. UNIFORMITY OF APPLICATION AND CON-STRUCTION.

This [Act] shall be applied and construed to effectuate its general purpose to make uniform the law with respect to the subject of this [Act] among States enacting it.

SECTION 1002. SHORT TITLE.

This [Act] may be cited as the Uniform Partnership Act (1994).

SECTION 1003. SEVERABILITY CLAUSE.

If any provision of this [Act] or its application to any person or circumstance is held invalid, the invalidity does not affect other provisions or applications of this [Act] which can be given effect without the invalid provision or application, and to this end the provisions of this [Act] are severable.

SECTION 1004. EFFECTIVE DATE.

This [Act] takes effect _____.

SECTION 1005. REPEALS.

Effective January 1, 199__, the following acts and parts of acts are repealed: [the State Partnership Act as amended and in effect immediately before the effective date of this Act].

SECTION 1006. APPLICABILITY.

(a) Before January 1, 199__, this [Act] governs only a partnership formed:

(1) after the effective date of this [Act], unless that partnership is continuing the business of a dissolved partnership under [Section 41 of the prior Uniform Partnership Act]; and

(2) before the effective date of this [Act], that elects, as provided by subsection (c), to be governed by this [Act].

(b) After January 1, 199__, this [Act] governs all partnerships.

(c) Before January 1, 199__, a partnership voluntarily may elect, in the manner provided in its partnership agreement or by law for amending the partnership agreement, to be governed by this [Act]. The provisions of this [Act] relating to the liability of the partnership's partners to third parties apply to limit those partners' liability to a third party who had done business with the partnership within one year preceding the partnership's election to be governed by this [Act], only if the third party knows or has received a notification of the partnership's election to be governed by this [Act].

SECTION 1007. SAVINGS CLAUSE.

This [Act] does not affect an action or proceeding commenced or right accrued before this [Act] takes effect.

FORM OF PARTNERSHIP AGREEMENT

[From M. Volz, C. Trower & D. Reiss, The Drafting of Partnership Agreements 65–85 (7th ed. 1986).]

General Partnership Agreement of

[Insert Name]

This is a general Partnership Agreement, made and entered into by and between [list partners' full names], (collectively, the "Partners").

SECTION 1

FORMATION OF PARTNERSHIP

The Partners hereby form a partnership (the "Partnership") pursuant to the [name of state] Uniform Partnership Act. The rights and duties of the Partners shall be as provided in that Act except as modified by this Agreement.

SECTION 2

NAME

The business of the Partnership shall be conducted under the name "[insert name]" or such other name as the Managing Partner shall hereafter designate in writing to the Partners.

SECTION 3

DEFINITIONS

"Act" means the [insert jurisdiction of formation] Uniform Partnership Act, [insert citation to official state statute].

"Agreement" means this Partnership Agreement, as amended, modified, or supplemented from time to time.

"Bankruptcy" shall be deemed to have occurred with respect to any Partner 60 days after the happening of any of the following: (1) the filing of an application by a Partner for, or a consent to, the appointment of a trustee of the Partner's assets; (2) the filing by a Partner of a voluntary petition in bankruptcy or the filing of a pleading in any court of record admitting in writing the Partner's inability to pay the Partner's debts as they become due; (3) the making by a Partner of a general assignment for the benefit of creditors; (4) the filing by a Partner of an answer admitting the material allegations of, or consenting to, or defaulting in answering a bankruptcy petition filed against the Partner in any bankruptcy proceeding; or (5) the entry of an order, judgment, or decree by any court of competent jurisdiction adjudicating a Partner a bankrupt or appointing a trustee of the Partner's assets, and that order, judgment, or decree continuing unstayed and in effect for a period of 60 days.

"Capital Account" means with respect to each Partner, the account established on the books and records of the Partnership for each Partner under Section 11.01. Each Partner's Capital Account shall initially equal the cash and the agreed value of property (net of liabilities assumed or to which the property is subject) contributed by the Partner to the Partnership, and during the term of the Partnership shall be (1) *increased* by the amount of (a) Taxable Income allocated to the Partner, other than Taxable Income attributable to the difference between the agreed value and adjusted basis of the property at contribution, and (b) any money and the agreed value of property (net of any liabilities assumed or to which the property is subject) subsequently contributed to the Partnership, and (2) *decreased* by the amount of (a) Tax Losses allocated to the Partner, *except* (i) Tax Losses attributable to depreciation of contributed property, which shall decrease Capital Accounts only to the extent of depreciation computed as if the property were purchased by the Partnership at its agreed value, and (ii) Tax Losses attributable to the difference between the agreed value and adjusted basis of property at contribution (which shall not decrease the contributing Partner's Capital Account), and (b) all cash and the agreed value of property (net of liabilities assumed or to which the property is subject) distributed to such Partner, and shall otherwise be kept in accordance with applicable Treasury Regulations.

"Capital Contribution" means the amount of money or the agreed value of other property contributed to the Partnership by a Partner.

"Code" means the Internal Revenue Code ... as amended, modified, or rescinded from time to time, or any similar provision of succeeding law.

"Incapacity" or "Incapacitated" means the incompetence, insanity, interdiction, death, disability, or incapacity, as the case may be, of any Partner.

"Interest" means the entire ownership interest of a Partner in the Partnership.

"Managing Partner" means [insert name] but in the event that he is at any time no longer a Partner, or is replaced by vote of the Partners, the term shall mean the party or parties then acting in that capacity.

"Net Cash Flow" with respect to any fiscal period means all cash revenues of the Partnership during that period (including interest or other earnings on the funds of the Partnership), *less* the sum of the following to the extent made from those cash revenues:

(1) All principal and interest payments on any indebtedness of the Partnership.

(2) All cash expenses incurred incident to the operations of the Partnership's business.

(3) Funds set aside as reserves for contingencies, working capital, debt service, taxes, insurance, or other costs or expenses incident to the conduct of the Partnership's business, which the Managing Partner deems reasonably necessary or appropriate.

"Partners" means [insert names]; any person admitted as a substituted Partner pursuant to Section 16; and, with respect to those provisions of this Agreement concerning a Partner's right to receive a share of profits or other compensation by way of income or the return of a Partner's contribution, any assignee of a Partner's Interest (except that an assignee who does not become a substituted Partner shall have only those rights specified in Section 27 of the Act).

"Partnership Percentage" means the following percentages:

Name	Percentage
[insert]	[insert]

Distributions or allocations made in proportion to or in accordance with the Partnership Percentages of the Partners shall be based upon relative Partnership Percentages as of the record date for distributions and in accordance with Section 706(c) and (d) of the Code for allocations.

"Taxable Income" and "Tax Losses," respectively, shall mean the net income or net losses of the Partnership as determined for federal income tax purposes, and all items required to be separately stated by Section 702 of the Code and the Regulations thereunder.

SECTION 4

BUSINESS OF THE PARTNERSHIP

The business of the Partnership is to [insert specific purposes] and to engage in any and all activities related or incidental thereto.

SECTION 5

NAMES AND ADDRESSES OF PARTNERS

The names and addresses of the Partners are:

[Insert name and addresses where partners wish to be contacted about partnership-related business.]

SECTION 6

TERM

The term of the Partnership shall begin [*or:* began] on [insert] and shall continue until the earlier of [date] or until dissolved by an act or event specified in this Agreement or by the law as one effecting dissolution.

SECTION 7

BUSINESS OFFICES

The principal place of business of the Partnership shall be [insert]. The Managing Partner may, from time to time, change the principal place of business of the Partnership, and in such event the Managing Partner shall notify the other Partners in writing within 30 days of the effective date of such change. The Managing Partner may in his discretion establish additional places of business of the Partnership.

SECTION 8

CAPITAL AND CONTRIBUTIONS

8.01. *Initial Capital Contributions.* The Partners shall initially make Capital Contributions totaling $_____ and among them in accordance with their Partnership Percentages. The Partners' initial Capital Contributions shall be made as soon as practicable after execution of this Agreement.

8.02. *Partners' Assessments.* In addition to the Capital Contributions required by Section 8.01, each Partner shall be obligated to make additional Capital Contributions, as called for by the Managing Partner. All additional Capital Contributions shall be made in accordance with the Partnership Percentages and within 30 days after the Partners have received notice thereof from the Managing Partner. The Managing Partner shall call these assessments based upon his estimate of all costs, expenses, or charges with respect to operation of the Partnership, *less* the expected revenues from such operations. Any increases in the Capital Contributions of the Partners pursuant to this Section 8.02 shall be noted on Annex A attached hereto and incorporated by reference.

8.03. *Default in Payment of Capital Contributions.* If any Partner fails to pay all or any portion of an additional assessment called pursuant to Section 8.02 (an "Assessment Payment") within 60 days after notification of the assessment, the remaining Partners shall advance an additional amount to the Partnership equal to the unpaid Assessment Payment (and as between them in accordance with their respective Partnership Percentages), which amount shall be deemed a loan to the defaulting Partner and a subsequent Capital Contribution to the Partnership. Thereafter, the Managing Partner shall withhold any distributions to which the defaulting Partner would otherwise be entitled and pay that amount to the other Partners in accordance with their respective Partnership Percentages, until the entire Assessment Payment, plus interest computed at _____ per cent shall have been repaid in full.

8.04. *Interest on Capital Contributions.* No Partner shall be paid interest on any Capital Contribution.

8.05. *Withdrawal and Return of Capital Contributions.* No Partner shall be entitled to withdraw any part of his Capital Contribution, or to receive any distributions from the Partnership except as provided by this Agreement.

8.06. *Loans by Partner.* The Partners may (but shall not be obligated to) [*or*: the Partners shall, in accordance with their

243

Partnership Percentages,] loan or advance to the Partnership such funds as they deem advisable [*or*: as are necessary for the Partnership's operations]; provided, however, that interest on those loans or advances shall not be in excess of _____ per cent.

SECTION 9

DISTRIBUTIONS

9.01.   Distributions as Between Partners.   Net Cash Flow shall be distributed among the Partners in accordance with their respective Partnership Percentages.

9.02.   Timing of Distributions and Discretion of Partners as to Reinvestment.   Partnership distributions, if any, will be made to those persons recognized on the books of the Partnership as Partners or as assignees of Interests on the day of the distribution. To the extent permitted by law and as permitted by any loan agreements entered into by the Partnership, the Partnership's Net Cash Flow may in whole or in part be reinvested in the Partnership's business or distributed to the Partners, as the Managing Partner determines.

SECTION 10

ALLOCATION OF PROFITS AND LOSSES FOR TAX PURPOSES

The Taxable Income and Tax Losses to be allocated among the Partners shall be allocated among them in accordance with their respective Partnership Percentages.

SECTION 11

BOOKS OF ACCOUNT, RECORDS, AND REPORTS

11.01.   Responsibility for Books and Records.   Proper and complete records and books of account shall be kept by the Managing Partner in which shall be entered fully and accurately all transactions and other matters relative to the Partnership's business as are usually entered into records and books of account maintained by persons engaged in businesses of a like character, including a Capital Account for each Partner.   The Partnership books and records shall be prepared in accordance with generally accepted accounting practices, consistently applied, and shall be kept on the cash [*or*: accrual] basis except in circumstances in which the

Managing Partner determines that another basis of accounting will be in the best interests of the Partnership [*or:* on the basis determined in the best interests of the Partnership by the Managing Partner]. The books and records shall at all times be maintained at the principal place of business of the Partnership and shall be open to the inspection and examination of the Partners or their duly authorized representatives during reasonable business hours.

11.02. Reports to Partners. As soon as practicable in the particular case, the Managing Partner shall deliver to every other Partner

(1) Such information concerning the Partnership after the end of each fiscal year as shall be necessary for the preparation by such a Partner of his income or other tax returns.

(2) An unaudited statement prepared by the Managing Partner setting forth, as of the end of and for each fiscal year, a profit and loss statement and a balance sheet of the Partnership and a statement showing the amounts allocated to or against each Interest during that year.

(3) If feasible, on or before October 15 of each year, a statement setting forth projected Taxable Income or Tax Losses to be generated by the Partnership for the fiscal year.

(4) Other information as in the judgment of the Managing Partner shall be reasonably necessary for the other Partners to be advised of the results of operations of the Partnership.

11.03. Additional Reports. The Managing Partner may prepare and deliver to the Partners from time to time during each fiscal year, in connection with distributions or otherwise, unaudited statements showing the results of operations of the Partnership to the date of that statement.

SECTION 12

FISCAL YEAR

The fiscal year of the Partnership shall end on the thirty-first day of December in each year.

SECTION 13

PARTNERSHIP FUNDS

The funds of the Partnership shall be deposited in such bank account or accounts, or invested in such interest-bearing or noninterest-bearing investments, as shall be designated by the Managing Partner. All withdrawals from any such bank accounts shall be made by the duly authorized agent or agents of the Managing Partner. Partnership funds shall be held in the name of the Partnership and shall not be commingled with those of any other person.

SECTION 14

RIGHTS OF PARTNERS

14.01. *Incapacity.* Within 90 days after a Partner becomes Incapacitated, his executor, administrator, committee, or analogous fiduciary (the "Representative") shall elect whether to retain the Incapacitated Partner's Interest in the Partnership or whether to sell that Interest to the remaining Partners. If the Representative elects to retain that Interest, the Interest shall remain bound by all the provisions of this Agreement, and the Partnership shall continue. If the Representative elects to sell the Incapacitated Partner's Interest to the other Partners, he shall so notify the other Partners in writing within the 90 day period and the other Partners must purchase the Incapacitated Partner's Interest. Any Interest shall be purchased by the remaining Partners in proportion to their respective Partnership Percentages at that time, or in such other proportion as they may mutually agree. The purchase price of an Interest sold pursuant to this Section 14.01 shall be the Contract Price as defined by Section 14.06, and payment for the Interest shall be made in the manner set forth in Section 14.07.

14.02. *Bankruptcy.* At the Bankruptcy of any Partner, that Partner (an "Inactive Partner") or his representative shall cease to have any voice in the conduct of the affairs of the Partnership and all acts, consents, and decisions with respect to the Partnership shall thereafter be made by the other Partners. The Inactive Partner shall, nonetheless, remain liable for his share of any losses of the Partnership or contributions to the Partnership as provided herein, and shall be entitled to receive his share of Taxable Income, Tax Losses, and Net Cash Flow. For six months from and after the date of the Bankruptcy of any Partner, the other Partners shall have the irrevocable option to purchase the Inactive Partner's Interest in the Partnership. That purchase shall be made in proportion to the respective Partnership Percentages of the other Partners at the time or in such other proportion as they may mutually agree. Should the other Partners exercise their option to purchase the Inactive Partner's Interest, they shall notify the Inactive Partner or his representative of their intention to do so within this six-month period. The purchase price of any Interest purchased pursuant to this Section 14.02 shall be the Contract Price as defined by Section 14.06 and shall be payable at the time and in the manner specified in Section 14.07. Should the other Partners not exercise the option to purchase the Inactive Partner's Interest, the Inactive Partner shall remain such in accordance with the provisions set forth above.

   14.03.   Limitation on Sale of Interests.   If a Partner desires to offer for sale his Interest in the Partnership, such Partner (the "Selling Partner") shall give written notice of all material terms and conditions of the offer to the other Partners (the "Buying Partners"). Within 30 days after receipt of the notice, the Buying Partners shall notify the Selling Partner of their intent to purchase the Interest of the Selling Partner upon the terms and conditions contained in the offer. The Buying Partners shall purchase the Interest of the Selling Partner in proportion to their respective Partnership Percentages, or in such other proportion as the Buying Partners may mutually agree. If the Buying Partners fail to notify the Selling Partner that they elect to purchase his Interest within the 30–day period, the Selling Partner shall have the right (1) to sell his Interest within 90 days to a third party on the same terms offered to the Buying Partners, *if* all Partners consent to the specific sale pursuant to Section 14.04, or (2) failing this consent, to withdraw from the Partnership.

   If a Partner withdraws pursuant to the immediately preceding sentence, the Partner shall be entitled to a payment from the Partnership equal to the Contract Price and payable at the time and in the manner set forth in Section 14.07. Any amounts received pursuant to this Section 14.03 shall constitute complete and full discharge of all amounts owing to the withdrawing Partner on account of his Interest as a Partner in the Partnership.

   14.04.   Assignment.   Subject to the right of first refusal in Section 14.03, a Partner may assign all or a portion of his Interest *provided that* the other Partners unanimously consent, in writing, to the assignment (which consent may be withheld in their absolute discretion). The assignment shall confer upon the assignee the right to become a substituted Partner, in the following manner and subject to the following conditions:

   (1) Each assignment shall be effective as of the day on which all Partners accept the transfer.

   (2) No assignment shall be effective if the assignment would, in the opinion of counsel to the Partnership, result in the termination of the Partnership for purposes of the then applicable provisions of the Code.

(3) No assignment to a minor or incompetent shall be effective in any respect except that this limitation shall not apply to a transfer in trust for the benefit of a minor or in custodianship under the Uniform Gifts to Minors Act or similar legislation.

Unless an assignee becomes a substituted Partner, the assignee shall have no right to interfere in the management or administration of the Partnership's business or affairs, or to require any information or account of Partnership transactions, or to inspect the Partnership's books. The assignment merely entitles the assignee to receive the share of distributions, income, and losses to which the assigning Partner would otherwise be entitled.

14.05. Transferees Bound by Agreement. Any assignee and any person admitted to the Partnership as a substituted Partner shall be subject to and bound by all the provisions of this Agreement as if originally a party to this Agreement.

14.06. Contract Price. The Contract Price shall be equal to the fair market value of the selling Partner's Interest as of the date of the event triggering the sale. The fair market value shall be determined within 60 days by (1) an appraisal (to be performed by [insert name]) of the fair market value of the Partnership's assets, less its liabilities, and (2) a valuation of the selling Partner's Interest as if the net assets of the Partnership were sold for cash and the cash distributed in accordance with Section 17.02 (dissolution).

14.07. Payment—Time and Manner.

(a) Any Interest transferred to other Partners or the Partnership pursuant to Sections 14.01, 14.02, or 14.03 of this Agreement shall be paid for, at the purchaser's option, either (1) all in cash at the time of transfer of the Interest, or (2) by a downpayment computed in accordance with Section 14.07(b) and delivery of a promissory note signed by the purchaser(s).

(b) If the purchaser(s) elects the second option in Section 14.07(a) above, he shall pay as a downpayment 33 per cent of the Contract Price. The remaining unpaid portion of the Contract Price shall be represented by a promissory note of the purchasers, in such form as shall be acceptable to the purchasers, and providing for four equal annual installments of the remaining unpaid portion of the Contract Price, each installment due on the anniversary of the transfer of the interest. The promissory note shall provide that interest at an annual rate of 9 per cent (compounded semi-annually) shall be paid with each payment of principal (or such higher interest rate as shall be necessary to avoid the imputation of interest pursuant to Section 483 of the Code), from the date of acquisition of the Interest on the portion of the note remaining unpaid from time to time.

14.08. *Adjustment of Partnership Percentages.* If a Partner withdraws pursuant to Section 14.03, the Partnership Percentages of the remaining Partners shall immediately be recalculated so that each Partner's Partnership Percentage is equal to (1) his Capital Contribution as stated on Annex A, *divided by* (2) the aggregate Capital Contributions of all remaining Partners. If the Partners or a third party purchases an Interest pursuant to Sections 14.01, 14.02, or 14.03, the Partnership Percentage of the selling Partner shall be added to that of the purchasing Partners, pro rata, or shall become the Partnership Percentage of the third-party purchaser, as the case may be.

14.09. *Voting.* All decisions required to be made or actions required to be taken by the Partners pursuant to this Agreement (including amendment hereof) shall be made or taken by the affirmative vote (at a meeting or, in lieu thereof, by written consent of the required percentage in Interest) of Partners having _____ per cent of the aggregate Partnership Percentages.

SECTION 15

MANAGEMENT AND ADMINISTRATION OF BUSINESS

15.01. *Authority of Managing Partner.* The Managing Partner shall have the authority to manage the day-to-day operations and affairs of the Partnership and to make decisions regarding the business of the Partnership. Any action taken by the Managing Partner shall constitute the act of and serve to bind the Partnership. In dealing with the Managing Partner acting on behalf of the Partnership, no person shall be required to inquire into the authority of the Managing Partner to bind the Partnership. Persons dealing with the Partnership are entitled to rely conclusively on the power and authority of the Managing Partner as set forth in this Agreement.

15.02. *Power of Managing Partner.* The powers of the Managing Partner shall include, but shall not be limited to, the power to

(1) Create, by grant or otherwise, easements and servitudes relating to the Partnership's property.

(2) Employ and dismiss from employment any and all employees, agents, independent contractors, real estate managers, brokers, attorneys, and accountants.

(3) To let or lease all or any portion of any Partnership property for any purpose and without limit as to the term thereof, whether or not that term (including renewal terms) shall extend beyond the date of termination of the Partnership and whether or not the portion so leased is to be occupied by the lessee or, in turn, subleased in whole or in part to others.

(4) Construct, alter, improve, repair, raze, replace, or rebuild any property.

(5) Obtain replacements of any mortgage or mortgages related in any way to the property owned by the Partnership, and to repay in whole or in part, refinance, recast, modify, consolidate, or extend any mortgages affecting any such property.

(6) Take such action on behalf of the Partnership as may be necessary to acquire real or personal property for the Partnership as the Partners deem advisable or beneficial to the purposes and goals of the Partnership.

(7) Sell or exchange Partnership property.

(8) Be reimbursed for all expenses incurred in conducting the Partnership business, all taxes paid by the Managing Partner in connection with the Partnership business, and all costs associated with the development, organization, and initial operation of the Partnership.

(9) Do any and all of the foregoing at such a price, rental or amount, for cash, securities, or other property and upon those terms as the Partners deem proper.

(10) Deposit Partnership funds in an account or accounts to be established at that time or times in such financial institutions (including any state or federally chartered bank or savings and loan association), and authorize withdrawals of those funds by such persons, at such times, and in those amounts, as the Managing Partner may designate.

(11) Place record title to any property in its name or in the name of a nominee or a trustee for the purpose of mortgage financing or any other convenience or benefit of the Partnership.

(12) Cause the Partnership to carry such indemnification insurance as the Managing Partner deems necessary to protect himself and any other persons entitled to indemnification by the Partnership under Section 15.06.

(13) Keep, or cause to be kept, full and accurate records of all transactions of the Partnership.

(14) Prepare, or cause to be prepared, all tax returns and reports for the Partnership and, in connection therewith, make any elections that the Partners deem advisable, including but not limited to the election referred to in Section 754 of the Code, and act as "tax matters partner" for the Partnership, within the meaning of Sections 6221 through 6232 of the Code.

(15) Prepare, or cause to be prepared, and deliver to each Partner (A) the reports and other information described by Section 11, and (B) such other information as in the Managing Partner's judgment shall be reasonably necessary for the Partners to be advised of the results of operations of the Partnership.

(16) Execute, acknowledge, and deliver any and all instruments to effectuate any and all of the foregoing.

15.03. *Time to Be Devoted to Business.* The Managing Partner shall devote such time to the Partnership's business as the Managing Partner, in his sole discretion, shall deem necessary [*or:* such time as is necessary] [*or:* all of his time and attention] to manage and supervise the Partnership business and affairs in an efficient manner. Nothing in this Agreement shall preclude the employment, at the expense of the Partnership, of any agent or third party to manage or provide other services with respect to the Partnership's property or administrative business, subject to the control of the Managing Partner.

15.04. *Other Activities and Competition.* The Partners shall not be required to manage the Partnership as their sole and exclusive functions. The Partners may have other business interests and may engage in other activities in addition to and in competition with those relating to the Partnership. Neither the Partnership nor any Partner shall have any right by virtue of this Agreement, or the partnership relationship created hereby, in or to such other ventures or activities of any Partner or to the income or proceeds derived therefrom.

15.05. *Liability.* No Partner shall be liable, responsible, or accountable in damages or otherwise to the Partnership or any Partner for any action taken or failure to act on behalf of the Partnership within the scope of the authority conferred on any Partner by this Agreement or by law unless the act or omission was performed or omitted fraudulently or in bad faith or constituted negligence.

15.06. *Indemnification.* The Partnership shall indemnify and hold harmless the Partners from and against any loss, expense, damage, or injury suffered or sustained by them by reason of any acts, omissions, or alleged acts or omissions arising out of their activities on behalf of the Partnership or in furtherance of the interests of the Partnership, including but not limited to any judgment, award, settlement, reasonable attorneys' fees, and other costs or expenses incurred in connection with the defense of any actual or threatened action, proceeding, or claim, if the acts, omissions, or alleged acts or omissions upon which the actual or threatened action, proceeding, or claims are based were for a purpose reasonably believed to be in the best interests of the Partnership and were not performed or omitted fraudulently or in bad faith or as a result of negligence by a Partner and were not in violation of the Partner's fiduciary obligation to the Partnership. Any such indemnification shall be first from the assets of the Partnership, and then from all Partners and borne among them in accordance with their Partnership Percentages.

*15.07. **Termination of Management Powers.*** The other Partners may terminate all management powers, duties, and responsibilities of the Managing Partner by a vote of Partners having _____ per cent or more of the aggregate Partnership Percentages.

*15.08. **Limits on Managing Partner's Powers.*** Anything in this Agreement to the contrary notwithstanding, the Managing Partner shall not cause or permit the Partnership to

(1) Commingle the Partnership's funds with those of any other person, or employ or permit another to employ those funds or assets in any manner except for the exclusive benefit of the Partnership (except to the extent that funds are temporarily retained by agents of the Partnership).

(2) Reimburse the Managing Partner for expenses incurred by the Managing Partner except for the actual cost to the Managing Partner of goods, materials, or services (including reasonable travel and entertainment expenses) used for or by the Partnership.

*15.09. **Employment and Compensation of Managing Partner.*** The Managing Partner shall receive $_____ per annum, payable in advance on January 1 of each year, for services performed in his capacity as a Managing Partner, which amount shall be deemed a payment to the Managing Partner for services not in his capacity as a Partner with the meaning of Section 707(c) of the Code.

SECTION 16

DISSOLUTION OF THE PARTNERSHIP

The happening of any one of the following events shall work an immediate dissolution of the Partnership:

(1) The sale or other disposition of all or substantially all of the assets of the Partnership.

(2) The affirmative vote for dissolution of the Partnership by Partners having at least _____ per cent of the aggregate Partnership Percentages.

(3) The Bankruptcy or Incapacity of any Partner; *provided that* the remaining Partners shall continue the business of the Partnership within the meaning of Section 38 of the Act unless the Partnership is dissolved under subparagraph (2) above.

(4) The expiration of the term of the Partnership.

SECTION 17

WINDING UP, TERMINATION, AND
LIQUIDATING DISTRIBUTIONS

17.01. *Winding Up.* If the Partnership is dissolved and its business is not continued under Section 16(3), the Managing Partner or his successor shall commence to wind up the affairs of the Partnership and to liquidate the Partnership's assets. The Partners shall continue to share profits and losses during the period of liquidation in accordance with Section 10. Following the occurrence of any of the events set forth in Section 16, the Partners shall determine whether the assets of the Partnership are to be sold or whether the assets are to be distributed to the Partners. If assets are distributed to the Partners, all such assets shall be valued at their then fair market value as determined by the Partners and the difference, if any, of the fair market value over (or under) the adjusted basis of such property to the Partnership shall be credited (or charged) to the Capital Accounts of the Partners in accordance with the provisions of Section 10. Such fair market value shall be used for purposes of determining the amount of any distribution to a Partner pursuant to Section 17.02. If the Partners are unable to agree on the fair market value of any asset of the Partnership, the fair market value shall be the average of two appraisals, one prepared by a qualified appraiser selected by Partners having 50 per cent or more of the aggregate Partnership Percentages, and the other selected by the remaining Partners.

17.02. *Distributions.* Subject to the right of the Partners to set up such cash reserves as may be deemed reasonably necessary for any contingent or unforeseen liabilities or obligations of the Partnership, the proceeds of the liquidation and any other funds of the Partnership shall be distributed.

253

(1) To creditors, in the order of priority as provided by law except those liabilities to Partners in their capacities as Partners.

(2) To the Partners for loans, if any, made by them to the Partnership, or reimbursement for Partnership expenses paid by them.

(3) To the Partners in proportion to their respective Capital Accounts until they have received an amount equal to their Capital Accounts immediately prior to such distribution, but *after* adjustment for gain or loss with respect to the disposition of the Partnership's assets incident to the dissolution of the Partnership and the winding up of its affairs, whether or not the disposition occurs prior to the dissolution of the Partnership.

(4) To the Partners in accordance with their Partnership Percentages.

17.03. Deficit Capital Account Restoration. If, upon the dissolution and liquidation of the Partnership, after crediting all income upon sale of the Partnership's assets that have been sold and after making the allocations provided for in Section 17.01, any Partner has a negative Capital Account, then the Partner shall be obligated to contribute to the Partnership an amount equal to the negative Capital Account for distribution to creditors, or to Partners with positive Capital Account balances, in accordance with this Section.

17.04. Final Reports. Within a reasonable time following the completion of the liquidation of the Partnership's properties, the Managing Partner shall supply to each of the other Partners a statement that shall set forth the assets and liabilities of the Partnership as of the date of complete liquidation, each Partner's portion of distributions pursuant to Section 17.02, and the amounts paid to the Managing Partner pursuant to Section 17.02.

17.05. Rights of Partners. Each Partner shall look solely to the assets of the Partnership for all distributions with respect to the Partnership and his Capital Contribution (including the return thereof), and share of profits, and shall have no recourse therefor (upon dissolution [or] otherwise) against any other Partner except as provided in Section 17.03.

17.06. Termination. Upon the completion of the liquidation of the Partnership and the distribution of all Partnership funds, the Partnership shall terminate.

SECTION 18

NOTICES

All notices and demands required or permitted under this Agreement shall be in writing and may be sent by certified or registered mail or similar delivery service, postage prepaid, to the Partners at their addresses as shown from time to time on the records of the Partnership, and shall be deemed given when mailed or delivered to the service. Any Partner may specify a different address by notifying the Managing Partner in writing of the different address.

. . .

IN WITNESS WHEREOF, the undersigned have executed this Agreement as of this _____ day of _____, 19__.

_____   _____
[Partner's signature]   [Partner's signature]

_____   _____
[Partner's signature]   [Partner's signature]

UNIFORM LIMITED PARTNERSHIP ACT (1976) WITH 1985 AMENDMENTS

ARTICLE 1. GENERAL PROVISIONS

ARTICLE 2. FORMATION; CERTIFICATE OF LIMITED PARTNERSHIP

ARTICLE 3. LIMITED PARTNERS

ARTICLE 4. GENERAL PARTNERS

ARTICLE 5. FINANCE

* Omitted.

256

* Omitted.

ARTICLE 1

GENERAL PROVISIONS

§ 101. Definitions

As used in this [Act], unless the context otherwise requires:

(1) "Certificate of limited partnership" means the certificate referred to in Section 201, and the certificate as amended or restated.

(2) "Contribution" means any cash, property, services rendered, or a promissory note or other binding obligation to contribute cash or property or to perform services, which a partner contributes to a limited partnership in his capacity as a partner.

(3) "Event of withdrawal of a general partner" means an event that causes a person to cease to be a general partner as provided in Section 402.

(4) "Foreign limited partnership" means a partnership formed under the laws of any state other than this State and having as partners one or more general partners and one or more limited partners.

(5) "General partner" means a person who has been admitted to a limited partnership as a general partner in accordance with the partnership agreement and named in the certificate of limited partnership as a general partner.

(6) "Limited partner" means a person who has been admitted to a limited partnership as a limited partner in accordance with the partnership agreement.

(7) "Limited partnership" and "domestic limited partnership" mean a partnership formed by two or more persons under the laws of this State and having one or more general partners and one or more limited partners.

(8) "Partner" means a limited or general partner.

(9) "Partnership agreement" means any valid agreement, written or oral, of the partners as to the affairs of a limited partnership and the conduct of its business.

* Omitted.

258

(10) "Partnership interest" means a partner's share of the profits and losses of a limited partnership and the right to receive distributions of partnership assets.

(11) "Person" means a natural person, partnership, limited partnership (domestic or foreign), trust, estate, association, or corporation.

(12) "State" means a state, territory, or possession of the United States, the District of Columbia, or the Commonwealth of Puerto Rico.

§ 102. Name

The name of each limited partnership as set forth in its certificate of limited partnership:

(1) shall contain without abbreviation the words "limited partnership";

(2) may not contain the name of a limited partner unless (i) it is also the name of a general partner or the corporate name of a corporate general partner, or (ii) the business of the limited partnership had been carried on under that name before the admission of that limited partner;

(3) may not be the same as, or deceptively similar to, the name of any corporation or limited partnership organized under the laws of this State or licensed or registered as a foreign corporation or limited partnership in this State; and

(4) may not contain the following words [here insert prohibited words]. . . .

§ 105. Records to Be Kept

(a) Each limited partnership shall keep at the office referred to in Section 104(1) the following:

(1) a current list of the full name and last known business address of each partner, separately identifying the general partners (in alphabetical order) and the limited partners (in alphabetical order);

(2) a copy of the certificate of limited partnership and all certificates of amendment thereto, together with executed copies of any powers of attorney pursuant to which any certificate has been executed;

(3) copies of the limited partnership's federal, state and local income tax returns and reports, if any, for the three most recent years;

(4) copies of any then effective written partnership agreements and of any financial statements of the limited partnership for the three most recent years; and

(5) unless contained in a written partnership agreement, a writing setting out:

(i) the amount of cash and a description and statement of the agreed value of the other property or services contributed by each partner and which each partner has agreed to contribute;

(ii) the times at which or events on the happening of which any additional contributions agreed to be made by each partner are to be made;

(iii) any right of a partner to receive, or of a general partner to make, distributions to a partner which include a return of all or any part of the partner's contribution; and

(iv) any events upon the happening of which the limited partnership is to be dissolved and its affairs wound up.

(b) Records kept under this section are subject to inspection and copying at the reasonable request and at the expense of any partner during ordinary business hours.

§ 106. Nature of Business

A limited partnership may carry on any business that a partnership without limited partners may carry on except [here designate prohibited activities].

§ 107. Business Transactions of Partner With Partnership

Except as provided in the partnership agreement, a partner may lend money to and transact other business with the limited partnership and, subject to other applicable law, has the same rights and obligations with respect thereto as a person who is not a partner.

ARTICLE 2

FORMATION; CERTIFICATE OF LIMITED PARTNERSHIP

§ 201. Certificate of Limited Partnership

(a) In order to form a limited partnership, a certificate of limited partnership must be executed and filed in the office of the Secretary of State. The certificate shall set forth:

(1) the name of the limited partnership;

(2) the address of the office and the name and address of the agent for service of process required to be maintained by Section 104;

(3) the name and the business address of each general partner;

(4) the latest date upon which the limited partnership is to dissolve; and

(5) any other matters the general partners determine to include therein.

(b) A limited partnership is formed at the time of the filing of the certificate of limited partnership in the office of the Secretary of State or at any later time specified in the certificate of limited partnership if, in either case, there has been substantial compliance with the requirements of this section.

Comment

The 1985 Act requires far fewer matters to be set forth in the certificate of limited partnership than did Section 2 of the 1916 Act and Section 201 of the 1976 Act. This is in recognition of the fact that the partnership agreement, not the certificate of limited partnership, has become the authoritative and comprehensive document for most limited partnerships, and that creditors and potential creditors of the partnership do and should refer to the partnership agreement and to other information furnished to them directly by the partnership and by others, not to the certificate of limited partnership, to obtain facts concerning the capital and finances of the partnership and other matters of concern. Subparagraph (b), which is based upon the 1916 Act, has been retained to make it clear that existence of the limited partnership depends only upon compliance with this section. Its continued existence is not dependent upon compliance with other provisions of this Act.

§ 202. Amendment to Certificate

(a) A certificate of limited partnership is amended by filing a certificate of amendment thereto in the office of the Secretary of State. The certificate shall set forth:

(1) the name of the limited partnership;

(2) the date of filing the certificate; and

(3) the amendment to the certificate.

261

(b) Within 30 days after the happening of any of the following events, an amendment to a certificate of limited partnership reflecting the occurrence of the event or events shall be filed:

(1) the admission of a new general partner;

(2) the withdrawal of a general partner; or

(3) the continuation of the business under Section 801 after an event of withdrawal of a general partner.

(c) A general partner who becomes aware that any statement in a certificate of limited partnership was false when made or that any arrangements or other facts described have changed, making the certificate inaccurate in any respect, shall promptly amend the certificate.

(d) A certificate of limited partnership may be amended at any time for any other proper purpose the general partners determine.

(e) No person has any liability because an amendment to a certificate of limited partnership has not been filed to reflect the occurrence of any event referred to in subsection (b) of this section if the amendment is filed within the 30–day period specified in subsection (b).

(f) A restated certificate of limited partnership may be executed and filed in the same manner as a certificate of amendment....

§ 204. Execution of Certificates

(a) Each certificate required by this Article to be filed in the office of the Secretary of State shall be executed in the following manner:

(1) an original certificate of limited partnership must be signed by all general partners;

(2) a certificate of amendment must be signed by at least one general partner and by each other general partner designated in the certificate as a new general partner; and

(3) a certificate of cancellation must be signed by all general partners.

(b) Any person may sign a certificate by an attorney-in-fact, but a power of attorney to sign a certificate relating to the admission of a general partner must specifically describe the admission.

(c) The execution of a certificate by a general partner constitutes an affirmation under the penalties of perjury that the facts stated therein are true.

§ 206. Filing in Office of Secretary of State

(a) Two signed copies of the certificate of limited partnership and of any certificates of amendment or cancellation (or of any judicial decree of amendment or cancellation) shall be delivered to the Secretary of State. A person who executes a certificate as an agent or fiduciary need not exhibit evidence of his [or her] authority as a prerequisite to filing. Unless the Secretary of State finds that any certificate does not conform to law, upon receipt of all filing fees required by law he [or she] shall:

(1) endorse on each duplicate original the word "Filed" and the day, month, and year of the filing thereof;

(2) file one duplicate original in his [or her] office; and

(3) return the other duplicate original to the person who filed it or his [or her] representative.

(b) Upon the filing of a certificate of amendment (or judicial decree of amendment) in the office of the Secretary of State, the certificate of limited partnership shall be amended as set forth therein, and upon the effective date of a certificate of cancellation (or a judicial decree thereof), the certificate of limited partnership is cancelled.

§ 207. Liability for False Statement in Certificate

If any certificate of limited partnership or certificate of amendment or cancellation contains a false statement, one who suffers loss by reliance on the statement may recover damages for the loss from:

(1) any person who executes the certificate, or causes another to execute it on his behalf, and knew, and any general partner who knew or should have known, the statement to be false at the time the certificate was executed; and

(2) any general partner who thereafter knows or should have known that any arrangement or other fact described in the certificate has changed, making the statement inaccurate in any respect within a sufficient time before the statement was relied upon reasonably to have enabled that general partner to cancel or amend the certificate, or to file a petition for its [judicial] cancellation or amendment . . . .

§ 208. Scope of Notice

The fact that a certificate of limited partnership is on file in the office of the Secretary of State is notice that the partnership is a limited partnership and the persons designated therein as general partners are general partners, but it is not notice of any other fact.

Comment

... By stating that the filing of a certificate of limited partnership only results in notice of the general liability of the general partners, Section 208 obviates the concern that third parties may be held to have notice of special provisions set forth in the certificate. While this section is designed to preserve by implication the limited liability of limited partners, the implicit protection provided is not intended to change any liability of a limited partner which may be created by his action or inaction under the law of estoppel, agency, fraud or the like.

§ 209. Delivery of Certificates to Limited Partners

Upon the return by the Secretary of State pursuant to Section 206 of a certificate marked "Filed," the general partners shall promptly deliver or mail a copy of the certificate of limited partnership and each certificate of amendment or cancellation to each limited partner unless the partnership agreement provides otherwise.

ARTICLE 3

LIMITED PARTNERS

§ 301. Admission of Limited Partners

(a) A person becomes a limited partner:

(1) at the time the limited partnership is formed; or

(2) at any later time specified in the records of the limited partnership for becoming a limited partner.

(b) After the filing of a limited partnership's original certificate of limited partnership, a person may be admitted as an additional limited partner:

(1) in the case of a person acquiring a partnership interest directly from the limited partnership, upon compliance with the partnership agreement or, if the partnership agreement does not so provide, upon the written consent of all partners; and

(2) in the case of an assignee of a partnership interest of a partner who has the power, as provided in Section 704, to grant the assignee the right to become a limited partner, upon the exercise of that power and compliance with any conditions limiting the grant or exercise of the power.

§ 302. Voting

Subject to Section 303, the partnership agreement may grant to all or a specified group of the limited partners the right to vote (on a per capita or other basis) upon any matter.

Comment

Section 302 first appeared in the 1976 Act, and must be read together with subdivision (b)(6) of Section 303. Although the 1916 Act did not speak specifically of the voting powers of limited partners, it was not uncommon for partnership agreements to grant such powers to limited partners. Section 302 is designed only to make it clear that the partnership agreement may grant such power to limited partners. If such powers are granted to limited partners beyond the "safe harbor" of subdivision (6) or (8) of Section 303(b), a court may (but of course need not) hold that, under the circumstances, the limited partners have participated in "control of the business" within the meaning of Section 303(a). Section 303(c) makes clear that the exercise of powers beyond the ambit of Section 303(b) is not ipso facto to be taken as taking part in the control of the business.

§ 303. Liability to Third Parties

(a) Except as provided in subsection (d), a limited partner is not liable for the obligations of a limited partnership unless he [or she] is also a general partner or, in addition to the exercise of his [or her] rights and powers as a limited partner, he [or she] participates in the control of the business. However, if the limited partner participates in the control of the business, he [or she] is liable only to persons who transact business with the limited partnership reasonably believing, based upon the limited partner's conduct, that the limited partner is a general partner.

(b) A limited partner does not participate in the control of the business within the meaning of subsection (a) solely by doing one or more of the following:

(1) being a contractor for or an agent or employee of the limited partnership or of a general partner or being an officer, director, or shareholder of a general partner that is a corporation;

(2) consulting with and advising a general partner with respect to the business of the limited partnership;

(3) acting as surety for the limited partnership or guaranteeing or assuming one or more specific obligations of the limited partnership;

(4) taking any action required or permitted by law to bring or pursue a derivative action in the right of the limited partnership;

(5) requesting or attending a meeting of partners;

(6) proposing, approving, or disapproving, by voting or otherwise, one or more of the following matters:

(i) the dissolution and winding up of the limited partnership;

(ii) the sale, exchange, lease, mortgage, pledge, or other transfer of all or substantially all of the assets of the limited partnership;

(iii) the incurrence of indebtedness by the limited partnership other than in the ordinary course of its business;

(iv) a change in the nature of the business;

(v) the admission or removal of a general partner;

(vi) the admission or removal of a limited partner;

(vii) a transaction involving an actual or potential conflict of interest between a general partner and the limited partnership or the limited partners;

(viii) an amendment to the partnership agreement or certificate of limited partnership; or

(ix) matters related to the business of the limited partnership not otherwise enumerated in this subsection (b), which the partnership agreement states in writing may be subject to the approval or disapproval of limited partners;

(7) winding up the limited partnership pursuant to Section 803; or

(8) exercising any right or power permitted to limited partners under this [Act] and not specifically enumerated in this subsection (b).

(c) The enumeration in subsection (b) does not mean that the possession or exercise of any other powers by a limited partner constitutes participation by him [or her] in the business of the limited partnership.

(d) A limited partner who knowingly permits his [or her] name to be used in the name of the limited partnership, except under circumstances permitted by Section 102(2), is liable to creditors who extend credit to the limited partnership without actual knowledge that the limited partner is not a general partner.

Comment

... The second sentence of Section 303(a) .... was adopted partly because of the difficulty of determining when the "control" line has been overstepped, but also (and more importantly) because of a determination that it is not sound public policy to hold a limited partner who is not also a general partner liable for the obligations of the partnership except to persons who have done business with the limited partnership reasonably believing, based on the limited partner's conduct, that he is a general partner. Paragraph (b) is intended to provide a "safe harbor" by enumerating certain activities which a limited partner may carry on for the partnership without being deemed to have taken part in control of the business. This "safe harbor" list has been expanded beyond that set out in the 1976 Act to reflect case law and statutory developments and more clearly to assure that limited partners are not subjected to general liability where such liability is inappropriate. Paragraph (d) is derived from Section 5 of the 1916 Act, but adds as a condition to the limited partner's liability the requirement that a limited partner must have knowingly permitted his name to be used in the name of the limited partnership.

§ 304. Person Erroneously Believing Himself [or Herself] Limited Partner

(a) Except as provided in subsection (b), a person who makes a contribution to a business enterprise and erroneously but in good faith believes that he [or she] has become a limited partner in the enterprise is not a general partner in the enterprise and is not bound by its obligations by reason of making the contribution, receiving distributions from the enterprise, or exercising any rights of a limited partner, if, on ascertaining the mistake, he [or she]:

(1) causes an appropriate certificate of limited partnership or a certificate of amendment to be executed and filed; or

(2) withdraws from future equity participation in the enterprise by executing and filing in the office of the Secretary of State a certificate declaring withdrawal under this section.

(b) A person who makes a contribution of the kind described in subsection (a) is liable as a general partner to any third party who transacts business with the enterprise (i) before the person withdraws and an appropriate certificate is filed to show withdrawal, or (ii) before an appropriate certificate is filed to show that he [or she] is not a general partner, but in either case only if the third party actually believed in good faith that the person was a general partner at the time of the transaction.

§ 305. Information

Each limited partner has the right to:

(1) inspect and copy any of the partnership records required to be maintained by Section 105; and

(2) obtain from the general partners from time to time upon reasonable demand (i) true and full information regarding the state of the business and financial condition of the limited partnership, (ii) promptly after becoming available, a copy of the limited partnership's federal, state, and local income tax returns for each year, and (iii) other information regarding the affairs of the limited partnership as is just and reasonable.

ARTICLE 4

GENERAL PARTNERS

§ 401. Admission of Additional General Partners

After the filing of a limited partnership's original certificate of limited partnership, additional general partners may be admitted as provided in writing in the partnership agreement or, if the partnership agreement does not provide in writing for the admission of additional general partners, with the written consent of all partners.

§ 402. Events of Withdrawal

Except as approved by the specific written consent of all partners at the time, a person ceases to be a general partner of a limited partnership upon the happening of any of the following events:

(1) the general partner withdraws from the limited partnership as provided in Section 602;

(2) the general partner ceases to be a member of the limited partnership as provided in Section 702;

(3) the general partner is removed as a general partner in accordance with the partnership agreement;

(4) unless otherwise provided in writing in the partnership agreement, the general partner: (i) makes an assignment for the benefit of creditors; (ii) files a voluntary petition in bankruptcy; (iii) is adjudicated a bankrupt or insolvent; (iv) files a petition or

answer seeking for himself [or herself] any reorganization, arrangement, composition, readjustment, liquidation, dissolution, or similar relief under any statute, law, or regulation; (v) files an answer or other pleading admitting or failing to contest the material allegations of a petition filed against him [or her] in any proceeding of this nature; or (vi) seeks, consents to, or acquiesces in the appointment of a trustee, receiver, or liquidator of the general partner or of all or any substantial part of his [or her] properties;

(5) unless otherwise provided in writing in the partnership agreement, [120] days after the commencement of any proceeding against the general partner seeking reorganization, arrangement, composition, readjustment, liquidation, dissolution, or similar relief under any statute, law, or regulation, the proceeding has not been dismissed, or if within [90] days after the appointment without his [or her] consent or acquiescence of a trustee, receiver, or liquidator of the general partner or of all or any substantial part of his [or her] properties, the appointment is not vacated or stayed or within [90] days after the expiration of any such stay, the appointment is not vacated;

(6) in the case of a general partner who is a natural person,

(i) his [or her] death; or

(ii) the entry of an order by a court of competent jurisdiction adjudicating him [or her] incompetent to manage his [or her] person or his [or her] estate;

(7) in the case of a general partner who is acting as a general partner by virtue of being a trustee of a trust, the termination of the trust (but not merely the substitution of a new trustee);

(8) in the case of a general partner that is a separate partnership, the dissolution and commencement of winding up of the separate partnership;

(9) in the case of a general partner that is a corporation, the filing of a certificate of dissolution, or its equivalent, for the corporation or the revocation of its charter; or

(10) in the case of an estate, the distribution by the fiduciary of the estate's entire interest in the partnership.

Comment

Section 402 expands considerably the provisions of Section 20 of the 1916 Act, which provided for dissolution in the event of the retirement, death or insanity of a general partner. Subdivisions (1), (2) and (3) recognize that the general partner's agency relationship is terminable at will, although it may result in a breach of the partnership agreement giving rise to an action for damages. Subdivisions (4) and (5) reflect a judgment that, unless the limited partners agree otherwise, they ought to have the power to rid themselves of a general partner who is in such dire financial straits that he is the subject of proceedings under the National Bankruptcy Code or a similar provision of law. Subdivisions (6) through (10) simply elaborate on the notion of death in the case of a general partner who is not a natural person. . . .

§ 403. General Powers and Liabilities

(a) Except as provided in this [Act] or in the partnership agreement, a general partner of a limited partnership has the rights and powers and is subject to the restrictions of a partner in a partnership without limited partners.

(b) Except as provided in this [Act], a general partner of a limited partnership has the liabilities of a partner in a partnership without limited partners to persons other than the partnership and the other partners. Except as provided in this [Act] or in the partnership agreement, a general partner of a limited partnership has the liabilities of a partner in a partnership without limited partners to the partnership and to the other partners.

§ 404. Contributions by General Partner

A general partner of a limited partnership may make contributions to the partnership and share in the profits and losses of, and in distributions from, the limited partnership as a general partner. A general partner also may make contributions to and share in profits, losses, and distributions as a limited partner. A person who is both a general partner and a limited partner has the rights and powers, and is subject to the restrictions and liabilities, of a general partner and, except as provided in the partnership agreement, also has the powers, and is subject to the restrictions, of a limited partner to the extent of his [or her] participation in the partnership as a limited partner.

§ 405. Voting

The partnership agreement may grant to all or certain identified general partners the right to vote (on a per capita or any other basis), separately or with all or any class of the limited partners, on any matter.

ARTICLE 5

FINANCE

§ 501. Form of Contribution

The contribution of a partner may be in cash, property, or services rendered, or a promissory note or other obligation to contribute cash or property or to perform services.

§ 502. Liability for Contribution

(a) A promise by a limited partner to contribute to the limited partnership is not enforceable unless set out in a writing signed by the limited partner.

(b) Except as provided in the partnership agreement, a partner is obligated to the limited partnership to perform any enforceable promise to contribute cash or property or to perform services, even if he [or she] is unable to perform because of death, disability, or any other reason. If a partner does not make the required contribution of property or services, he [or she] is obligated at the option of the limited partnership to contribute cash equal to that portion of the value, as stated in the partnership records required to be kept pursuant to Section 105, of the stated contribution which has not been made.

(c) Unless otherwise provided in the partnership agreement, the obligation of a partner to make a contribution or return money or other property paid or distributed in violation of this [Act] may be compromised only by consent of all partners. Notwithstanding the compromise, a creditor of a limited partnership who extends credit or otherwise acts in reliance on that obligation after the partner signs a writing which reflects the obligation, and before the amendment or cancellation thereof to reflect the compromise, may enforce the original obligation.

§ 503. Sharing of Profits and Losses

The profits and losses of a limited partnership shall be allocated among the partners, and among classes of partners, in the manner provided in writing in the partnership agreement. If the partnership agreement does not so provide in writing, profits and losses shall be allocated on the basis of the value, as stated in the partnership records required to be kept pursuant to Section 105, of the contributions made by each partner to the extent they have been received by the partnership and have not been returned.

§ 504. Sharing of Distributions

Distributions of cash or other assets of a limited partnership shall be allocated among the partners and among classes of partners in the manner provided in writing in the partnership agreement. If the partnership agreement does not so provide in writing, distributions shall be made on the basis of the value, as stated in the partnership records required to be kept pursuant to Section 105, of the contributions made by each partner to the extent they have been received by the partnership and have not been returned.

ARTICLE 6

DISTRIBUTIONS AND WITHDRAWAL

§ 601. Interim Distributions

Except as provided in this Article, a partner is entitled to receive distributions from a limited partnership before his [or her] withdrawal from the limited partnership and before the dissolution and winding up thereof to the extent and at the times or upon the happening of the events specified in the partnership agreement.

§ 602. Withdrawal of General Partner

A general partner may withdraw from a limited partnership at any time by giving written notice to the other partners, but if the withdrawal violates the partnership agreement, the limited partnership may recover from the withdrawing general partner damages for breach of the partnership agreement and offset the damages against the amount otherwise distributable to him [or her].

§ 603. Withdrawal of Limited Partner

A limited partner may withdraw from a limited partnership at the time or upon the happening of events specified in writing in the partnership agreement. If the agreement does not specify in writing the time or the events upon the happening of which a limited partner may withdraw or a definite time for the dissolution and winding up of the limited partnership, a limited partner may withdraw upon not less than six months' prior written notice to each general partner at his [other] address on the books of the limited partnership at its office in this State.

§ 604. Distribution Upon Withdrawal

Except as provided in this Article, upon withdrawal any withdrawing partner is entitled to receive any distribution to which he [or she] is entitled under the partnership agreement and, if not otherwise provided in the agreement, he [or she] is entitled to receive, within a reasonable time after withdrawal, the fair value of his [or her] interest in the limited partnership as of the date of withdrawal based upon his [or her] right to share in distributions from the limited partnership.

§ 605. Distribution in Kind

Except as provided in writing in the partnership agreement, a partner, regardless of the nature of his [or her] contribution, has no right to demand and receive any distribution from a limited partnership in any form other than cash. Except as provided in writing in the partnership agreement, a partner may not be compelled to accept a distribution of any asset in kind from a limited partnership to the extent that the percentage of the asset distributed to him [or her] exceeds a percentage of that asset which is equal to the percentage in which he [or she] shares in distributions from the limited partnership.

§ 606. Right to Distribution

At the time a partner becomes entitled to receive a distribution, he [or she] has the status of, and is entitled to all remedies available to, a creditor of the limited partnership with respect to the distribution.

§ 607. Limitations on Distribution

A partner may not receive a distribution from a limited partnership to the extent that, after giving effect to the distribution, all liabilities of the limited partnership, other than liabilities to partners on account of their partnership interests, exceed the fair value of the partnership assets.

§ 608. Liability Upon Return of Contribution

(a) If a partner has received the return of any part of his [or her] contribution without violation of the partnership agreement or this [Act], he [or she] is liable to the limited partnership for a period of one year thereafter for the amount of the returned contribution, but only to the extent necessary to discharge the limited partnership's liabilities to creditors who extended credit to the limited partnership during the period the contribution was held by the partnership.

(b) If a partner has received the return of any part of his [or her] contribution in violation of the partnership agreement or this

[Act], he [or she] is liable to the limited partnership for a period of six years thereafter for the amount of the contribution wrongfully returned.

(c) A partner receives a return of his [or her] contribution to the extent that a distribution to him [or her] reduces his [or her] share of the fair value of the net assets of the limited partnership below the value, as set forth in the partnership records required to be kept pursuant to Section 105, of his contribution which has not been distributed to him [or her].

ARTICLE 7

ASSIGNMENT OF PARTNERSHIP INTERESTS

§ 701. Nature of Partnership Interest

A partnership interest is personal property.

§ 702. Assignment of Partnership Interest

Except as provided in the partnership agreement, a partnership interest is assignable in whole or in part. An assignment of a partnership interest does not dissolve a limited partnership or entitle the assignee to become or to exercise any rights of a partner. An assignment entitles the assignee to receive, to the extent assigned, only the distribution to which the assignor would be entitled. Except as provided in the partnership agreement, a partner ceases to be a partner upon assignment of all his [or her] partnership interest.

§ 703. Rights of Creditor

On application to a court of competent jurisdiction by any judgment creditor of a partner, the court may charge the partnership interest of the partner with payment of the unsatisfied amount of the judgment with interest. To the extent so charged, the judgment creditor has only the rights of an assignee of the partnership interest. This [Act] does not deprive any partner of the benefit of any exemption laws applicable to his [or her] partnership interest.

§ 704. Right of Assignee to Become Limited Partner

(a) An assignee of a partnership interest, including an assignee of a general partner, may become a limited partner if and to the extent that (i) the assignor gives the assignee that right in accordance with authority described in the partnership agreement, or (ii) all other partners consent.

(b) An assignee who has become a limited partner has, to the extent assigned, the rights and powers, and is subject to the restrictions and liabilities, of a limited partner under the partnership agreement and this [Act]. An assignee who becomes a limited partner also is liable for the obligations of his [or her] assignor to make and return contributions as provided in Articles 5 and 6. However, the assignee is not obligated for liabilities unknown to the assignee at the time he [or she] became a limited partner.

(c) If an assignee of a partnership interest becomes a limited partner, the assignor is not released from his [or her] liability to the limited partnership under Sections 207 and 502.

§ 705. Power of Estate of Deceased or Incompetent Partner

If a partner who is an individual dies or a court of competent jurisdiction adjudges him [or her] to be incompetent to manage his [or her] person or his [or her] property, the partner's executor, administrator, guardian, conservator, or other legal representative may exercise all of the partner's rights for the purpose of settling his [or her] estate or administering his [or her] property, including any power the partner had to give an assignee the right to become a limited partner. If a partner is a corporation, trust, or other entity and is dissolved or terminated, the powers of that partner may be exercised by its legal representative or successor.

ARTICLE 8

DISSOLUTION

§ 801. Nonjudicial Dissolution

A limited partnership is dissolved and its affairs shall be wound up upon the happening of the first to occur of the following:

(1) at the time specified in the certificate of limited partnership;

(2) upon the happening of events specified in writing in the partnership agreement;

(3) written consent of all partners;

(4) an event of withdrawal of a general partner unless at the time there is at least one other general partner and the written provisions of the partnership agreement permit the business of the limited partnership to be carried on by the remaining general

partner and that partner does so, but the limited partnership is not dissolved and is not required to be wound up by reason of any event of withdrawal, if, within 90 days after the withdrawal, all partners agree in writing to continue the business of the limited partnership and to the appointment of one or more additional general partners if necessary or desired; or

(5) entry of a decree of judicial dissolution under Section 802.

§ 802. Judicial Dissolution

On application by or for a partner the [designate the appropriate court] court may decree dissolution of a limited partnership whenever it is not reasonably practicable to carry on the business in conformity with the partnership agreement.

§ 803. Winding Up

Except as provided in the partnership agreement, the general partners who have not wrongfully dissolved a limited partnership or, if none, the limited partners, may wind up the limited partnership's affairs; but the [designate the appropriate court] court may wind up the limited partnership's affairs upon application of any partner, his [or her] legal representative, or assignee.

§ 804. Distribution of Assets

Upon the winding up of a limited partnership, the assets shall be distributed as follows:

(1) to creditors, including partners who are creditors, to the extent permitted by law, in satisfaction of liabilities of the limited partnership other than liabilities for distributions to partners under Section 601 or 604;

(2) except as provided in the partnership agreement, to partners and former partners in satisfaction of liabilities for distributions under Section 601 or 604; and

(3) except as provided in the partnership agreement, to partners first for the return of their contributions and secondly respecting their partnership interests, in the proportions in which the partners share in distributions....

ARTICLE 10

DERIVATIVE ACTIONS

§ 1001. Right of Action

A limited partner may bring an action in the right of a limited partnership to recover a judgment in its favor if general partners with authority to do so have refused to bring the action or if an effort to cause those general partners to bring the action is not likely to succeed.

§ 1002. Proper Plaintiff

In a derivative action, the plaintiff must be a partner at the time of bringing the action and (i) must have been a partner at the time of the transaction of which he [or she] complains or (ii) his [or her] status as a partner must have devolved upon him [or her] by operation of law or pursuant to the terms of the partnership agreement from a person who was a partner at the time of the transaction.

§ 1003. Pleading

In a derivative action, the complaint shall set forth with particularity the effort of the plaintiff to secure initiation of the action by a general partner or the reasons for not making the effort.

§ 1004. Expenses

If a derivative action is successful, in whole or in part, or if anything is received by the plaintiff as a result of a judgment, compromise, or settlement of an action or claim, the court may award the plaintiff reasonable expenses, including reasonable attorney's fees, and shall direct him [or her] to remit to the limited partnership the remainder of those proceeds received by him [or her].

ARTICLE 11

MISCELLANEOUS

§ 1105. Rules for Cases Not Provided for in This [Act]

In any case not provided for in this [Act] the provisions of the Uniform Partnership Act govern.

DELAWARE LIMITED LIABILITY PARTNERSHIP ACT

(Excerpts)
[Delaware Code Annotated, Title 6, Chapter 15]

§ 1502. Definitions ...

(6) "Registered limited liability partnership" means a partnership formed pursuant to an agreement governed by the laws of this State, registered under § 1544 of this title and complying with §§ 1545, 1546 and 1549 of this title.

§ 1515. Nature of partner's liability

(a) Except as provided in Subsection (b) of this Section, all partners are liable:

(1) Jointly and severally for everything chargeable to the partnership under §§ 1513 and 1514 of this title [UPA §§ 13, 14]; and

(2) Jointly for all other debts and obligations of the partnership;

but any partner may enter into a separate obligation to perform a partnership contract.

(b) Subject to Subsection (c) of this Section, a partner in a registered limited liability partnership is not liable either directly or indirectly, by way of indemnification, contribution, assessment or

---

* Omitted.

278

otherwise, for debts, obligations and liabilities of or chargeable to the partnership, arising from negligence, wrongful acts or misconduct whether characterized as tort, contract or otherwise, committed while the partnership is a registered limited liability partnership and in the course of the partnership business by another partner or an employee, agent or representative of the partnership.

(c) Subsection (b) of this Section shall not affect the liability of a partner in a registered limited liability partnership for his own negligence, wrongful acts or misconduct or that of any person under his direct supervision and control. . . .

§ 1544. Registered Limited Liability Partnerships

(a) To become and to continue as a registered limited liability partnership, a partnership shall file with the Secretary of State an application or a renewal application, as the case may be, stating the name of the partnership; the address of its principal office; the address of a registered office and the name and address of a registered agent for service of process required to be maintained by Section 1549 of this title; the number of partners; a brief statement of the business in which the partnership engages; that the partnership thereby applies for status or renewal of this status, as the case may be, as a registered limited liability partnership and any other matters the partnership determines to include therein. A partnership becomes a registered limited liability partnership at the time of the filing of the initial application in the Office of the Secretary of State or at any later date or time specified in the application if, in either case, there has been substantial compliance with the requirements of this chapter. A partnership continues as a registered limited liability partnership if there has been substantial compliance with the requirements of this chapter.

(b) The application or renewal application shall be executed by a majority in interest of the partners or by one or more partners authorized to execute an application or renewal application. . . .

(e) Registration is effective for one year after the date an application is filed. . . . Registration, whether pursuant to an original application or a renewal application, as a registered limited liability partnership is renewed if, during the sixty-day period preceding the date the application or renewal application otherwise would have expired, the partnership files with the Secretary of State a renewal application. . . . .

§ 1545. Name of Registered Limited Liability Partnerships

The name of a registered limited liability partnership shall contain the words "Registered Limited Liability Partnership" or the abbreviation "L.L.P." or the designation "LLP" as the last words or letters of its name. . . .

§ 1546. Insurance or Financial Responsibility of Registered Limited Liability Partnerships

(a) A registered limited liability partnership shall carry at least $1,000,000 of liability insurance of a kind that is designed to cover the kinds of negligence, wrongful acts, and misconduct for which liability is limited by § 1515(b) of this title and which insures the partnership and its partners.

(b) If, in any proceeding, compliance by a partnership with the requirements of subsection (a) of this section is disputed, (1) that issue shall be determined by the court, and (2) the burden of proof of compliance shall be on the person who claims the limitation of liability in § 1515(b) of this title.

(c) If a registered limited liability partnership is in compliance with the requirements of subsection (a) of this section, the requirements of this section shall not be admissible or in any way be made known to a jury in determining an issue of liability for or extent of the debt or obligation or damages in question.

(d) A registered limited liability partnership is considered to be in compliance with subsection (a) of this section if the partnership provides $1,000,000 of funds specifically designated and segregated for the satisfaction of judgments against the partnership or its partners based on the kinds of negligence, wrongful acts, and misconduct for which liability is limited by § 1515(b) of this title by:

> (1) deposit in trust or in bank escrow of cash, bank certificates of deposit, or United States Treasury obligations; or

> (2) a bank letter of credit or insurance company bond.

§ 1547. Applicability of Chapter to Foreign and Interstate Commerce

(a) A partnership, including a registered limited liability partnership, formed and existing under this chapter, may conduct its business, carry on its operations, and have and exercise the powers granted by this chapter in any state, territory, district, or possession of the United States or in any foreign country.

(b) It is the policy of this state that the internal affairs of partnerships, including registered limited liability partnerships, formed and existing under this chapter, including the liability of partners for debts and obligations of partnerships, shall be subject to and governed by the laws of this state.

§ 1553. Limited Partnerships as Registered Limited Liability Limited Partnerships

A domestic limited partnership may become a registered limited liability limited partnership by complying with the applicable provisions of the Delaware Revised Uniform Limited Partnership Act....

TEXAS LIMITED LIABILITY PARTNERSHIP ACT

[TEXAS REVISED PARTNERSHIP ACT]

Section 1.01.   General Definitions

In this Act: . . .

(10) "Partnership" means an entity created as described by Section 2.02(a). The term includes a registered limited liability partnership formed under Section 3.08 or under the Texas Uniform Partnership Act and its subsequent amendments. . . .

Section 3.08.   Liability in and Registration of Registered Limited Liability Partnership

(a) LIABILITY OF PARTNER.   (1) A partner in a registered limited liability partnership is not individually liable for debts and obligations of the partnership arising from errors, omissions, negligence, incompetence, or malfeasance committed while the partnership is a registered limited liability partnership and in the course of the partnership business by another partner or a representative of the partnership not working under the supervision or direction of the first partner unless the first partner:

(A) was directly involved in the specific activity in which the errors, omissions, negligence, incompetence, or malfeasance were committed by the other partner or representative; or

(B) had notice or knowledge of the errors, omissions, negligence, incompetence, or malfeasance by the other partner or representative at the time of occurrence and then failed to take reasonable steps to prevent or cure the errors, omissions, negligence, incompetence, or malfeasance.

(2) Subsection (a)(1) does not affect:

(A) the joint and several liability of a partner for debts and obligations of the partnership arising from a cause other than the causes specified by Subsection (a)(1);

(B) the liability of a partnership to pay its debts and obligations out of partnership property; or

(C) the manner in which service of citation or other civil process may be served in an action against a partnership.

(3) In this subsection, "representative" includes an agent, servant, or employee of a registered limited liability partnership.

(b) REGISTRATION. (1) In addition to complying with Subsections (c) and (d)(1), to become a registered limited liability partnership, a partnership must file with the secretary of state an application stating:

(A) the name of the partnership;

(B) the federal tax identification number of the partnership;

(C) the street address of the partnership's principal office in this state and outside this state, as applicable;

(D) the number of partners at the date of application; and

(E) in brief, the partnership's business.

(2) The application must be executed by a majority-in-interest of the partners or by one or more partners authorized by a majority-in-interest of the partners.

(3) Two copies of the application must be filed, accompanied by a fee of $100 for each partner.

(4) A partnership is registered as a registered limited liability partnership on filing a completed initial or renewal application, in duplicate with the required fee, or on a later date specified in the application. A registration is not affected by later changes in the partners of the partnership.

(5) An initial application filed under this subsection and registered by the secretary of state expires one year after the date of registration or later effective date unless earlier withdrawn or revoked or unless renewed in accordance with Subdivision (7).

(6) A registration may be withdrawn by filing in duplicate with the secretary of state a written withdrawal notice executed by a majority-in-interest of the partners or by one or more partners authorized by a majority-in-interest of the partners. A withdrawal notice must include the name of the partnership, the federal tax identification number of the partnership, the date of registration of the partnership's last application under this section, and a current street address of the partnership's principal office in this state and outside this state, if applicable. A withdrawal notice terminates the status of the partnership as a registered limited liability partnership as of the date of filing the notice or a later date specified in the notice, but not later than the expiration date under Subdivision (5).

(7) An effective registration may be renewed before its expiration by filing in duplicate with the secretary of state an application

containing current information of the kind required in an initial application and the most recent date of registration of the partnership. The renewal application must be accompanied by a fee of $200 for each partner on the date of renewal. A renewal application filed under this section continues an effective registration for one year after the date the effective registration would otherwise expire....

(c) NAME. A registered limited liability partnership's name must contain the words "registered limited liability partnership" or the abbreviation "L.L.P." as the last words or letters of its name.

(d) INSURANCE OR FINANCIAL RESPONSIBILITY. (1) A registered limited liability partnership must:

(A) carry at least $100,000 of liability insurance of a kind that is designed to cover the kinds of errors, omissions, negligence, incompetence, or malfeasance for which liability is limited by Subsection (a)(1); or

(B) provide $100,000 of funds specifically designated and segregated for the satisfaction of judgments against the partnership based on the kinds of errors, omissions, negligence, incompetence, or malfeasance for which liability is limited by Subsection (a)(1) by:

(i) deposit in trust or in bank escrow of cash, bank certificates of deposit, or United States Treasury obligations; or

(ii) a bank letter of credit or insurance company bond.

(2) If the registered limited liability partnership is in compliance with Subdivision (1), the requirements of this subsection shall not be admissible or in any way be made known to the jury in determining an issue of liability for or extent of the debt or obligation or damages in question.

(3) If compliance with Subdivision (1) is disputed:

(A) compliance must be determined separately from the trial or proceeding to determine the partnership debt or obligation in question, its amount, or partner liability for the debt or obligation; and

(B) the burden of proof of compliance is on the person claiming limitation of liability under Subsection (a)(1).

(e) LIMITED PARTNERSHIP. A limited partnership may become a registered limited liability partnership by complying with applicable provisions of the Texas Revised Limited Partnership Act and its subsequent amendments.

[TEXAS REVISED LIMITED PARTNERSHIP ACT]

Section 2.14.   Limited Partnership as Registered Limited Liability Partnership

(a) A limited partnership is a registered limited liability partnership as well as a limited partnership if it:

(1) registers as a registered limited liability partnership as provided by Section 3.08(b), Texas Revised Partnership Act, as permitted by its partnership agreement or, if its partnership agreement does not include provisions for becoming a registered limited liability partnership, with the consent of partners required to amend its partnership agreement;

(2) complies with Section 3.08(d), Texas Revised Partnership Act; and

(3) has as the last words or letters of its name the words "Limited Partnership" or the abbreviation "Ltd." followed by the words "registered limited liability partnership" or the abbreviation "L.L.P."

(b) In applying Section 3.08(b), Texas Revised Partnership Act, to a limited partnership:

(1) an application to become a registered limited liability partnership or to withdraw a registration must be executed by at least one general partner; and

(2) all other references to partners mean general partners only.

(c) If a limited partnership is a registered limited liability partnership, Section 3.08(a), Texas Revised Partnership Act, applies to its general partners and to any of its limited partners who, under other provisions of this Act, are liable for the debts or obligations of the limited partnership.

*

INDEX

References are to Pages

†